The Case Files
of the
Oriental
Sleuths

The Case Files of the
Oriental Sleuths:
Charlie Chan, Mr. Moto & Mr. Wong

by David Rothel

BearManor Media
2011

The Case Files of the Oriental Sleuths:
Charlie Chan, Mr. Moto, and Mr. Wong

© 2011 David Rothel

Photo credits and acknowledgments: 20th Century-Fox, Monogram Pictures, United Artists, ABC, CBS, NBC.

Please note that while every attempt has been made to identify the copyright holders of the photos published herein, some omissions or errors may have occurred. Please send any corrections to the publisher at the address listed for correction in subsequent reprints.

For information, address:

BearManor Media
P. O. Box 71426
Albany, GA 31708

bearmanormedia.com

Typesetting, cover and layout by John Teehan

Published in the USA by BearManor Media

ISBN—1-59393-642-7
978-1-59393-642-6

Table of Contents

The Case Files of Mr. Moto

The Case Files of Mr. Wong

Foreword

DURING THE GOLDEN AGE of magazine fiction, motion pictures, and radio—roughly the 1920s through the late 1940s—three Oriental crime fighters were introduced to the American public. Through the media which they inhabited they became fictional icons in American popular culture: Honolulu Police Inspector Charlie Chan, International Secret Agent Mr. I. A. Moto, and Justice Department Agent Mr. James Lee Wong—the Oriental Sleuths.

Created by established and respected authors Earl Derr Biggers, Pulitzer Prize-winner John P. Marquand, and Hugh Wiley, the three Oriental sleuths' adventures first appeared in a serialized format in such popular slick magazines as *The Saturday Evening Post* and *Collier's* and then were quickly snapped up by Hollywood to sate the appetites of film-goers for detective thrillers on the silver screen. Charlie Chan carried his case loads over into radio, television, television animation, newspaper comic strips, comic books, Better Little Books, and games. Mr. Moto followed with radio adventures and a graphic novel, and Mr. Wong added comic book exploits to his résumé.

During the past couple of years while examining the careers of these super sleuths, I have had the opportunity to explore the dark alleys, the exotic locales, the clues, the red herrings, and the sinister suspects these Oriental sleuths encountered in their murder investigations through the decades—the case files of Charlie Chan, Mr. Moto, and Mr. Wong. I invite you now to join them in their exploits, whether for the first time or for a return visit. It looks as if it's going to be a dark and stormy night in the mysterious environs where these capers will take you, so put on your trench coat and snap-brim fedora as you join the Oriental sleuths in their fascinating murder investigations.

– David Rothel
Dahlonega, Georgia

The Case Files of Charlie Chan

Earl Derr Biggers
and the Novels

LATE IN HIS LIFE Earl Derr Biggers (1884-1933) commented that he never expected to become a mystery writer—especially a mystery writer with a Chinese-American detective as his hero. It just didn't seem to be in the cards. But life takes one down a circuitous path, in Biggers' case a path that began in Warren, Ohio, where he was born in 1884, then on to Harvard with graduation in 1907, then back to Ohio where he first worked for the state's leading newspaper, *The Cleveland Plain Dealer*, and then the publishing house of Bobbs-Merrill. But these jobs didn't last very long for the restless Biggers, and by 1908 he had relocated to Boston and was writing a humorous column for the *Boston Traveler*, and shortly thereafter became the paper's drama critic—which eventually got him fired because of his frequent acerbic reviews.

By 1913 he had completed his first novel, *Seven Keys to Baldpate*, which soon came to the attention of showman George M. Cohen who purchased the dramatic rights for a Broadway production. Over time *Baldpate* was filmed seven times with the original title and twice with a different one—and Earl Derr Biggers secured a place in American literature as well as becoming a wealthy man. With his newfound fame and fortune, the young writer married the girl from Boston that he originally had met while at the *Traveler*.

With another successful novel, *Love Insurance*, under his belt, after which he turned it into a play entitled *See-Saw*, Biggers and his wife decided to vacation in Hawaii; they could now well-afford it. And it was there on the beach of Waikiki that he heard about a Chinese-Ameri-

Earl Derr Biggers

can police detective, Chang Apana, who had acquired a reputation in the Islands. Although Biggers claimed that he never modeled Charlie Chan on any one person in real life, there is little denying that he got his idea at that time for a murder mystery featuring a Chinese–American detective located in Honolulu who would eventually become Charlie Chan. The first Chan novel, *The House without a Key*, was serialized in the *Saturday Evening Post* magazine in 1925 and then published by Bobbs-Merrill as a novel.

Chang Apana, a real-life Chinese-American police detective in Hawaii was most likely Biggers' inspiration for the character of Charlie Chan.

With the success of the first Chan novel, Biggers and his wife decided to relocate permanently in San Marino, California, and he was encouraged to write a sequel, *The Chinese Parrot* (1926), and eventually six novels in all, adding *Behind That Curtain* (1928), *The Black Camel* (1929), *Charlie Chan Carries On* (1930), and *Keeper of the Keys* (1932) to the list. In the novels the Chan character is not central in the plot; he is presented as a subordinate character involved in solving a murder that takes place among the main characters in the story. It has been noted that in the original publication of *The House without a Key*, the Chan character is not even mentioned in the dust jacket comments.

Biggers was well aware of the "yellow peril," evil, and sinister Oriental characters that frequently populated the pages of literature of the times, but he created his Charlie Chan character in a different mold—affable, compassionate, and wise, a family man on the side of law and order. (See Sax Rohmer's *The Mystery of Dr. Fu Manchu* (1913), Charles Beecham's "Ah Sing" in the 1920 novel *The Yellow Spider*, Edgar Wallace's "Fing-Su" in the 1926 novel *The Yellow Snake*, as examples of the "yellow peril.") He never envisioned the character in the stylized, tough, slap-'em-around-type of leading-man detectives such as Sam Spade, Phillip Marlowe, or Michael Shayne. No, Charlie always talked softly, was polite in the extreme, never chased after the *femme fatales*, and seemed troubled and somewhat sad when he had to utter the fateful words, "*You* are murderer" at the end of a case.

Earl Derr Biggers was not to live long enough to see the enduring quality of his fictional creation, Charlie Chan. On April 5, 1933, Biggers died in a Pasadena, California, hospital of a heart attack. He was only forty-nine years old.

The Charlie Chan Novels

The House without a Key (1925)
Publisher: Bobbs-Merrill (First edition).

PLOT/COMMENT: East meets West in this first novel in the Charlie Chan series. Wealthy Bostonian society figure John Quincy Winterslip goes to Hawaii to bring back his elderly aunt Minerva who is visiting members of the Winterslip family who live on the island paradise. Aunt Minerva's planned short visit has turned into many months. The strait-laced, somewhat stuffy, young John Quincy is eager to return to his fiancée Agatha, his successful investment business, and his family roots, but the murder of his uncle, Dan Winterslip, changes his plans and brings Inspector Charlie Chan of the Honolulu police into the lives of the Western branch of the Winterslips. Soon, John Quincy falls under the spell of Hawaii, breaks off his engagement to the similarly straitlaced Agatha, and, after Charlie Chan solves the murder, resolves to make Hawaii his new home.

Earl Derr Biggers first visited the Hawaiian Islands in 1919, but didn't get around to writing *The House without a Key* until four years later. Biggers was one of the early American writers who attempted to cast the "spell of the Islands" into words as he created his mystery novel. An example can be found early in the novel as he provides this description of the "best" hour of the day:

> It was the hour at which she [Minerva Winterslip] liked Waikiki best, the hour just preceding dinner and the quick tropic darkness. The shadows cast by the tall coconut palms lengthened and deepened, the light of the falling sun flamed on Diamond Head and tinted with gold the rollers sweeping in from the coral reef. A few late swimmers, reluctant to depart, dotted those waters whose touch is like the caress of a lover.

Present-day readers are surprised by the late appearance of the Honolulu Police detective. John Quincy Winterslip and the Winterslip family carry most of the story, and Charlie doesn't enter or speak his first words until almost one hundred pages of plot have transpired. As stated before, the novel was twice adapted for films.

The Chinese Parrot (1926) Publisher: Bobbs-Merrill (First edition).

PLOT/COMMENT: Honolulu heiress Sally Jordan has fallen upon hard times and must sell her valuable string of pearls. She does so through the well-known jeweler Alexander Eden. Eden's son Bob and old friend Charlie Chan are asked to hand deliver the precious jewels to their new owner, millionaire businessman P. J. Madden, who resides in a desert area of Southern California in a town called Eldorado. Madden has purchased the pearls for his daughter Evelyn, but Bob and Charlie soon become wary because things do not appear as they should. Then two mysterious deaths occur—a Chinese parrot and a Chinese employee of Madden—causing Charlie to go undercover as a cook named Ah Kim as he investigates. By the time the situation is resolved, Bob has found love with a young lady named Paula Wendell who works as a location scout for a film company.

Again, Charlie Chan is a secondary character in the novel; Bob Eden is the focus of much of the plot. Bob and other key players in the book solve the murder *with* Charlie rather than Charlie conducting his own solo investigation to discover the murderer. We readers of the novels—almost a hundred years after Biggers penned them—are conditioned by the many Charlie Chan movies, radio, and television episodes we have experienced and expect the venerable detective to show up on the scene early in the plot development and be the central character. Biggers had a bigger picture in mind and was less concerned with this Chinese supporting character.

Behind That Curtain (1928) Publisher: Bobbs-Merrill (First edition)

PLOT/COMMENT: Charlie Chan is vacationing in San Francisco when he gets a telegram from his Honolulu home that Mrs. Chan has just given birth to the couple's eleventh child and that he is to return as soon as possible. On his last evening in San Francisco Charlie is invited to a dinner party by businessman Barry Kirk, a man whose acquaintance Charlie has made while in the city. The guests at the lavish party include a famous Hollywood actress; an explorer who has just returned from Tibet with a film of his adventures; and Sir Frederic Bruce, the retired head of Scotland Yard, who has been in San Francisco researching an old case that he never solved. During the dinner party he discusses the case which involved a British solicitor who fifteen years before in London was murdered with the only clue being a pair of Chinese slippers which the victim had donned just before the murder. Bruce believes that the disappearance of several women during the intervening years is somehow connected to the solicitor's murder. After the dinner party while the guests are viewing the explorer's film of Tibet, a gunshot rings out in Kirk's living quarters below the room where the film is being shown. Sir Frederic Bruce's body is discovered there, murdered in cold blood and wearing a pair of Chinese slippers. The stunned Barry Kirk asks Charlie to stay on in San Francisco long enough to clear up the mystery of Bruce's murder and the previous murders.

Earl Derr Biggers, somewhat sensitive as to how his writings were received by some reviewers, dedicated this third book in his Charlie Chan series to "The only critic I love—My wife." Fittingly, with the novel set in San Francisco, the 1929 filmed version of *Behind That Curtain* was the debut film when the Fox Theatre in San Francisco opened on June 28 in 1929.

The Black Camel (1929) Publisher: Bobbs-Merrill (First edition)

PLOT/COMMENT: "Death is a black camel that kneels unbidden at every gate. Tonight black camel has knelt here," says Charlie Chan to the usual suspects after the body of beautiful Hollywood actress Sheila Fane is discovered with a knife through her heart. Ms. Fane, we learn, has just completed shooting a film in Hawaii and has invited guests to a dinner party at her rented Waikiki beach house. Just before dinner is to be served, screams are heard on the garden pavilion and the horrified guests and servants discover the actress's body. Charlie Chan soon arrives and begins an investigation that leads him to a mysterious psychic named Tarneverro that the actress has recently consulted regarding her troubled past and future marriage plans. An ex-husband, a beach bum, an unsolved Hollywood murder from a few years previous, the enigmatic psychic, and others are all tangled up in the mystery of Sheila Fine's murder, a murder case that Honolulu's finest detective must solve.

Readers of Earl Derr Biggers' novels frequently comment on how beautifully he sets the scene for his characters. In *The Black Camel* he begins chapter two with this description of the oncoming night on the Hawaiian beach:

> After a brief twilight, the dark sweeps over Waikiki Beach like Old Man Mystery himself. In the hours before the moon, like a climbing torch, ascends the purple sky, the sense of hearing comes into its own. Blackness covers the coco-palms, yet they may be heard rustling at the trade-wind's touch; the white line of the breakers is blotted out, yet they continue to crash on that unseen shore with what seems an added vigor. This is night in the real sense of the word, intriguing, awe-inspiring, but all too short, for the moon is waiting an early cue.

The Charlie Chan aphorisms, which became so popular and prevalent in the films, also dotted the pages of the novels. Charlie closes his *Black Camel* case with a desire for peace and rest, but acknowledges to the character of Wu Kno-Ching that there is, of course, much more to life:

"I am weary," sighed Chan, "I want peace now. A very trying case, good Wu Kno-ching. But"—he nodded, and a smile spread over his fat face—"as you know, my friend, a gem is not polished without rubbing nor a man perfected without trials."

Charlie Chan Carries On (1932)
Publisher: Bobbs-Merrill (First edition)

PLOT/COMMENT: The title of this novel refers to Charlie's taking over an investigation from Inspector Duff of Scotland Yard (who was first introduced in *Behind That Curtain*). Inspector Duff has been investigating the murder of Hugh Morris Drake, a wealthy automobile manufacturer from Detroit who was murdered at his hotel in London. Drake has been a member of an around-the-world cruise club, and Duff believes the murderer may be a member of the club. Before Drake's murder is solved, the tour group moves on from London, continuing their journey with Sergeant Welby of Scotland Yard on board. When Welby is subsequently murdered on the docks in Yokohama, Inspector Duff journeys to Honolulu to join the tour. Duff suspects that the same killer is responsible for additional murders committed in London, France, Italy, and Japan. While the ship is in port in Honolulu, Duff is shot and wounded by the mysterious killer and is unable to continue the voyage and the investigation, so Charlie carries on. Charlie solves the case before the ship makes port in San Francisco, the last leg of the tour, but not before more murders occur.

In this fifth Charlie Chan novel Charlie is still pretty much a supporting character, but he finally gets his name in the title. Even so, because of the structure of the novel, Charlie again does not come on the scene until well into the book. Inspector Duff and the murder victims and suspects carry the earlier parts of the novel. As stated previously, the 1931 filmed version with Warner Oland is considered lost; however, a Spanish version filmed at the same time and using many of the same sets is available. The 1940 film *Charlie Chan's Murder Cruise* is also based on the novel, but in the film Inspector Duff dies from his wounds.

Keeper of the Keys (1932) Publisher: Bobbs-Merrill (First edition)

PLOT/COMMENT: Once again the setting is California, a beautiful remote area with snow-capped mountains in the distance, where Charlie Chan encounters murder. Charlie has been invited to be a houseguest on the estate of Dudley Ward. Ward's other guests include his ex-wife, world-famous soprano Ellen Landini; three of her other ex-husbands; and her current inamorato Hugh Beaton—and there are others present, including servants. Ward wants Charlie there because he hopes to discover if rumors of a son he did not know about are true. As a plane piloted by Michael Ireland, who also had an affair with Landini and was later rebuffed, makes a noisy landing on the estate, Ellen Landini is shot dead, murdered by person or persons unknown. Presently, a second murder occurs, raising the stakes for Charlie and the local authority, young Sheriff Holt.

This last novel by Earl Derr Biggers was never made into a film, but did have a short run on Broadway in 1933 with William Harrigan essaying the role of Charlie Chan. The novel was also adapted into thirty-nine fifteen-minute episodes for the Charlie Chan radio series on the Mutual Broadcasting System under the title *The Case of the Madame Landini Murder*.

The Charlie Chan Films

FOLLOWING THE SUCCESSFUL publication of the first Earl Derr Biggers novel, Hollywood immediately took notice and made a deal with the author for the film rights. Pathé Pictures quickly filmed a silent serialized version of *The House without a Key* in the same year the book was published, 1925, with Japanese actor George Kuwa as Chan. (In 1932 it was filmed again with Warner Oland as Charlie under the title *Charlie Chan's Greatest Case*.) In 1928 another Japanese actor, Kamiyama Sojin, played Charlie Chan in a silent feature version of *The Chinese Parrot*, produced by Universal Pictures. Both the first version of *House without a Key* and *The Chinese Parrot* are now considered lost. Then, as sound came into movies, Fox studio produced *Behind That Curtain* in 1929 with Korean-American actor E. L. Park playing the role of Chan in the picture. (Not much is known about Park, and some sources list him as British.) In 1931 *Charlie Chan Carries On* was produced by Fox, this time starring Swedish actor Warner Oland in the leading role he would go on to play for sixteen feature films. The success of this film quickly led to the filming of *Black Camel* (1931), the last of the films based on Biggers' novels. *Keeper of the Keys* was produced on Broadway as a

Chang Apana and Charlie Chan (Warner Oland) shared real and reel adventures during the actor's visit to Hawaii.

mystery play but was not successful, and perhaps that is the reason that Fox opted out of producing the last novel as a film. Detailed coverage of the films will begin with *Behind That Curtain*, the first surviving Charlie Chan Film.

Behind That Curtain (Fox, 1929) 91m.

Producer: William Fox, Director: Irving Cummings, Screenplay: Clarke Silvernail based on the novel by Earl Derr Biggers.

CAST: Warner Baxter, Lois Moran, Gilbert Emery, Claude King, Philip Strange, Boris Karloff, Jamiel Hasson, Peter Gawthorne, John Rogers, Edgar Norton, Frank Finch Smiles, Mercedes De Valasco, E. L. Park.

E. L. Park [Charlie Chan] *had the charisma and charm of a bag of lint.* –gftbiloxi

PLOT/COMMENT: Wealthy Sir George Mannering (Claude King) is displeased, to say the least, with his niece Eve's (Lois Moran) relationship with Eric Durand (Philip Strange), a suspected bounder. Finally his frustration grows to the point where he hires Hilary Galt (Edgar Norton), a private detective, to investigate Durand's background. Soon Galt is found murdered, and Eve tells her father that she and Durand have married and are moving to India, leaving Sir George and American explorer Col. John Beetham (Warner Baxter), a former suitor of Eve's, distraught. Sir Frederick Bruce (Gilbert Emory), a Scotland Yard inspector heading up the investigation, suspects that Durand is guilty of the murder and pursues him to India. By this time Eve is disenchanted with husband Durand and seeks comfort with Beetham who is about to start a desert expedition from India to Persia. Later, fearing the investigation might implicate Beetham in some way and that Durand is pursuing her for the information she has about the murder, Eve flees to San Francisco. It is at this point near the end of the film that Charlie Chan (E. L. Park), a San Francisco Police officer, becomes involved in the case. The investigation leads to a lecture hall when Beecham is speaking (now months later) and where Durand shows up with the intention of killing Eve. At this juncture in the case, Sir Frederick Bruce of Scotland Yard and Charlie resolve the situation, but only after some final bloodshed.

The movie can hardly be called a Charlie Chan film in that Charlie, played by Korean-American E. L. Park, only appears for a couple of short scenes near the end of the film. The film is very slow moving with actors exhibiting the over-articulated speaking style that was prevalent in the very earliest sound films.

The Warner Oland Films

When Warner Oland (1879-1938) assumed the role of Chinese detective Charlie Chan in *Charlie Chan Carries On* in 1931, he already had a considerable history of playing Oriental characters, although the earlier roles were mostly despicable in nature. During his initial years in films, Oland's physical features seemed to adapt easily toward ethnic and villain roles (at least in the eyes of directors), so with a little application of "yellowface" makeup, he was ready to perform Oriental skullduggery. His first portrayal of

Warner Oland as Charlie Chan.

an Asian character came in the Pearl White serial entitled *The Lightning Raider* in 1919 where he played the dastardly Wu Fang. Other such roles continued on a semi-regular basis throughout the 1920s, including the role of Li Hsun in *Mandarin's Gold* (1919), Charley Yong in *East Is West* (1922), Fu Shing in *The Fighting American* (1924), and Shanghai Dan in *Curlytop* (1924). During these same years Warner Oland, of course, played many non-Asian roles, too, including Cantor Rabinowitz in *The Jazz Singer* (1927), with Al Jolson, and the Duke in *Dream of Love* (1928), with Nils Asther and Joan Crawford.

Oland became a star with his portrayal of the sinister title character in *The Mystery of Dr. Fu Manchu* (1929) and continued playing the role in two sequels, *The Return of Dr. Fu Manchu* (1930) and *Daughter of the Dragon* (1931). He did a spoof of the character in *Paramount on Parade* (1930). With his fame and familiarity in Oriental roles, it came as little surprise when Fox announced in 1931 that Warner Oland was to become Charlie Chan in their planned series based on the Earl Derr Biggers character.

Oland's pre-Hollywood background did not seem a likely precursor to the Chan role. Born in Sweden, the young Johan Verner Ölund immigrated to the United States with his family when he was thirteen years old and attended schools in Boston, Massachusetts. Always fascinated by the theatre, Oland studied all aspects of theatre work, but eventually concentrated on acting as his primary focus. By 1906 his skills as an actor were realized by the great and famous actress Alla Nazimova, and he toured the country as a member of her theatre troupe. In 1907 he met Edith Gardner Shearn, a well-known portrait painter and playwright, and soon married her. During the early years of their marriage, the two worked together to translate Strindberg's works into English. The marriage was by all accounts a success and lasted until his death, only faltering during Oland's last years when he succumbed to alcoholism. With his success as a trained stage actor, it was only a matter of time before Hollywood beckoned, and eventually the role of Charlie Chan took over the actor's professional life.

During the first few years after Oland became Charlie Chan on screen, he continued to appear frequently in other roles on screen, including playing General Yu in *The Painted Veil* (1934), with Greta Garbo and Herbert Marshall (future Number One Son Keye Luke was also in the cast), and Dr. Yogami, a werewolf, in *Werewolf of London* (1935) with Henry Hull and Valerie Hobson. It wasn't until he had completed eight Charlie Chan films, half of his total output, that he then left other roles and portrayed the Chinese detective exclusively for the rest of his career.

Despite his fame and fortune as an actor (it was reported that he was eventually making thirty thousand dollars a picture for the Chan films), Warner Oland increasingly suffered from alcoholism, which threatened his acting career and his marriage, and eventually took over his life. On the set of his Chan movies, the directors learned that key dialogue scenes needed to be shot in the morning because, after drinking his lunch, Oland would be pretty much incapacitated. In a Cloverland film documentary by John Cork on Oland, Kay Linaker, leading lady in several of the Fox Charlie Chans, commented that he "drank with chasers, both alcohol… By eleven o'clock he might as well go home." By 1937 Oland's wife Edith filed for divorce.

During the filming of *Charlie Chan at the Ringside*, Oland walked off the set suddenly one day and never came back. (The film was later converted into a Mr. Moto film, *Mr. Moto's Gamble,* by Fox with Keye Luke appearing as Number One Son Lee Chan opposite Peter Lorre.) It was also during this time that Oland frequently appeared delusional and was hospitalized for several weeks. Upon his release in early 1938, Twentieth Century-Fox, in hopes that the actor had gotten his life together, signed Oland to a new contract for three more Chan films and suggested that he take a vacation before production began on the first film.

The actor decided to go alone on an extended trip to his homeland of Sweden. While there he contracted bronchial pneumonia which was complicated by early-stage emphysema. Warner Oland died in a Stockholm hospital on August 6, 1938. His wife Edith had his body cremated and returned to Southborough in Massachusetts where they had maintained a farm throughout their marriage. A large roughhewn stone marks Warner Oland's gravesite in the town's cemetery.

Charlie Chan Carries On (Fox, 1931) 76m.

Director: Hamilton MacFadden, Screenplay: Philip Klein based on the novel by Earl Derr Biggers.

CAST: Warner Oland; John Garrick; Marguerite Churchill; Warren Hymer; Marjorie White; C. Henry Gordon; William Holden; George Brent; Peter Gawthorne; John T. Murray; John Swor; Goodee Montgomery; Jason Robards, Sr.; Lumsden Hare; Zeffie Tilbury; Betty Francisco; Harry Beresford; John Rogers.

The only regret one has while watching this film is that the amiable Oriental sleuth and philosopher does not appear until the picture is half over. –Mordaunt Hall, *NY Times*

PLOT/COMMENT: This is one of four Warner Oland/Charlie Chan films that is considered lost. As a result of a Fox Studio fire in 1937, no prints of this film are known to exist. The closest thing that we have to the actual movie is a Portuguese-language version entitled *Eran Trece* (*There Were Thirteen*) that was shot on the same sets and aimed at the Brazilian film market. (It can be viewed in the Twentieth Century-Fox boxed DVD set of Charlie Chan movies.) The story, with considerable rewriting, was filmed in 1940 as *Charlie Chan's Murder Cruise* with Sidney Toler playing the role of the venerable detective. In *Charlie Chan Carries On* Charlie does not appear in the film until more than halfway through when Inspector Duff of Scotland Yard seeks his help on a murder that took place in a

London hotel and three more since then, with all the suspects now aboard a cruise ship docking in Honolulu before carrying on to its destination, San Francisco. (In *Murder Cruise* Inspector Duff is strangled and dies right after explaining the case to Charlie; in this original he is shot but survives.) Since the film is unavailable for viewing, I will defer to an excerpt from the *New York Times* review by Mordaunt Hall that appeared on March 21, 1931:

> In the group of world tourists is Max Minchin, who has made a pot of money as a bootlegger. Now and again he receives an opportunity to offer a little underworld philosophy and on one occasion he tells Chan, "When a guy double-crosses me, I re-cross him." Max also suggests that Chan had better wear iron underclothes if he wants to live through the search for the murderer. The man responsible for the killing is known to be among the little group, but who he is nobody knows. A man has been killed in a London hotel and there are all sorts of complications, so that any one of half a dozen men are looked upon with suspicion. When Chan takes up the case, he is in Honolulu. A mysterious gloved hand appears while he is talking to Inspector Duff, of Scotland Yard, and a second later the Englishman falls from a bullet wound. That same night Chan announces that he is going to San Francisco aboard the ship with the tourist party.
>
> How he succeeds in trapping the killer and who the killer is must of course be left untold in these columns.
>
> John Garrick appears as the sympathetic young man who helps Chan. Marguerite Churchill does very well as Pamela. Warren Hymer furnishes good fun as the bootlegger. Peter Gawthorne makes the most of the role of the Scotland Yard inspector. Marjorie White plays the bootlegger's wife, and William Holden [no, not *that* William Holden] interprets one of the several men suspected of the crime.

The Black Camel (Fox, 1931) 71m.

Producer: William Sistrom, Director: Hamilton MacFadden, Screenplay: Barry Conners, Philip Klein, Dudley Nichols, Adaptation: Hugh Stanislaus Strange, based on the novel by Earl Derr Biggers.

CAST: Warner Oland; Sally Eilers; Bela Lugosi; Dorothy Revier; Victor Carconi; Murray Kinnell; William Post, Jr.; Robert Young; Violet Dunn; J. M. Kerrigan; Mary Gordon; Rita Rozelle; Otto Yamaoka; Dwight

Frye; C. Henry Gordon; Robert Homans; Hamilton MacFadden; Louise Mackintosh; Richard Tucker; James Wang; Marjorie White.

It was good to see Charlie in Honolulu and in charge. So often in later movies he's in another city and humbly helping another police department. Here, he's the boss, and people do what he says—definitely more assertive. –jonfrum2000

PLOT/COMMENT: The only Chan film to be shot on a faraway location, *The Black Camel* concerns movie star Shelah Fayne (Dorothy Revier) who is in Honolulu filming a movie and carrying on an affair with her new boyfriend. Hesitant to commit to marrying the wealthy Alan Jaynes (William Post, Jr.) until she has had a chance to discuss it with her psychic Tanaverro the Great (Bela Lugosi), she is surprised and greatly disturbed when Tanaverro confronts her with questions about a Hollywood murder that took place three years before. Later that evening Shelah is shot to death in her room at a posh beachfront hotel. Charlie, who is present to speak at a rotary convention, must now look into the mysterious murder.

The Honolulu filming adds considerably to the overall exotic look and feel of the film. While the film is frequently praised as one of the best pictures in the series—and it is a very good little mystery—the annoying, frequent reappearances of Chan's bumbling assistant Kashimo (Otto Yamaoka) soon grate on the viewer and pull down every scene that he enters. Also, there is a plot hole that is also hard to ignore. Part of the resolution of the murder plot concerns the close resemblance between the earlier murdered actor and one of the suspects—most of whom knew the dead actor. If I had been one of the suspects, I would have pointed out the one who looked like the murdered actor. Unfortunately, nobody does.

Charlie Chan's Chance (Fox, 1932) 73m.

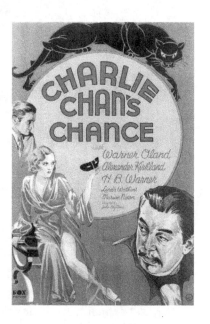

Producer: Joseph H. August, Director: John G. Blystone, Screenplay: Barry Conners, Philip Klein, based on the novel *Behind That Curtain* by Earl Derr Biggers.

CAST: Warner Oland; Alexander Kirkland; H. B. Warner; Marian Nixon; Linda Watkins; James Kirkwood; Ralph Morgan; James Todd; Herbert Bunston; James Wang; Joe Brown; Charles McNaughton; Edward Peil, Sr.; William P. Carleton; Thomas A. Curran; Tom Kennedy.

The soft-spoken and sagacious Chinese sleuth, Charlie Chan, again proves himself to be the king-pin of criminologists in the current film. –NY Times

PLOT/COMMENT: *Charlie Chan's Chance* is the second of the lost Chan films. The screenplay is loosely based on Biggers' *Behind That Curtain*, which was produced three years previously as an early sound film with Charlie (E. L. Park) only showing up for a couple of minutes at the end of the film. *Charlie Chan's Chance* would later have elements taken from it for the 1940 Sidney Toler Chan film *Murder Over New York*.

At one point Charlie is the intended murder victim in this film, and only by the chance intervention of a cat does Charlie avoid death. The film critic for the *New York Times* covered it this way in the January 23, 1932, edition, an excerpt of which follows:

Although this tale is somewhat confused, it has the virtue of a very pleasant time with Charlie Chan. In it there are some ingenious scenes, particularly one in which a vengeful Oriental hopes to kill Charlie Chan but is foiled by a cat. It is through observing a dead cat in the room that Chan decides that Sir Lionel has been slain. The physician declares it to be a case of heart disease and the observant Mr. Chan desires to know who or what stopped the heart.

The murder takes place in New York at a time when Chan was expecting to leave for his Honolulu home, into which had come another son, his eleventh child. There is the girl who confesses to having broken a necklace of pearls while on a stairway in the building in which Sir Lionel met his death, and then Chan has the happy idea of looking into an inkwell and is rewarded by finding a single pearl [one of the incidents later in *Murder Over New York*]. This might be called a link in the evidence, but it offers Chan more information than it does anybody else. Assuredly, in the course of his work on the crime, he has some very good luck.

No Charlie Chan film is complete without its romance, and it stands to reason that for a while the personable young man, known here as John Douglas, must be suspected of the crime. Here there is also a masked dancer named Shirley Marlowe, impersonated by Marian Nixon, who is quite fond of Douglas. The criminals, who snuff out lives by gas bombs, try to kill Shirley, but she escapes through sending her chauffeur on an errand, and he, poor fellow, is a victim of the murderous crew.

As in the book, Chan goes about finding the main criminal by rather shrewd means. This results in suspense, for there are several characters on whom one has an eye during the proceedings. For instance, Garrick Enderly, who treats his wife harshly and, because he says "Bah!" to everything, is likened to a sheep by Chan. The Chinese sleuth is not in the least troubled by Enderly, but others are.

H. B. Warner is efficient as a Scotland Yard inspector. James Kirkwood, another old favorite, handles the American police work. Herbert Bunston is capital as the excitable Enderly. Edward Peil, Sr. strikes one as having but little conception of a Chinese in his role of one Li Gung. Linda Watkins is the girl who arouses suspicion by breaking her necklace. But Warner Oland is the mainstay of this picture.

Charlie Chan's Greatest Case (Fox, 1933) 71m.

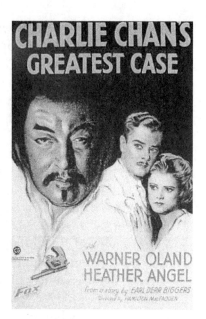

Director: Hamilton MacFadden, Screenplay: Lester Cole, Marion Orth, based on the novel *The House without a Key* by Earl Derr Biggers.

CAST: Warner Oland; Heather Angel; Roger Imhof; John Warburton; Walter Byron; Ivan F. Simpson; Virginia Cherrill; Francis Ford; Robert Warwick; Frank McGlynn, Sr.; Clara Blandick; Claude King; William Stack; Gloria Roy; Cornelius Keefe; Frances Chan; Alan Dong; David Dong; Frank Dong.

Always polite and using the word "most" in every other sentence, he [Charlie Chan] eventually shows that he has noticed a great deal more than one thinks. –NY Times

PLOT/COMMENT: All of the lost films, this being another of the four, are based on the Earl Derr Biggers novels and not on original screenplays. This Chan episode is based on the first Derr Biggers novel, *The House without a Key*, and from what little we can deduce from available reviews written at the time, follows the original novel better than most of the films. Again, lacking the actual film as a reference point, I'll defer to an excerpt from the *New York Times* review of October 7, 1933:

Chan enters the picture owning a ramshackle flivver and leaves it in an expensive car, which is a gift for the work he has done meanwhile. Here he is not called upon to leave his wife and seven children, for the murders are committed in his habitat, Honolulu. He may be a sound sleeper, which is revealed by the fact that the constant ringing of the telephone does not awaken him for some time. But when he starts to work on a crime, even though he may seem slow, he overlooks nothing.

As far as the mystery of these particular murders is concerned, it is not difficult for the audience to decide on the identity of the slayer, but the manner in which Chan makes his deductions is always interesting. When something is said about his easygoing manner, this wise Chinese declares that haste is only necessary when withdrawing one's hand from a tiger's mouth or when catching a flea. He hazards that theories are like fingerprints—"everybody had them. Only facts and motives lead to a murderer." He also says he cannot hasten and adds that a cat which tries to catch two mice at one time goes without supper.

The murdered men are Dan and Amos Winterslip, and judging by the number of persons who smoke a certain brand of cigarettes, many individuals had a part in the crime. But Chan in his leisurely fashion puts two and two together.

The cast is composed of popular leading and character actors of the period along with several children who play Charlie's offspring. Francis Ford, John Ford's older brother, would show up in several of the Chan films over the years and is Captain Hallett in this episode. Frances Chan plays the youngest Chan daughter, and three brothers, Alan, David, and Frank Dong, play three Chan sons in the film.

Charlie Chan's Courage (Fox, 1934) 71m.

Director: George Hadden, Eugene Forde, Screenplay: Seton I Miller, based on the novel *The Chinese Parrot* by Earl Derr Biggers.

CAST: Warner Oland, Drue Leyton, Donald Woods, Paul Harvey, Murray Kinnell, Reginald Mason, Virginia Hammond, Si Jenks, Harvey Clark, Jerry Jerome, Jack Carter, James Wang, DeWitt Jennings, Francis Ford, Lucille Miller, Mary MacLaren, Gail Kay, Larry Fisher, Paul Hurst.

Just why this film should have been called "Charlie Chan's Courage" is as great a mystery as that which he succeeds in solving during the course of the story. Chan, as usual, is not so much courageous as cautious. As he remarks, "Hen squats with caution on thin egg." – F.S.N. *NY Times*

PLOT/COMMENT: This is the last of the four lost films in the Chan series and again is based on an Earl Derr Biggers novel, *The Chinese Parrot*. The *Variety* critic at the time found the proceedings a bit slow, a criticism that percolated among critics and patrons about a number of these early Chan episodes. The title of the novel would have worked better in this instance since Charlie showed courage in all of his films, but this was a frequent happenstance with many movie series entries of the thirties and forties: *After Midnight with Boston Blackie*, *The Gay Falcon*, *Crime Doctor's Warning*, and *The Lone Wolf Strikes*. These are all generic titles that could be swapped around from series to series with their main point being to get the detective's name in the title; everything else was incidental.

So for one final time I defer to an excerpt of the *New York Times* review of August 25, 1934, to provide some comments on this film that we will likely never get to see.

There is a $300,000 pearl necklace which has been sold to a gruff financier. The seller is a woman for whom Chan worked, years before, as a houseboy. Charlie brings the pearls from Honolulu and is commissioned to deliver them to the buyer at his lonely desert ranch house.

"Large sugar bowl tempts many flies," remarks Chan as young Bob Crawford (Donald Woods) reports that he has been followed. Crawford volunteers to proceed to the ranch house ahead of Chan to get the lay of the land. He meets the traditional young woman during the journey and arrives at the ranch just in time to hear the report of two shots.

Mystery mounts upon mystery during the course of the next forty-five minutes. A Chinese Parrot, which may have seen too much and talked too freely, is done to death. A harmless old servant is killed. There is an abundance of suggestion that more dirty work may be done at the cross-roads.

Through the smoke and fire Chan prowls about, finding clues here and shedding proverbs there. "Hunting needle in haystack only requires careful inspection of hay," he decides. "Anxious man hurries too fast, often stubs big toe," he pronounces. But, for the sake of the record, credit for the solution must go to the young man and his young woman. Chan merely supplies the finishing touches.

As may be inferred, "Charlie Chan's Courage" is a good baffler, with Mr. Oland keeping faith with his public.

And now we move unfettered to the Charlie Chan films which have not been lost, and we can hope that in the dark recesses of some old barn in Poughkeepsie—maybe under a burlap bag and an empty box of Gummy Bears—the missing films will suddenly turn up, and we Chan film aficionados will rejoice.

Charlie Chan in London (Fox, 1934) 79m.

Producer: John Stone, Director: Eugene Forde, Screenplay: Phillip MacDonald.

CAST: Warner Oland, Drue Leyton, Raymond Milland, Mona Barrie, Douglas Walton, Alan Mowbray, George Barraud, Paul England, Madge Bellamy, Walter Johnson, Murray Kinnell, E. E. Clive, Elsa Buchanan, Reginald Sheffield, Perry Ivins, John Rogers, Helena Grant, C. Monague Shaw, Phyllis Coghlan, David Torrence, Claude King, Mary Gordon.

Warner Oland is clearly at the top of his game here as he attempts to save an innocent man from the gallows with only hours to spare. Really well done and a must for a Chan fan. –pbalos

PLOT/COMMENT: Young socialite Pamela Gray (Drue Leyton) is distraught over the fact that her brother Paul (Douglas Walton) has been convicted of the murder of a weapon's inventor and is scheduled to be hanged in only a few days. To make matters even worse, the lawyer who defended her brother, Neil Howard (Raymond Milland), is Pamela's fiancé—and he deep down feels that Paul is guilty. Pamela desperately seeks out Charlie Chan, who happens to be in London, and pleads with him to take the case—and, of course, he agrees and eventually finds the real culprit.

This is a taut little mystery that, thankfully, does not have the bumbling, comic distractions of an assistant such as Kashimo (as in the earlier *Black Camel*). The script stays focused on resolving the mystery of who really committed the murder. The production values (sets, costuming, editing, and camerawork) suggest a larger budget than was usually afforded a Chan picture. This is especially evident in the number of extras, horses, and dogs that were employed for the well-staged fox hunt scene. As with many pictures of this early sound era, the acting is played a bit broadly and in an overly dramatic manner, especially by leading lady Drue Leyton. Future Academy Award-winner Ray Milland (still billed as Raymond at this time) has the rather thankless role of the ineffectual lawyer/fiancé. The film benefits from the performances of such talented English character actors as Alan Mowbray, Paul England, and E. E. Clive. Clive, as the none-too-swift Detective Sergeant Thacker, lends some gentle humor to the proceeding without getting too much in the way. Viewers will immediately remember him from such films as *The Invisible Man* and *Bride of Frankenstein*. Overall, this is a very good entry in the Chan series.

Charlie Chan in Paris (Fox, 1935) 72m.

Producer: John Stone, Sol M. Wurtzel, Director: Lewis Seiler and Hamilton MacFadden (first week's shooting only), Screenplay: Edward T. Lowe and Stuart Anthony and based on a story by Philip MacDonald.

CAST: Warner Oland, Mary Brian, Thomas Beck, John Miljan, Erik Rhodes, Murray Kinnell, Minor Watson, John Qualen, Keye Luke, Henry Kolker, Dorothy Appleby, Ruth Peterson, Perry Ivins, Eddie Vitch, Lynn Bari, Harry Cording, Gino Corrado, Martin Faust, Richard Kipling, Wilfred Lucas, Paul McVey, Rolfe Sedan, August Tollaire.

All the great fictional gumshoes suffer from a curious weakness. They never begin to function on all six until someone has been assassinated. – NY Times

PLOT/COMMENT: Charlie arrives in Paris supposedly for a vacation, but we soon learn that he is there on business. It seems some English investors have sent him to Paris to investigate the possibility that certain French bonds from the highly respected Lamartine Bank are forgeries. Soon after his arrival Charlie's female contact in Paris, an Apache dancer named Nardi (Dorothy Appleby), is murdered. Then later a bank official is also murdered, and the bank president's daughter, Yvette (Mary Brian), is accused of the murder. Through all of this turmoil, a mysterious and troublesome beggar on crutches named Xavier weaves his presence in and out of the situations that arise and eventually becomes the number one suspect. Charlie is assisted by his college-educated son Lee (Keye Luke), who is in Europe on personal business and takes a side trip to Paris hoping to vacation with his Pop. Lee soon finds himself involved with the murder case.

Like the previous film this episode is also a swift-moving little mystery with a plot that is intricate but never loses the viewer along the way. When at the conclusion Charlie explains to the police official what clues led him to the murderer, the director wisely does the recap visually to help the viewer recall the specific scenes where the clues were dropped. This was the first appearance of Keye Luke as son Lee, and the boy actually helps his old man rather than just getting in the way—as would frequently be the case in some of the later episodes. The cast includes some excellent character actors who lend weight to the characters in the plot. Among them are Minor Watson as the police inspector, John Qualen as the hotel concierge, and Erik Rhodes as a frequently intoxicated sketch artist. Rhodes appeared notably in a couple of Astaire/Rogers musicals and other films during this era, frequently as a comic cuckold. Production values are first rate as usual for these early Charlie Chan pictures, even though they were considered low-budget affairs by the Fox Company.

———

KEYE LUKE (1904-1991) played the role of Number One Son Lee in eight of the Oland films, only leaving the series upon the death of Oland in 1938. He would return to the role in 1948 for the last two Chan films starring Roland Winters. Luke is probably most remembered for his performance as Lee Chan, but he had a long and successful career beyond the confines of that one role.

Warner Oland and Keye Luke portrayed father and son in eight Chan films. Keye Luke first appeared as Number One Son Lee Chan in *Charlie Chan in Paris*.

Luke was born in Gjuangzhou, China, to a father who ran an art shop. Early on the family moved to Seattle, Washington, where he received most of his education. A natural artist and possessing a love of art, Luke got a foothold in the Hollywood scene through his artwork, little envisioning an acting career. He entered the movie business as a commercial artist designing posters and other advertising materials—he worked on the artwork for the original *King Kong* pressbook. Then his ability as a muralist led him to painting several of the murals at Grauman's Chinese Theater in Hollywood, and in later years he did murals for several major big-budget films, including *The Shanghai Gesture* (1941) with Gene Tierney and Walter Huston and *Macao* (1952) with Robert Mitchum and Jane Russell. Because of his Chinese heritage he was asked to be technical advisor on a number of Asian-themed films, and this led to his entrance in films as an actor where he made his uncredited debut in *The Painted Veil* (1934) with Greta Garbo. (Interestingly, Warner Oland was also in the cast.)

From that point on Luke became the go-to young Asian actor when such roles became available—and the first one, right after *The Painted Veil*, was Lee Chan in *Charlie Chan in Paris*. From 1935 through 1938, between production of the eight films in which he played Lee Chan, Keye Luke was kept busy in other films such as *Mad Love* (1935) playing the assistant to Peter Lorre's "Dr. Gogol" prior to Lorre's becoming Mr. Moto in films, *The Good Earth* (1937) with Paul Muni, and *International Settlement* (1938) with Dolores del Rio. With the death of Warner Oland, Keye Luke played Lee Chan in the reworked Chan film now Mr. Moto film, *Mr. Moto's Gamble* (1938), and then retired from the role until the two 1948 Roland Winters Chan films.

A highlight of his later acting career in the 1940s included the on-going role of Dr. Lee Wong Howe in the Dr. Gillespie film series at MGM starring Lionel Barrymore. In the 1950s Luke added television roles to his résumé, playing guest roles in many of the popular television series of the day. In the late 1950s he created the role of Master Wang in the original Broadway production of Rodgers and Hammerstein's hit musical *Flower Drum Song*. Luke played the role for two years on Broadway and then toured with the show for another two years, never missing a performance.

Luke increased his television acting agenda in the early 1970s with guest roles in many programs and continuing roles in three series: *Kung Fu* (1972) as Master Po for forty-four episodes, *Anna and the King* (1972) as Kralahome for thirteen episodes, and playing Charlie Chan in fourteen episodes in the animated Saturday morning kids' show *The Amazing Chan and the Chan Clan* (1972), making the first time that a Chinese actor had played the role. It was reported that George Lucas considered Luke seriously for the Obi-Wan Kenobi role in *Star Wars*.

Luke continued to take acting roles in films and television well into his eighties. His last two appearances were featured roles in the films *Gremlins 2: The New Batch* (1990) and the Woody Allen comedy *Alice* (1990). Keye Luke died of a stroke on January 12, 1991.

Charlie Chan in Egypt (Fox, 1935) 72m.

Producer: Edward T. Lowe, Director: Louis King, Screenplay: Robert Ellis and Helen Logan.

CAST: Warner Oland, Pat Paterson, Thomas Beck, Rita Hayworth, Stepin Fetchit, Jameson Thomas, Frank Conroy, Nigel De Brulier, Paul Porcasi, Arthur Stone, James Eagles, Frank Reicher, George Irving, Anita Brown, John Davidson, John George, Gloria Roy.

The latest adventure out of Charlie Chan's casebook lifts the sage of Honolulu several notches above the Philo Vances and the Perry Masons. – NY Times

PLOT/COMMENT: Charlie finds himself in Egypt at the behest of the French Archeological Society to investigate the smuggling of excavated treasures from the opened tomb of High Priest Ameti that later show up on the antiquities black market. Professor Arnold (George Irving), the head of the expedition that uncovered the tomb, mysteriously disappears but is later found by Charlie in a mummy case with a bullet in his chest. Charlie tries to comfort the professor's grieving daughter Carol (Pat Paterson) and her mentally troubled brother Barry (James Eagles), a violinist, as he conducts his investigation. Among the suspects are Dr. Thurston (Frank Conroy), who Chan finds out knew that certain artifacts were being sold, as he claims, to financially support the project; Tom Evans (Thomas Beck), an archaeologist in love with Carol who was earlier fired by the dead Professor Arnold; Dr. Racine (Jameson Thomas), who has financially supported the project and wants to see a return on his investment; Edfu Ahmed (Nigel De Brulier), a local Egyptian who has objected to the excavation of the tomb; and Snowshoes (Stepin Fetchit), a black American servant who believes that he may be descended from Ameti. Before all is said and done, Carol's brother Barry is mysteriously murdered by a poison gas placed in a glass phial in his violin that breaks when a certain note is played, and Tom Evans is shot but survives while exploring the tomb with Charlie.

The film, while exuding an exotic ambience through the excavations of the tomb and its artifacts; the costuming with pith helmets and white linen suits; and the sets with their Egyptian-styled architecture and etchings, ultimately comes down to a middling, fairly slow-moving entry in the series. Undoubtedly the most troubling aspect of the film for today's audience is the shuffling, drawling, ultra-subservient performance of Stepin Fetchit as "Snowshoes," one of the few working black actors in film at this time but relegated to a then cultural stereotype (even called upon to flash a razor when frightened and bearing the ridiculous character name of "Snowshoes"). Of course, the popular actor was just giving his expected performance, the one that had made him famous, but it had to be demeaning for him even with the solace of picking up a check when he finished. While the film has some intriguing and clever moments (the poison in the glass phial, for instance), it nevertheless is not one of the stellar episodes in the Charlie Chan canon and is, at times, uncomfortable to watch in this day and age.

Charlie Chan in Shanghai
(Fox, 1935) 70m.

Producer: John Stone, Director: James Tinling, Screenplay: Gerard Fairlie and Edward T. Lowe from their story.

CAST: Warner Oland, Irene Hervey, Charles Locher, Russell Hicks, Keye Luke, Halliwell Hobbes, Frederick Vogeding, Neil Fitzgerald, Max Wagner, Harry Strang, Max Wagner, Pat O'Malley, Lynn Bari, Luke Chan, Jack Chefe, Frank Darien, David Torrence, Guy Usher, Joan Woodbury.

It is reasonably safe to predict that the next of the series (there will be a next, of course) will be called "Charlie Chan and Son in Peoria," or wherever the next mystery happens to pop up. –NY Times

PLOT/COMMENT: Considering Charlie Chan's ancestry, it's surprising that this is the only film in which Charlie returns to his homeland—and then only with stock footage. Upon his return to China (with the Fox back lot standing in for the ancient city), Charlie is met by Diana Woodland (Irene Hervey) and Philip Nash (Charles Locher), her boyfriend. Their task is to see that Charlie makes it to a banquet that evening which is being held in his honor and where Diana's father, Sir Stanley Woodland (David Torrence), will be in attendance—and is the man Charlie has come to Shanghai to see. During the celebration he tells Charlie that he needs to see him alone to discuss some activities that are under investigation. Before the meeting can take place, Sir Stanley is shot when he opens a booby-trapped box. Working with Colonel Watkins (Halliwell Hobbes), the Shanghai police commissioner, and an American G-Man named James Andrews (Russell Hicks), who has been sent to Shanghai, Charlie is on the case. Also adding to the mix is Charlie's son Lee (Keye Luke) who (as in *Charlie Chan in London*) explains that he found out that "Pop" was going to Shanghai and since he was on business in Asia, he decided to make a side trip to visit his dad—and he, too, of course, "helps" with the investigation. The evidence soon points to an international opium-smuggling ring that is operating out of Shanghai with the head man of the ring, we learn later, working as an undercover agent right under Charlie's nose.

As usual the production values Fox provided for the Chan series are first rate. Director James Tinling keeps the action flowing, and Fairlie and Lowe's script is suitably gimmicky, thus enabling the mystery aspects to flourish as we examine the clues and seek out the criminal mastermind along with Charlie. Many in the supporting cast are not as well known as we've come to expect in the Chan films. Among the cast is young Charles Locher who soon became Jon Hall to filmgoers in the later 1930s and then starred in "sex and sandal" films in the 1940s with Maria Montez and even later was *Ramar of the Jungle* in the 1950s television series.

Charlie Chan's Secret (Twentieth Century-Fox, 1936) 72 m.

Producer: John Stone, Director: Gordon Wiles, Screenplay: Robert Ellis from a story by Ellis and Helen Logan, Additional dialogue: Joseph Hoffman.

CAST: Warner Oland, Rosina Lawrence, Charles Quigley, Henrietta Crosman, Edward Trevor, Astrid Allwyn, Herbert Mundin, Jonathan Hale, Egon Brecher, Gloria Roy, Ivan Miller, Arthur Edmund Carewe, William

Bailey, Francis Ford, Bud Geary, Chuck Hamilton, James T. Mack, Jerry Miley, Landers Stevens, Brick Sullivan.

There is nothing in it (including Warner Oland) to surprise or disappoint the Chan addict, whose name, apparently, is still legion.
–NY Times

PLOT/COMMENT: A ship sinks off the coast of Honolulu and Allen Colby (Jerry Miley), long missing heir to millions of Colby dollars, is thought to have drowned, but no body is found in the wreckage. Charlie Chan questions whether Colby is really dead and decides he must take the Clipper to San Francisco to confer with Henrietta Lowell (Henrietta Crosman) regarding Colby. The situation is this: If Colby should be alive, Henrietta and her family would lose the Colby inheritance they came into upon his disappearance and would have to make an accounting of the money that has been spent during his long absence. It soon develops that Colby *is* alive and arrives at the old family mansion before Chan can get there. As Colby searches for the caretaker Ulrich (Egon Brecher), a secret panel opens and a knife is thrown, stabbing him in the back. Later that night Henrietta, a devout spiritualist, is having a séance in the Colby house with other family members and their lawyer Warren Phelps (Jonathan Hale) in attendance. The family includes daughter Alice Lowell (Rosina Lawrence) and her fiancé Dick Williams (Charles Quigley), daughter Janice Gage (Astrid Allwyn) and her husband Fred (Edward Trevor). Charlie arrives before the séance and brings them up to date regarding Allen Colby. As Henrietta's spiritual advisors Carlotta (Gloria Roy) and Professor Bowen (Arthur Edmund Carewe) are conducting the séance, the body of Allen Colby suddenly appears, stopping the séance and revealing to Charlie and all those in attendance that a murder has been committed. It's up to Charlie now to find the killer.

The plot contains many of the standard elements that make for a satisfying little mystery: the dark, shadowy, deserted mansion with secret passages and sliding panels; spiritualists conducting a séance in a darkened room with apparitions appearing in ghostly light; characters seeking spiritual guidance and the future through fingers pressed on a Ouija board; a final gathering of the usual suspects for the smart detective to reveal the murderer; and a comic, frightened butler, Baxter (Herbert Mundin), who panics/hyperventilates when anything mysterious or spooky occurs—much in the manner of a Caucasian Mantan Moreland. The director, Gordon Wiles, brings a sense of style and flair to the typical mystery maneuverings and a quick-moving pace that holds the attention. *Charlie Chan's Secret* rates near the top of the Warner Oland episodes.

Charlie Chan at the Circus (Twentieth Century-Fox, 1936) 72m.

Producer: John Stone, Director: Harry Lachman, Screenplay: Robert Ellis and Helen Logan.

CAST: Warner Oland, Keye Luke, George Brasno, Olive Brasno, Francis Ford, Maxine Reiner, John McGuire, Shirley Deane, Paul Stanton, J. Carrol Naish, Boothe Howard, Drue Leyton, Wade Boteler, Shia Jung, Han Hsiang Li, John Aasen, John Dilson, Franklyn Farnum, Faye Lee, Annie Mar, Paul McVey, Richard Ung.

So the Chan family, all 14 of them, go to the circus and wouldn't you know it, the guy who hires Charlie winds up murdered. And Charlie's got a whole circus full of suspects. –bkoganbing

PLOT/COMMENTS: Charlie receives fourteen passes to the circus for his whole brood from circus co-owner Joe Kinney (Paul Stanton). (This is the first time all fourteen family members have shown up on the screen, outside of a photo that is seen in a couple of previous episodes.) Kinney seeks the assistance of the famous sleuth because he has been receiving threatening, anonymous letters. Before Charlie can confer with him, Kinney is strangled in the circus business wagon. Upon investigation it is learned that just about everyone who knew Kinney had a grievance against him: the other co-owner John Gaines (Francis Ford), the Hindu snake charmer Tom

Charlie, Mrs. Chan, and the whole Chan clan went to the circus.

Holt (J. Carrol Naish), the show animal trainer Hal Blake (John McGuire), his jealous wife Nellie Farrell (Drue Leyton), and an assortment of other circus hangers-on who had it in for Kinney in one way or another—including the ape Caesar who has been beaten by Kinney.

The circus setting makes for a fascinating backdrop for this Charlie Chan adventure—the circus performers and the animals going about their daily routine and the staging of actual circus shows makes for considerable audience enjoyment. The episode was filmed in January of 1936 while the real Barnes Circus was in winter quarters, and some of their performers doubled for cast members during the filming, especially for the high-wire acrobatic shots. The brother and sister "little people" team of George and Olive Brasno perform a delightful and entertaining dance as one of the sideshow attractions at the circus and then contribute to the plot as they assist Charlie and son Lee in the search for evidence.

As in most of the Chan pictures, outstanding character actors are utilized that give the production a depth and flair that many other lower-budgeted films do not have. In this episode the former silent film director, actor, and older brother of John Ford, Francis Ford, offers a well-rounded portrait of the circus co-owner who has a caring and compassionate manner with his big top performers. J. Carrol Naish, known for playing just about every ethnic type, plays a Hindu snake charmer and general roustabout—at once warm and appealing and then an angry malcontent. Twenty-one years later Naish would himself become Charlie Chan in the 1957 television series, *The New Adventures of Charlie Chan.*

Many fans of the Charlie Chan/Warner Oland films feel that the series hit its stride with this film and continued at this high level of production and performance until the death of Oland in 1938. Certainly, *Charlie Chan at the Circus* is one of the most charming and intriguing of the entire series.

Charlie Chan at the Race Track (Twentieth Century-Fox, 1936) 70m.

Associate Producer: John Stone, Director: H. Bruce Humberstone, Screenplay: Robert Ellis, Helen Logan, Edward T. Lowe from a story by Lou Breslow, Saul Elkins.

CAST: Warner Oland; Keye Luke; Helen Wood; Thomas Beck; Alan Dinehart; Gavin Muir, Gloria Roy; Jonathan Hale; G. P. Huntley; George Irving; Frank Coghlan, Jr.; Frankie Darro; John Rogers; John Henry Allen; Harry Jans; Paul Fox; Sam Flint.

...the film follows Hollywood's latest adaptation from Greek trag-edy, dictated for all we know by the Hays office, of having its mur-ders done offstage somewhere. – NY Times

PLOT/COMMENT: A race horse named Avalanche and owned by Major Gordon Kent (George Irving) is given to George Chester (Alan Dinehart) at the time of his wedding to Kent's daughter Catherine (Gloria Roy). When the horse races in the Melbourne Sweepstakes, it is disquali-fied because jockey "Tip" Collins (Frankie Darro) fouls another horse in the race. Kent, convinced that the foul was deliberate and that a gambling ring is responsible for the loss, plans to seek legal help in going after the racetrack fixers when he returns to America.

On the ship back to the United States, Kent is found dead in Ava-lanche's stall. At first thought to be an accident, Charlie Chan, brought onto the case in Honolulu, establishes that it is murder and, with son Lee, continues on the voyage back to Los Angeles where the horse is scheduled to race again. Among the suspects are son-in-law Chester; a fellow horse owner and friend of Chester and the late Major Kent, Warren Fenton (Jon-athan Hale); a gambler named Denny Barton (G. P. Huntley, Jr.); Kent's male secretary Bruce Rogers (Thomas Beck), who is in love with Fenton's daughter Alice (Helen Wood); and horse trainer Badley (Gavin Muir).

Charlie suspects that during a small fire in the stable portion of the ship, Avalanche and another race horse, Gallant Lad, are switched by opera-tors from the gambling ring in an attempt to fix the odds for the upcom-ing Santa Juanita [Anita] race in California—a white star on one horse is disguised by paint and the reverse is done on the other horse, otherwise the horses are identical in conformation. Charlie has his hands full un-disguising the two horses and returning them to their proper stalls before the race and then revealing the murderer of Major Kent before the final credits.

Charlie Chan at the Race Track has a huge cast for a film of its type. In addition to the credited cast members, there are forty-nine uncredited members—some of them well-known actors such as Paul Fix, James Flavin, and Sam Flint. Director H. Bruce Humberstone even appears briefly in one scene as a gambler. The film is an excellent episode in the Chan series: fast moving, exciting, and sufficiently complex in the mystery department so that the viewer is enticed to pay close attention.

The picked up pace of the Chan plots starting with the previous film, *Charlie Chan at the Circus,* is very evident—and welcome. Director Humberstone uses an editing device, a sweeping pan from scene to scene, during the last portion of the film that gives added pace to the climactic scenes. One weakness in the plot is the horse switching bit. As one who has owned horses will tell you, there is more than just a physical marking that identifies a horse. No trainer who has worked with a particular horse would confuse him for another horse.

This is Thomas Beck's third appearance in a Chan film; he will make two more during the Oland series. Beck acknowledged that part of the reason for so many roles in Oland's films was the fact that the two of them got on well off camera and enjoyed each other's company. It was also thought that Beck's distraction kept Oland from imbibing too much during the filming.

Charlie Chan at the Opera (Twentieth Century-Fox, 1936) 70m.

Associate Producer: John Stone, Director: H. Bruce Humberstone, Screenplay: Charles Belden and Scott Darling from a story by Bess Meredyth.

CAST: Warner Oland, Boris Karloff, Keye Luke, William Demarest, Guy Usher, Margaret Irving, Gregory Gaye, Nedda Harrigan, Charlotte Henry, Thomas Beck, Maurice Cass, Tom McGuire, Stanley Blystone, Benson Fong, Tudor Williams, Joan Woodbury.

The movie is a very accomplished piece of work. Its theatre and backstage atmosphere give it a feeling of a show within a show, and it's a pretty good one whichever way you look at it. –telegonus

PLOT/COMMENT: Gravelle (Boris Karloff), a former operatic star believed to be dead as a result of a theatre fire years before when he was locked in his dressing room, is now an anonymous resident of the Rockland State Sanitarium, insane and suffering from amnesia. He regains his memory upon seeing a newspaper report that the opera *Carnival* is opening that evening in Los Angeles with his former costar Mme. Lili Rochelle (Margaret Irving) and baritone Enrico Borelli (Gregory Gaye), either or both of whom he suspects of locking his dressing room door that fateful night. Gravelle overpowers his guard and escapes. In an aside situation, Lili Rochelle has been receiving anonymous threatening letters and has gone to the police. Who could be sending the letters? We soon discover that Lili's husband (Frank Conroy) is annoyed by the attention playboy Borelli is showing Lili and that Borelli's wife Lucretia (Nedda Harrigan) is also angry and jealous of her husband's suspected affair with Lili. The insane Gravelle, seeking revenge, sneaks into the theatre and steals one of Borelli's costumes and informs him that he is taking over the role for this performance.

Charlie and Lee get involved when they visit old friend Inspector Regan (Guy Usher) prior to taking a ship back to Honolulu and hear about the threatening letters. It is then that they meet Sergeant Kelly (William Demarest), a stereotypical dimwitted, and in this case, racist cop who takes an immediate dislike to the Chinese detective and his son. To provide Lili with some protection, it is decided that the theatre will be surrounded by cops and that Regan, Kelly, Charlie, and Lee will be backstage during the performance to keep an eye on things. Needless to say, the opera debut that evening is fraught with intrigue and, eventually, murder. The stage manager (Maurice Cass) delivers an inside-joke line that the opera "will go on even if Frankenstein walks in!" By the end of the first act, Mme. Lili and baritone Borelli have been murdered, stabbed with the knife that is part of Borelli's costume. Now Charlie goes to work to discover if the obvious suspect, the insane Gravelle, is the murderer or if it is someone else taking advantage of Gravelle's presence.

This is another Chan episode where the studio spent money freely to get an outstanding product, using some leftover sets from *Café Metropole* (1937 starring Tyrone Power and Loretta Young) for the opera scenes, commissioning Oscar Levant to write the music for the opera, and again employing a very large cast to tell the story—forty-four uncredited cast members beyond those listed in the credits.

Playing on Karloff's star power in horror films, the above-the-title credits proclaim, Charlie Chan *vs.* Boris Karloff in *Charlie Chan at the Opera*, as if it were an encounter much like Frankenstein meets the Wolf Man, a to-the-death struggle! Karloff's very theatrical—almost over the top "creepy"—performance as the insane opera singer gives the episode a mystery/horror film feeling that was not typical of the Chan series, but works well here. William Demarest, a top character actor at the time (and years later Uncle Charlie on *My Three Sons*), provides most of the comedy for the film, some of it slapstick and some a bit racist as when he refers to Charlie as "Chop Suey." Many moviegoers were surprised by the operatic voice that Boris Karloff displayed in the film. In reality, he was pantomiming to the voice of singer Tudor Williams. The film is considered by many to be the best in the entire Chan series and, despite its convoluted plot, certainly does deliver the mystery and entertainment goods during its seventy-minute running time.

Charlie Chan at the Olympics (Twentieth Century-Fox, 1937) 71m.

Associate Producer: John Stone, Director: H. Bruce Humberstone, Screenplay: Robert Ellis and Helen Logan from a story by Paul Burger.

CAST: Warner Oland; Katherine DeMille; Pauline Moore; Allan Lane; Keye Luke; C. Henry Gordon; John Eldredge; Layne Tom, Jr.; Jonathan Hale; Morgan Wallace; Fredrik Vogeding; Andrew Tombes; Arno Frey; David Horsley; Howard C. Hickman.

Stock footage of the dirigible Hindenburg was retouched, frame by frame, to blot out the swastikas emblazoned on the airship's tail.
–IMDb

PLOT/COMMENT: The story begins with the theft of a military guidance system that allows a plane to be flown by remote control without a pilot. Chan becomes involved when the pilot controlling the test plane is murdered. The search for the murderer and the missing device takes Charlie halfway around the world—from Honolulu to San Francisco to New York and then on the dirigible Hindenburg to Berlin where the 1936 Olympics is being held and son Lee is a member of the American swim team. If the remote control device should fall into enemy hands (never identified, but we *are* in Berlin) the result could be disastrous in a war situation.

Among the suspects Charlie has to deal with are the inventor Mr. Cartwright (John Eldredge); his business partner Mr. Hopkins (Jonathan Hale); war profiteer Arthur Hughes (C. Henry Gordon); a mysterious adventuress named Yvonne Roland (Katherine DeMille), who may just be trying to lure Olympic athlete and romantic interest Richard Masters (Allan Lane) from Betty Adams (Pauline Moore) or may be a Mata Hari working for Charles Zaraka (Morgan Wallace), a ruthless foreign agent. Once Charlie gets to Berlin, he has the assistance of Police Inspector Strasser (Fredrik Vogeding), a none-too-smart but dedicated officer who is proud of the efficiency of his German police. Whenever there is some mishap in the proceedings, he declares with Germanic passion, "Ziss kind of thing cannot happen in BERLIN!!"

This is a very different type of Charlie Chan film. Usually there is a murder of a prominent person during the first few minutes and Charlie begins his investigation to determine the killer. In this case there are two murders that take place off camera and the victims are the pilot and the man who hijacked the plane carrying the remote control device, two men whom we have only seen for a few moments and who are not mentioned again for much of the film. The script seems to be saying it's too bad they got murdered, but the most important thing is to find the remote control device before it falls into enemy hands! So the bulk of the story concerns Charlie's search for the remote control device—an Alfred Hitchcock "McGuffin" in that it pushes the story along, helps build suspense, and once Charlie gets it back, is of no further consequence to the story.

During the early part of the film when Charlie is still in Honolulu, we meet Charlie Chan, Jr. as played by Layne Tom, Jr. The delightful child actor was ten years old when this film was made, and he would appear in two more Chan films: *Charlie Chan in Honolulu*, where he would be

Number Five Son Tommy, and *Charlie Chan's Murder Cruise*, where he would play Number Seven Son Willie. Interestingly, in an interview for a filmed featurette for the DVD release of *Charlie Chan at the Olympics*, Layne Tom refers to his role in *at the Olympics* as playing Number Three Son, but Charlie in the film clearly identifies him as Number Two Son Charlie, Jr.—leaving later Number Two Son Jimmy (Victor Sen Yung) somewhere in limbo. But then, in the TV series *The New Adventures of Charlie Chan* with J. Carrol Naish, he has Number One Son Barry with him. It's too bad that over the years the scriptwriters did not do some checking on the genealogy of Mr. Chan and family.

This would be the last of the three Charlie Chan films directed by H. Bruce Humberstone, and the series would quickly miss him. *Charlie Chan at the Race Track, at the Opera,* and *at the Olympics* are generally considered the best of the Chan films, fast-paced episodes with none of the stodginess that had encroached on the series prior to his arrival. He reinvigorated the series and, according to Keye Luke and others who worked with him, Humberstone was a perfectionist who demanded the best out of his cast and crew.

There is a bit of inside-the-studio promotion for those who look closely and quickly during a scene on the dirigible Hindenburg. While Charlie and Mr. Hopkins are talking, Mr. Cartwright (John Eldredge) is looking at a magazine. As he turns a page, we see momentarily that the story in the magazine (it had to be the *Saturday Evening Post*) is "Think Fast, Mr. Moto" by John P. Marquand, the movie version of which was about to be filmed on the Twentieth Century-Fox lot with Peter Lorre.

Charlie Chan on Broadway (Twentieth Century-Fox, 1937) 68m.

Producer: John Stone, Director: Eugene Forde, Screenplay: Charles S. Belden, Jerome Cady from a story by Art Arthur, Robert Ellis, Helen Logan.

CAST: Warner Oland; Keye Luke; Joan Marsh; J. Edward Bromberg; Douglas Fowley; Harold Huber; Donald Woods; Louise Henry; Joan Woodbury; Leon Ames; Marc Lawrence; Toshia Mori; Charles Williams; Eugene Borden; Lon Chaney, Jr.; James Flavin; Robert Lowery.

The hunt is on for a missing diary that could blow the lid off the mobs. Loads of fun! – admjtk1701

PLOT/COMMENT: Mob girlfriend Billie Bronson (Louise Henry) returns from an enforced exile in Europe with plans to blackmail her former lover Johnny Burke (Douglas Fowley), owner of the Hottentot Club, with a diary packed with "enough information on the rackets and politics to blow this whole town higher than a kite." Charlie and Lee briefly meet Billie on shipboard as they are returning, presumably from the Olympics, and Billie, afraid that someone may try to steal the diary, hides it in Charlie's luggage.

Billie has plans to sell the diary to newspaper editor Murdock (J. Edward Bromberg) of the *New York Bulletin*. Ace reporter Speed Patten (Donald Woods) and photographer Joan Wendell (Joan Marsh) of the *Bulletin* go to the Hottentot Club in hopes of getting an exclusive story and photos when Billie shows up there. Billie has an encounter with Burke and his current flame Marie Collins (Joan Woodbury) and then shortly thereafter is found dead in Burke's office.

While Charlie is enjoying a banquet in his honor given by the New York Police Department, news arrives of Billie's murder. With that, Charlie is on the case, assisting hyper Chief Inspector James Nelson (Harold Huber). During the investigation it soon becomes apparent that the diary is missing, and Lee suspects that it might be in their hotel room because Lee had seen Billie trying to get into their room. When Charlie and the Inspector arrive at the hotel, they find the body of Thomas Mitchell (Marc Lawrence), a gangland figure who has also been after the diary. With two murders to solve and a diary to be found, Charlie has a busy time during his short stay in New York.

It has been said that this Charlie Chan episode plays like a Warner Bros. gangster picture, and there's some truth in that. It certainly is fast paced with a production design that features the Hottentot pseudo-sophisticated night spot that's brimming with gangster and gun-moll types for our delectation. Douglas Fowley as low-life Johnny Burke is just barely beyond a "dees, does, and dem" vocabulary in his verbal exchanges with Charlie and the law and is delightful, as usual. Many seem to find Harold Huber over the top and annoying in his role of Inspector Nelson, but the powers that be at the studio apparently liked him enough to recast him in the next Chan film in basically the same role only French—and there he is definitely irritating.

The title of the film is something of a misnomer in that the script has nothing to do with Broadway theatre, and the under-the-credits music of "Give My Regards to Broadway" adds to that expectation. A better title would have been *Charlie Chan in New York City*, but there is little in the plot to even nail it to the Big Apple; it could just as easily have taken place in Chicago or Philadelphia. The film may not be up to the level of the three previous films directed by H. Bruce Humberstone, and the script may be more loosely wrapped, but it's still a pleasing entry in the series.

Charlie Chan at Monte Carlo (Twentieth Century-Fox, 1937) 71m.

Producer: John Stone, Director: Eugene Forde, Screenplay: Jerry Cady based upon a story by Robert Ellis and Helen Logan.

CAST: Warner Oland, Keye Luke, Virginia Field, Sidney Blackmer, Harold Huber, Kay Linaker, Robert Kent, Edward Raquello, George Lynn,

Louis Mercier, George Davis, John Bleifer, Georges Renavent, George Sorel.

The plot stumbles along and seems to move in aimless directions.
–pbalos

PLOT/COMMENT: Charlie and Lee plan a brief stop in Monte Carlo before they continue on their way to Paris where Lee has a painting that will be on display at an art exhibit. They soon encounter Police Inspector Jules Joubert (Harold Huber) who has never met Charlie but knows his reputation as a detective and desires to spend some time with him. Joubert insists that he show Charlie and son a Monte Carlo casino at which Charlie observes the animosity between two gamblers, Victor Karnoff (Sidney Blackmer) and Paul Savarin (Edward Raquello), who are also business rivals. Later, Charlie and Lee are stranded when the taxi that Joubert has arranged for them breaks down on the road, forcing them to walk. While walking they come upon the murdered body of Karnoff's courier who was delivering a million dollars in bonds for his boss. In addition, the chauffeur's body is found a short distance from the car. These murders are enough to get Charlie on the case

Charlie and Lee return to Monte Carlo where they help Inspector Joubert with the investigation. Soon there is a long line of suspects that include Karnoff himself who stands to collect the insurance money for the bonds; Savarin who would be hurt financially if Karnoff's plan for the bonds was carried out; Karnoff's wife Joan (Kay Linaker) who is being blackmailed by a shady bartender named Al Rogers (George Lynn)—who later on shows up dead with some of the bonds; the beautiful Evelyn Gray (Virginia Field) who drives an expensive car, wears lavish clothes and jewelry, but has no visible means of support; and Gordon Chase (Robert Kent), Karnoff's secretary, who seems to be in love with the high-living Evelyn. Through obvious clues and some that only Charlie discovers (and that aren't revealed to the viewer) the guilty party is soon brought to justice—and Charlie and Lee are off to Paris and the art exhibit.

This was the last of the Warner Oland films, and it is not generally considered among the best of his Chan films. Critics of the film frequently carp about the overblown performance of Harold Huber as the police inspector and that he is a comic distraction at times—and he certainly is, at times. But the film does have a vigor about it that is enticing (partly a result of Huber's exuberant Inspector Joubert), and the plot is one that the viewer can follow through its many ins and outs without too much difficulty. In addition, the production design is elegant in its display of the elaborate casino room, opulent hotel lobby, and the decorous home of Karnoff—all of which give the production a look far beyond its allotted budget. The film is also enhanced by the acting skills of such capable performers as Sidney Blackmer, Kay Linaker, Robert Kent, and the before-mentioned Harold Huber. I think perhaps the critics are a bit too harsh on the film and should give it another viewing.

The Sidney Toler Films for Twentieth Century-Fox

Many moviegoers only remember Sidney Toler (1874-1947) as Charlie Chan and are surprised to learn that he had a long and successful career on Broadway as an actor, director, and playwright before going to Hollywood and costarring with some of filmdom's biggest stars. He was born in Warrensburg, Missouri, but the family soon moved to Wichita, Kansas, where Toler first demonstrated his talent on stage at the age of seven performing in a production of *Tom Sawyer*—at a time when its author Mark Twain was still alive! After spending a brief period of time in college, the restless Toler took off for New York to seek his fortune and over the next few years became associated with several acting companies, playing roles ranging from romantic leads to villains to singing baritone with an operatic company.

Sidney Toler played Charlie Chan in eleven films for Twentieth Century-Fox.

Sidney Toler (his real name, by the way) made his first appearance on Broadway in 1902 in a show entitled *The Office Boy*. Soon he was working with such future stars as Humphrey Bogart, John Barrymore, and Edward G. Robinson. During the early years of the new century until the late 1920s, Toler not only acted in Broadway shows but also had his own stock company of actors and became a successful director and playwright. Bruce Eder states in *All Movie Guide* that one of his shows, *The Man They Left Behind*, became a regional success and was at one time being performed simultaneously by eighteen companies around the country and that two of his plays, *Golden Days* and *The Exile*, were produced on Broadway.

With the arrival of sound in motion pictures in 1929, Toler, now an established stage actor who knew how to "talk," was sought by Hollywood, mainly for supporting roles. His first significant role was that of an Englishman in *Madame X* (1929), directed by Lionel Barrymore and starring Ruth Chatterton and Lewis Stone for MGM. Later films included *Blonde Venus* (1932) with Marlene Dietrich and Cary Grant, *Call of the Wild* (1935) starring Clark Gable and Loretta Young, and *If I Were King* (1938) with Ronald Colman and Basil Rathbone—just before the opportunity to play Charlie Chan arrived.

With the death of Warner Oland in August of 1938, Twentieth Century-Fox was faced with finding a suitable replacement for the popular actor who had made the Charlie Chan series a moneymaker for the studio. It is said that thirty-four actors were auditioned for the role before Toler was selected to carry on the role. Over the next five years he would make eleven Charlie Chan films for the studio, starting with *Charlie Chan in Honolulu* (1938) and concluding with *Castle in the Desert* in 1942. At that point, whether because of World War II and the loss of many film markets outside the United States or just a change in studio policy, Twentieth Century-Fox made a conscious decision to cancel all of its B-picture units at the studio. (Other series affected by this decision included the Jane Withers pictures, the Michael Shayne detective films with Lloyd Nolan and the Cisco Kid adventures with Cesar Romero. Only the Laurel and Hardy pictures continued until 1944.)

Not wanting to leave the character that had become a signature role for him, Toler tried to purchase the screen rights to the character of Charlie Chan. Some confusion exists as to whether Toler succeeded in getting the rights and then taking them to Monogram Pictures or whether Fox sold the rights to Monogram; whatever the case, when the deal was complete, Monogram picked up the series—albeit at a much lower budget per picture—and Sidney Toler continued as Chan. The new series started with *Charlie Chan in the Secret Service* (1944) and continued for eleven features (the same number Toler had completed for Fox) through *The Trap* (1947), completed just a few months before Toler's death. It has been reported that he was so ill during the last two films that he had difficulty walking on the sets. Sidney Toler died on February 12, 1947, of intestinal cancer. He was seventy-two years old.

Charlie Chan in Honolulu (Twentieth Century-Fox, 1938) 67m.

Producer: John Stone, Director: H. Bruce Humberstone, Screenplay: Charles Belden, Chandler Sprague.

CAST: Sidney Toler; Phyllis Brooks; Sen Yung; Eddie Collins; John "Dusty" King; Claire Dodd; George Zucco; Robert Barrat; Marc Lawrence; Richard Lane; Layne Tom, Jr.; Philip Ahn; Paul Harvey; Richard Alexander; David Dong; James Flavin.

It is the usual, red-herring scented, passably diverting mystery film. – NY Times

PLOT/COMMENT: When a murder is committed on the freighter *Susan B. Jennings* in the Honolulu harbor, Charlie Chan is called to action, though his personal thoughts are on the impending birth of his first grandchild in a Honolulu hospital. Charlie soon learns that Judy Hayes (Phyllis Brooks) has been sent by her boss, an attorney in Shanghai, to deliver three hundred thousand dollars in cash to a man who is to meet her in Honolulu. He is to identify himself with a wedding ring. The man arrives at the ship, but before the money can be delivered, he is shot dead.

Charlie begins to interrogate the few passengers who made the trip from Shanghai on the cargo ship. They include the mysterious Dr. Cardigan (George Zucco) who keeps a living human brain in a suitcase in order to conduct experiments on it, a police detective who identifies himself as Detective Joe Arnold (Richard Lane) with the San Francisco Police Department, and his prisoner, murderer Johnny McCoy (Marc Lawrence). In addition, there is Mrs. Carol Wayne (Claire Dodd), a widow whose husband recently died, she says, while she was seeking a divorce from him. She claims to be traveling on the ship just to get away from it all. There is also an odd fellow named Al Hogan (Eddie Collins) who is overseeing a large contingent of wild animals below deck on the ship, all but one of them in cages. Oscar the lion seems to be a personal pet of Hogan's.

Before Charlie's investigation can be concluded, the three hundred thousand dollars disappears from a locked case in Judy's cabin, and Carol Wayne is found strangled to death in Judy's cabin. During all of this intrigue and murder, Captain Johnson (Robert Barrat) and the owner of the ship company are pressuring Charlie and his boss, Inspector Rawlins (Paul Harvey), to let them release the ship so that the cargo goods can be delivered before the shipping company loses too much money. When Charlie calls all of the suspects into the Captain's cabin, you know that justice is on the way.

This first of the Sidney Toler episodes is markedly different from any of the Warner Oland Chan films, even though H. Bruce Humberstone, one of the best directors in the Chan series (*at the Race Track, at the Opera, at the Olympics*), was at the helm. The difference is the amount of comedy that is brought into the plot by the screenwriters and director Humberstone. The first twenty minutes is almost totally comedic as the Chan clan is having breakfast at their home prior to son-in-law Wing Foo (Philip Ahn) arriving at the house to tell the them that his wife (Daughter Number One, Ling) is about to have her baby, causing Charlie and the family, except for Number Two Son Jimmy (Victor Sen Yung) and Number Five Son Tommy (Layne Tom, Jr.), to rush to the hospital. The humor continues as Jimmy, a fledgling detective, gets the call about the murder and hastens to the *Susan B. Jennings* to conduct the investigation under the assumption by everyone (not too bright!) that the young man is really the famous Charlie Chan. By the time Charlie leaves the hospital and gets to the ship, Jimmy has been chased by the free-roving Oscar the lion and is about to be thrown overboard by the ship's crew in what comes close to slapstick humor. Throughout the film there are comic scenes interspersed with serious investigative scenes. Eddie Collins, the actor playing the wild animal overseer Al Hogan, mugs unabashedly throughout every scene he inhabits and there are more scenes than he merits. Much of the episode, in fact, seems to be aimed at a more juvenile audience than the previous Warner Oland pictures.

Regarding the new Charlie Chan, Sidney Toler brings a more vigorous and overtly humorous Chan to the screen (at least in this episode) as compared with Oland. And while he is very polite when speaking to others in that Charlie Chan manner, there is an occasional bite of sarcasm in some of the politeness that makes Toler's Chan less passive than Oland's. During the investigative portions of the film, Toler handles the police work much in the manner and style of Oland. Beyond that, the viewer can make his/her choice of a favorite Chan; they both were certainly fine actors who caught the flavor of the Oriental character they were destined to play—much more so, let's say, than the later Roland Winters and the much later J. Carrol Naish.

Charlie Chan in Reno (Twentieth Century-Fox, 1939) 70m.

Producer: John Stone, Director: Norman Foster, Screenplay: Frances Hyland, Albert Ray, Robert E. Kent from the story "Death Makes a Decree" by Philip Wylie.

CAST: Sidney Toler, Ricardo Cortez, Phyllis Brooks, Slim Summerville, Kane Richmond, Sen Yung, Pauline Moore, Eddie Collins, Kay Linaker, Louise Henry, Robert Lowery, Charles D. Brown, Iris Wong, Morgan Conway, Hamilton MacFadden.

There are more suspects than you could throw a red-herring at…
– NY Times

PLOT/COMMENT: At the time the movie was made Reno was the divorce capital of the United States, and the plot plays upon that point. We immediately meet up with Mary Whitman (Pauline Moore) who is in Reno to get a divorce from her husband Curtis (Kane Richmond). Soon after her arrival at the Hotel Sierra, she encounters boozy, bitchy Jeanne Bentley (Louise Henry) who announces loudly that she plans to marry Curtis as soon as the divorce becomes final. A row ensues and Bentley is asked to leave the hotel by owner Mrs. Russell (Kay Linaker). Later that evening Bentley's maid Choy Wong (Iris Wong) discovers Mary Whitman standing over the dead body of Jeanne Bentley in Bentley's hotel suite. Mary is arrested and held on murder charges by the Reno Sheriff, Tombstone Fletcher (Slim Summerville).

Charlie is brought onto the case at the request of Curtis Whitman because he and his wife Mary have been friends with Charlie in Honolulu, and neither believes that Mary could have committed murder. Charlie agrees to go to Reno with Curtis to see what he can do for Mary. Number Two Son Jimmy, who is a student at USC studying criminology, is on Easter break and decides to join his pop on the case.

Charlie soon has a hotel full of suspects that have reason and/or motive to wish Jeanne dead. Jeanne had broken up the marriage of hotel owner Mrs. Russell five years before. Doctor Ainsley (Ricardo Cortez), the hotel physician, may have been blackmailing Jeanne regarding the death certificate on her previous husband (previously Mrs. Russell's husband). Wally Burke (Robert Lowery) had been rudely dumped by the gold-digging Jeanne on the night she was murdered. Vivian Wells (Phyllis Brooks), the hotel social director, is in love with Doctor Ainsley and feared that Jeanne was on the make for him, too. Finally, there is Jeanne's present husband who she was divorcing at the time she was murdered. Did his hatred cause him to kill her?

This second outing for Sidney Toler and Victor Sen Yung is a nice improvement over *Charlie Chan in Honolulu*. They seem more comfortable in the roles and their interaction—as when Jimmy appears in a police lineup after having been mugged and minus clothes—is a delightfully comic moment in the film. And they actually work together as a team when Jimmy helps his pop identify the murderer in the final moments—and not just in a bumbling manner as is so often the case. Director Norman Foster, who had cut his teeth on the more fast-moving and action-full Mr. Moto films, helms this Chan episode, and his influence can be felt in this film and the next one, *at Treasure Island*, generally acknowledged to be one of the finest Toler films. As usual this Chan film boasts a list of supporting players that adds enormously to the quality of the production: Ricardo Cortez, Phyllis Brooks, Kane Richmond, Eddie Collins, Kay Linaker, Robert Lowery, and even a former Chan director, Hamilton MacFadden (*Charlie Chan Carries On, Black Camel, and Charlie Chan's Greatest Case*).

Slim Summerville's Sheriff Tombstone Fletcher was a special delight in the film when it was released in 1939, and I'm sure it is still funny to many of today's viewers of the film. But times have changed, and I'm not sure that today's audiences are as willing to suspend disbelief and view the comic, bumbling antics of a police officer (or anyone else or especially the Harold Huber lunacy in several other Chan films) that are the antithesis of the way a real person in the real world would behave. Back in the 1930s and '40s, simpler times for sure, audiences had the same fun and enjoyment watching the slapstick, almost moronic behavior of western film sidekicks such as Smiley Burnette or Fuzzy St. John, but today those same antics seem over the top and incongruous to audiences when juxtaposed with the "serious plot" in the rest of the film. I enjoyed Slim Summerville's performance very much, but, of course, I grew up watching "dumb" cops and "goofy" sidekicks in a plethora of detective and western films.

Charlie Chan at Treasure Island (Twentieth Century-Fox, 1939) 59m.

Producer: Edward Kaufman, Director: Norman Foster, Screenplay: John Larkin.

CAST: Sidney Toler, Sen Yung, Cesar Romero, Douglas Fowley, Pauline Moore, Donald MacBride, Wally Vernon, Douglass Dumbrille, Sally Blane, Charles Halton, Billie Seward, June Gale, Trevor Bardette, Louis Jean Heydt, Kay Linaker (uncredited), Gerald Mohr ((uncredited).

With Chan's gumshoeing abilities now well known to film audiences after about 25 episodes, solution is secondary to the story unwinding through maze of weird and spooky episodes. – Variety

PLOT/COMMENT: On a Honolulu Clipper headed for San Francisco and the 1939 World's Fair, Charlie and son Jimmy are present at the sudden death of their friend, writer Paul Essex (Louis Jean Heydt). While the death at first appears to be a suicide, Charlie will have none of it and suspects murder. The clues lead him to a shady spiritualist named Zodiac. Charlie gets help in his investigation of Zodiac from a stage magician named Fred Rhadini (Cesar Romero) who works with a psychic named Eve Cairo (Pauline Moore) and who has been publicly challenging Zodiac to meet him on stage where Rhadini says he will prove that Zodiac is a fake. As usual there are a couple of other murders along the way before Charlie begins to pull the plot strings together and reveals the murderer. It all comes down to the Rhadini/Zodiac confrontation on stage at Treasure Island in San Francisco at the 1939 World's Fair.

Charlie Chan at Treasure Island is almost universally credited with being the best of the Sidney Toler Chan films by fans and critics alike. Director Norman Foster, in his second Chan outing, keeps the film moving briskly through its brief fifty-nine-minute running time, and John Larkin's compact script contains elements that have served mystery plots well over the years: an old, dark house; the supernatural; a séance with visions appearing in the semi-darkness; and a mind reader revealing future events from a crystal ball, just to name a few. The high contrast black-and-white photography also adds a mysterious and spooky quality to the goings-on that sets the appropriate atmosphere for murder. In addition, the film boasts a fine list of character actors who can be counted on to acquit themselves well, people like Cesar Romero, Douglas Fowley, Douglass Dumbrille, Wally Vernon, Louis Jean Heydt, and Donald MacBride as Charlie's police cohort. All of the elements of *Treasure Island* work well, and you get a chance to see some of the 1939 World's Fair. You can't ask for much more!

Charlie Chan in City in Darkness (Twentieth Century-Fox) 75m.

Associate Producer: John Stone, Director: Herbert I. Leeds, Screenplay: Robert Ellis and Helen Logan, based on a play by Ladislaus Fodor and Gina Kaus.

CAST: Sidney Toler; Lynn Bari; Richard Clarke; Harold Huber; Pedro de Cordoba; Dorothy Tree; C. Henry Gordon; Douglass Dumbrille; Noel Madison; Leo G. Carroll; Lon Chaney, Jr.; Louis Mercier; George Davis; Barbara Leonard; Adrienne D'Ambricourt; Frederick Vogeding.

City in Darkness *is decidedly weak in story factors and slow in proceeding through to the eventual finish. It's one of the weakest in the Chan series. –Variety*

PLOT/COMMENT: It's 1939 and a new world war threatens as Charlie is in Paris for a reunion with friends from World War I, including the Prefect of Police, J. Romaine (C. Henry Gordon). When the murder of a prominent industrialist, B. Petroff (Douglass Dumbrille), is discovered, Charlie finds himself participating in the investigation with Marcel Spivak (Harold Huber), the secretary to the Prefect, son of the Bucharest chief of Police, and wannabe detective. A disparate group of suspects is soon rounded up, including locksmith and forger Louis Santelle (Leo G. Carroll); the former secretary of the victim, Tony Madero (Richard Clarke) and his fiancée Marie Dubon (Lynn Bari); a war profiteer and cohort of the victim, Belescu (Noel Madison); Charlotte Ronnell, a foreign agent working with Petroff to get clearance papers for a shipload of munitions going to an unnamed enemy country; and the victim's butler Antoine (Pedro de Cordoba). Charlie does not have the assistance of a son on this case, but he does have to put up with the "assistance" of Marcel Spivak.

Harold Huber strikes again! Making his third appearance in Chan films—previously mucking up the proceedings as police inspectors in *Charlie Chan in Monte Carlo* and *in New York*—he returns in this film, totally out of control and over the top as Marcel. Huber's Marcel so overpowers the plot that Charlie soon becomes a supporting player in the story. Apparently, Huber's performances in the previous films were deemed successful and, thus, his role was strengthened for *City in Darkness*. One critic described Huber's performances as "running wild spouting a lot of nonsense in a loud voice." One has to wonder what first-time Chan director Herbert I. Leeds was thinking in letting a second-lead actor take over the film. And even more puzzling is why veteran Chan screenwriters Robert Ellis and Helen Logan—who were responsible for some of the best Chan films—would not see their error when they created the role.

Beyond the inexplicable dominance of the Huber role, the film opens with an excellent montage of stock footage and voiceover narration that sets the prewar scene in France—blackouts and gas masks, etc.—in preparation for the war with Germany that was on the horizon. This is one of the few Chan films where the murdered man, Petroff, really deserves to be murdered. He is a despicable character who is unconcerned about the suffering victims of war; his only interest is to make a profit. Surprisingly, the role of Petroff—only one brief scene—is performed by Douglass Dumbrille, a highly respected character actor who would be expected to get more screen time in a film.

The mystery aspects are handled with enough clues and shady suspects to keep the plot pot stirred sufficiently. This time the observant viewer might even be able to come up with the murderer right along with Charlie. That said, though, *Charlie Chan in City in Darkness* is generally regarded by Chan fans and critics as the weakest in the series that Twentieth Century-Fox produced.

Charlie Chan in Panama (Twentieth Century-Fox, 1940) 67m.

Producer: Sol M. Wurtzel, Director: Norman Foster, Screenplay: John Larkin, Lester Ziffren.

CAST: Sidney Toler, Jean Rogers, Lionel Atwill, Mary Nash, Sen Yung, Kane Richmond, Chris-Pin-Martin, Lionel Royce, Helen Ericson, Jack La Rue, Edwin Stanley, Donald Douglas, Frank Puglia, Addison Richards, Edward Keane, Charles Stevens, Eddie Acuff, Lane Chandler, Edward Gargan, Jimmy Aubrey.

While other members of the cast fall around him like flies, Charlie Chan proceeds in his customary leisurely fashion to unravel the mystery of attempted sabotage... – NY Times

PLOT/COMMENT: In this first Chan episode dealing with matters directly related to the oncoming war with Nazi Germany, Charlie is in Panama undercover masquerading as a hat shop owner but really searching for saboteurs that may be planning to blow up the Panama Canal just as the U.S. Navy fleet is passing through. Sure enough, Number Two Son Jimmy shows up to help his pop solve the mystery. Charlie's search is for a person named Ryner who is the ringleader of the saboteurs. Soon, Charlie's contact man R. J. Godley (Addison Richards) is murdered in the hat shop by a poisonous cigarette, and then a mysterious-acting English novelist is shot in his hotel room. Charlie soon learns that the novelist was an undercover British government agent who was also after Ryner. Finally, a cabaret owner by the name of Manolo (Jack La Rue) is discovered to be part of the plot to blow up the canal, but he too is murdered after planting the explosive device and, thus, is not Ryner.

Charlie has a list of suspects to draw upon to find Ryner but only a few hours before the fleet passes through the canal. There is Dr. Rudolph Grosser (Lionel Royce), a Viennese scientist and expert on tropical diseases and plagues, who is discovered to have Bubonic Plague-infected rats in his possession. Cabaret singer Kathi Lenesch (Jean Rogers) has recently sneaked into the country with no passport and has, it appears, foreign connections that may involve her with the plot. Middle-aged Chicago school teacher Miss Finch (Mary Nash) seems innocent enough, but she turns up constantly where unsavory things are happening. Richard Cabot (Kane Richmond), the superintendent for the Miraflores Power Control at the canal, would seem to be an innocent participant in the operations of the canal, but he, perhaps, is too friendly with Kathi Lenesch and her illegal entry into the country. Any way you look at it, Charlie has his work cut out for him.

This is an excellent entry in the series, one of my favorites, and much of the credit must go to the excellent script by Larkin and Zeffren and the fast-paced direction again of Norman Foster. There is much praise due also for the production design with its tropical milieu and many in the cast trying to stay cool in straw Panama hats and white linen suits. In one scene you can see the sweat on Charlie's forehead when he is working in his humid hat shop. The viewer may be caught off guard by the murders that occur later in the plot, the victims being characters who seemed likely to be the guilty party. The observant viewer, however, should pick up a couple of clues along the way that will lead to the same person Charlie identifies in the final moments—a conclusion, by the way, that is very suspenseful since all the subjects are being held by Charlie in the room where the explosives are about to go off. This one is a must-see Charlie Chan film.

Charlie Chan's Murder Cruise (Twentieth Century-Fox, 1940) 75m.

Producer: John Stone, Director: Eugene Forde, Screenplay: Robertson White, Lester Ziffren based on the Earl Derr Biggers novel *Charlie Chan Carries On* adapted by Robert Ellis, Helen Logan.

CAST: Sidney Toler; Sen Yung; Robert Lowery; Marjorie Weaver; Lionel Atwill; Don Beddoe; Leo G. Carroll; Cora Witherspoon; Leonard Mudie; Harlan Briggs; Charles Middleton; Claire Du Brey; Kay Linaker; James Burke; Richard Keene; Layne Tom, Jr.; C. Montague Shaw.

Even with three murders by strangulation in the story, the Honolulu detective hardly becomes perturbed and never seems to want for a 'Confucius Say. –Scho. Variety

PLOT/COMMENT: Charlie Chan's old friend from Scotland Yard, Inspector Duff (C. Montague Shaw), stops by Charlie's office shortly after having arrived on a cruise ship that has stopped off in Honolulu. The inspector, working incognito on a murder case involving a ruthless strangler that has already murdered one person on shipboard during the around-the-world cruise, says he thinks he is close to apprehending the murderer but would like Charlie to assist him. During the short time Charlie is out of the room, the strangler strikes again, badly wounding the Inspector who later dies. Shortly after this there is a call for police assistance at the hotel where the cruise passengers are staying. There has been another strangling; the victim this time is the uncle of another cruise member, Dick Kenyon (Robert Lowery), a young lawyer who worked closely with his uncle on business matters. The body is found clutching a bag with thirty dimes in it—thirty pieces of silver. Charlie deduces that the strangler must be one of the passengers on the cruise ship, so the next day when the ship leaves Honolulu to complete its voyage in San Francisco, Charlie and Number Two Son Jimmy are on board—Charlie to investigate and Jimmy to work as a steward undercover.

In established mystery fashion, Charlie has a goodly number of suspects from which to determine his murderer. There is Dick Kenyon who stands to inherit a fortune from his uncle with whom he has very recently quarreled over his impending marriage to Paula Drake (Marjorie Weaver). The suitcase strap used for the hotel strangling matches a second strap on Dr. Suderman's (Lionel Atwill) luggage; he is the conductor of the cruise. Charlie discovers that archaeologist Professor Gordon (Leo G. Carroll) does not seem to know enough about archaeology. James Ross (Don Beddoe), a seemingly rich glad-hander, may in fact be a wholesale jeweler who's fencing stolen jewels and does a little strangling on the side. There is the excitable and scatterbrained society matron Susie Watson (Cora Witherspoon) who could be smarter and more devious than she appears. The mysterious Mr. and Mrs. Walters (Charles Middleton and Claire Du Brey), a puritanical, blue-nosed couple, she with a claimed connection with the spirit world, may not be who they appear to be. Finally, before the ship arrives in port, the nervous and frightened Gerald Pendleton, who feared for his life and had wired his wife not to meet the ship, is found strangled with a leather shoestring, a bag of thirty silver coins at his side.

Just as the ship docks in San Francisco, a telegram arrives stating that Mrs. Pendleton has been in a serious accident. All the suspects leave for the morgue where an inquest on the murders is to be held prior to any of them being released. Later Charlie arrives at the inquest with the wheelchair-bound Mrs. Pendleton, the lady who may hold the answers to many of the questions still unanswered about the murders.

The film is based on the Biggers novel *Charlie Chan Carries On*, which was first produced by Fox in 1931 but is now considered a "lost" film. This version is much changed from the original and incorporates additional elements from several Chan films. *Charlie Chan's Murder Cruise* is a very fine entry in the series and exhibits a deepened relationship—father and son—between Toler and Sen Yung in their roles. They come across in a very caring and loving way. The film is very atmospheric, cloaked in dark shadows and heavy deck fog as the ship travels through the night to its destination in San Francisco. Add to that a black-garbed, mysterious man in a slouch hat and beard who we know is the strangler in disguise (or his henchman) lurking in the shadows, waiting for his chance.

There is the usual list of outstanding character actors the studio drew upon to flesh out the casts of the Chan mysteries. The only note of dissonance to be found is Cora Witherspoon's outlandish characterization of the middle-aged, flighty matron Susie Watson. Her screams and frantic behavior when anything untoward occurs remind one of the excesses of Harold Huber in his several roles as police inspectors in other Chan films. As noted elsewhere, these roles in 1930s and '40s films seem to be variations of the comic sidekick roles in westerns and today seem dated and out of place.

Charlie Chan at the Wax Museum (Twentieth Century-Fox, 1940) 67m.

Associate Producers: Ralph Dietrich, Walter Morosco, Director: Lynn Shores, Screenplay: John Larkin.

CAST: Sidney Toler, Sen Yung, C. Henry Gordon, Marc Lawrence, Joan Valerie, Marguerite Chapman, Ted Osborne, Michael Visaroff, Hilda Vaughn. Charles Wagenheim, Archie Twitchell, Eddie Marr, Joe King, Harold Goodwin.

It's all flimsy, muddled, absurd, and never for an instant believable. But frequently it's just preposterous enough to be amusing.
–Hobe. *Variety*

PLOT/COMMENT: Convicted murderer Steve McBirney (Marc Lawrence) makes a brazen escape after his sentencing and seeks the aid of Dr. Cream (C. Henry Gordon) who owns and operates a Museum of Crime, a wax museum of famous murderers down through time. Dr. Cream also has a side business in the basement of providing plastic surgery for those outside the law who need a new face to avoid capture—people like Steve McBirney. Recovering from the surgery with his entire head wrapped in bandages, McBirney now seeks revenge on Charlie Chan, the man who provided the evidence that convicted him.

Charlie is challenged to appear on the weekly "Crime League" radio broadcast by Dr. Otto Von Brom (Michael Visaroff), formerly with the Berlin Police and now a noted criminologist who had differences with Charlie regarding an old case where Joe Rocke was found guilty of murder and executed. Charlie believes Rocke was improperly convicted and that the real murderer was a fellow named Butcher Dagan, who also had dealings with McBirney. The broadcast is to be held at the Museum of Crime, and McBirney has rigged the chair that Charlie is to sit in so that he will be electrocuted.

The broadcast, of course, takes place on a dark and stormy night in the eerie confines of the museum with scary waxed figures hovering all around. Just prior to airtime a spooky lady dressed in black appears for the broadcast and turns out to be Mrs. Joe Rocke (Hilda Vaughn), the wife of the man wrongfully executed (according to Charlie) for murder. Tom Agnew (Ted Osborne), the director and announcer on the program, and his engineer Edwards (Harold Goodwin) are almost ready to go on the air when lawyer Carter Lane (Archie Twitchell) arrives representing Mrs. Rocke and tries to stop the broadcast but is unsuccessful.

Everyone takes his seat for the broadcast, Charlie momentarily in the electrified chair until Dr. Von Brom insists that he should sit in the chair assigned to Charlie. The change is made and almost immediately there are sparks and flames as the lights dim from the electrical overcharge (or so it appears) and Dr. Von Brom rises and then crumples to the floor, dead. Surprise of surprises, Charlie discovers that Von Brom has not died of electrocution (the wires to the chair had been cut) but from a poisoned dart that somebody present had blown from a quill shooter. Within the hour the dead body of McBirney is also found in one of the recesses of the museum. Charlie believes that Butcher Dagan is the murderer and that he is one of the people at the broadcast.

Almost the entire film takes place in the atmospheric Museum of Crime which, of course, is a great place to stage a murder mystery. It also allows for a savings in set costs for the production, and this Charlie Chan opus has the look and feel (for the first time) of a lower-budget picture. For the average viewer this is of little significance, but it becomes more noticeable as we move on to the three remaining Twentieth Century-Fox episodes.

There are the usual clues and red herrings as the plot weaves its way to the climactic revelation of who is Butcher Dagan, some of it being a bit hard to accept on face value. For instance, while we all know Charlie's knowledge is boundless, would he really recognize that the murder dart was covered with "Tonga" poison that was used by Dayak headhunters of Borneo and that in this case the dart was probably shot from a quill toothpick, several of which just happen to also be in Jimmy's pocket, thus making it more difficult to decipher who actually used one in the dark to commit the murder?

Despite my carping about a few matters, the film is an enjoyable and atmospheric chapter in the Charlie Chan canon and is well worth a look-see.

Murder Over New York (Twentieth Century-Fox, 1940) 65m.

Producer: Sol M. Wurtzel, Director: Harry Lachman, Screenplay: Lester Ziffren.

CAST: Sidney Toler, Marjorie Weaver, Robert Lowery, Ricardo Cortez, Donald MacBride, Melville Cooper, Joan Valerie, Kane Richmond, Sen Yung, John Sutton, Leyland Hodgson, Clarence Muse, Frederick Worlock, Lal Chand Mehra.

Charlie Chan wades through murders, plane saboteurs, and spies. Mysterious goings-on under the nose of Chan fail to upset his stoic pose. – Walt. Variety

PLOT/COMMENT: Charlie meets an old friend from Scotland Yard, Hugh Drake (Frederick Worlock), as he is flying to New York to attend an annual police convention (where he's to receive the key to the city). On the flight Drake tells Charlie that he is on a case for military intelligence and looking for Paul Narvo who murdered an official in the British Air Ministry three years ago and since then acts of sabotage have occurred in which he is the main suspect. Drake has been in search of Narvo's actress wife who has been eluding him for some time, but he thinks he will find her in New York and that she will lead him to Narvo. Drake suspects that Narvo may attempt to sabotage an upcoming test flight for the bomber TR4, an experimental plane. The TR3 bomber was recently sabotaged on a similar test flight. Before they land, Drake asks Charlie to help him on the case while he is in New York.

Charlie gets his key to the city and then with son Jimmy (who has shown up at the airport eager to assist his pop) heads for a party that George Kirby (Ricardo Cortez), president of the Metropolitan Aircraft Corporation, is having for Drake. When they get there, Charlie finds Drake on the floor of Kirby's office dead, poisoned by a gas released from a glass pellet found broken on the floor. Charlie, after summoning police Inspector Vance (Donald MacBride), tells Kirby to ask all of the guests to stay so that the investigation may begin with questioning all those present.

The guests include actress June Preston (Joan Valerie) who has performed in many different countries and who has lost a pearl from her necklace, later found in the inkwell in the office where Drake was murdered; Herbert Fenton, a fellow Englishman who had attended Oxford with Drake years before; Ralph Percy (Kane Richmond), chief designer at Metropolitan Aircraft Corporation; Keith Jeffrey (John Sutton), Kirby and Percy's stockbroker; Robert Boggs (Leyland Hodgson), Kirby's butler, who Jimmy discovers steaming open a cablegram from Scotland Yard meant for the dead Drake. A bit later in the plot we meet David Elliott (Robert Lowery), principal of a chemical research company that makes the poisonous gas that killed Drake and doubly suspicious because his fingerprints were found in the room where Drake was killed. Mrs. Narvo, it turns out, is Elliott's girlfriend Patricia Shaw (Marjorie Weaver) and is actually on the run from her husband because she fears for her safety.

Before Charlie can identify the saboteur Narvo, Gorge Kirby is found dead of poison placed in his brandy glass. In a final attempt to ferret out

Narvo, Charlie tricks all the suspects onto the test flight of the TR4 bomber where Narvo has hidden an explosive on board. Charlie believes he will reveal his hand before the plane is allowed to explode with him on it—and it sort of works.

This is the first Charlie Chan film since 1931 that does not to use the Chan name in the title of the film, and two of the final three Fox Chan episodes don't. It suggests that the studio might be losing confidence in the Chan name to bring in the customers. This ploy has been noted in some other film series when there seemed to be a lessening of interest in the main character (see later Sherlock Holmes series, for example).

The title *Murder over New York* is intriguing and perhaps would lure patrons into the theatre without the Chan name, but New York plays no real significance in the plot; it could have been Pittsburg just as easily. Then, too, the picture has some plot holes that even the least engaged viewer would possibly spot. Jimmy is a criminology student (never mind that in the last film he had switched to pre-law), and even though he is an undergraduate, he instantly recognizes the smell of a new poison gas that was only invented a few months before—maybe he's a better student than we thought! At the climax of the plot in front of Charlie and the police, the real Narvo, still unrevealed, gives a cohort a poisoned drink of water to shut him up. Wouldn't it be obvious to even the "dumb" police inspector that the carrier of the poisoned water would have to be Narvo—and how did this smart international saboteur expect to escape from this situation with Charlie and the police standing there? In addition, when Charlie reveals Narvos's identity, we discover that it is a person who has had a longstanding job in New York that would have precluded his ability to be a world-traveling saboteur. Holy plot holes, Batman!

The film has a fine cast that does its best to keep the story moving along with the usual clues and red herrings, but there seem to be even more distractions than usual—Shemp Howard of The Three Stooges, for instance, is disguised as a Hindu mystic in a comic police lineup bit that goes on for too long. Believability is also strained in the closing scenes by the poor use of airplane models during the test flight of the new bomber. If you haven't guessed by now, this is not one of the better Chan episodes.

Dead Men Tell (Twentieth Century-Fox, 1941) 60m.

Producers: Ralph Dietrich and Walter Morosco, Director: Harry Lachman, Screenplay: John Larkin.

CAST: Sidney Toler, Sheila Ryan, Robert Weldon, Sen Yung, Don Douglas, Katharine Aldridge, Paul McGrath, George Reeves, Truman Bradley, Ethel Griffies, Lenita Lane, Milton Parsons, Stanley Andrews.

Picture is a 'Grand Hotel' aboard the docked ship and played close to shore—with the four-piece map another familiar piece of story construction. – Walt. *Variety*

PLOT/COMMENT: Elderly Patience Nodbury (Ethel Griffies) has a treasure map that was left to her by a pirate ancestor, Black Hook, and she has chartered a voyage to Cocos Island to locate the pirate's treasure. Because the treasure is estimated to be worth sixty million dollars and a thief has already tried to steal it, Patience has taken the precaution of cutting the map into four sections and giving three sections to fellow passengers booked on the voyage of the *Suva Star*, an old, wooden sailing ship. Charlie encounters Miss Nodbury on the ship while seeking son Jimmy who wants to stowaway on the ship so that he can go on the treasure hunt (not a very well-motivated excuse for his involvement in the plot). In the conversation with the eccentric old lady, she tells Charlie that she believes, according to family tradition, that at the time of her death the ancestral pirate Black Hook will visit her. And sure enough, later that night when a peg-legged, hook-handed "ghost" pirate scrapes at her cabin door, Patience Nodbury opens the door and promptly suffers a fatal heart seizure.

Because of clues—including peg marks in the carpet and the hook scratches on the cabin door—Charlie declares that Patience Nodbury was scared to death, thus making it a crime of murder. Soon Charlie is surrounded by a treasure-trove of suspects from which to ferret out the murderer. Bill Lydig (George Reeves) seems to be a likely candidate because we soon learn that he is an escaped murderer looking to get out of the country and to the treasure, but before Charlie can question him, he turns up dead in a diving bell. There is Steve Daniels (Robert Weldon) who organized the treasure hunt and would have to return the money he received from passengers booked for the voyage—money he has already spent. Steve's girlfriend Kate Ransome (Sheila Ryan) screams once or twice but otherwise just seems to be along for the ride. Jed Thomasson (Don Douglas) is a seemingly nondescript member of the passenger list but one who received a portion of the map from Patience. Laura (Katharine Aldridge) and Charles Thursday (Paul McGrath) are newlyweds who have chosen a strange way to spend their honeymoon. Later we discover that Charles has been to Cocos Island previously, and might, therefore, be the man that Captain Kane (Truman Bradley) seeks revenge on for having been left to die on the island years before in a previous treasure hunt. Then there is psychoanalyst Dr. Anne Bonney (Lenita Lane) and her patient Gene LaFarge (Milton Parsons) who first found Nodbury's body and who suffers from an anxiety neurosis, so they say, and also has received a portion of the treasure map. The inscrutable Chinese detective has his work cut out for him.

Dead Men Tell probably comes the closest to *film noir* of any Charlie Chan film to this time. With stunning high-contrast black-and-white photography by cameraman Charles Clarke, Charlie and the rest of the cast move in and out of the deep shadows in one of the most atmospheric episodes in the series. In addition, director Harry Lachman effectively utilizes close-up camera work throughout the film to punch up the dramatic impact of scenes and to capture the expressive faces of the actors. Most of the action takes place on the *Suva Star* at night with thick fog hovering around the harbor and the ship's deck for a chilling effect that adds to the intrigue and air of mystery in the film. The whole film looks and feels different from any of the other Twentieth Century-Fox Chan episodes. Ken Hanke in his fine book *Charlie Chan at the Movies* comments, "Every shot, every composition is meticulously chosen and lit in a style that is almost the physical equal of a James Whale film. . . ." This is high praise, indeed, when you consider Whale's direction of such films as *Frankenstein*, *The Invisible Man*, and *Bride of Frankenstein*.

The supporting cast includes several young performers who would go on to successful careers as leading men and women in films and television. George Reeves would toil in mysteries, Hopalong Cassidy westerns, and jungle films for several more years until he donned the blue and red costume of Superman for films and television. Kay Aldridge was about to become a Saturday afternoon serial queen in *Perils of Nyoka* for Republic Pictures. Sheila Ryan would become a leading western film heroine, especially in the films and TV shows starring and/or produced by Gene Autry. In fact, Sheila eventually married Autry comic sidekick Pat Buttram.

Dead Men Tell may not have the best plot or as effective a climax as many of the other Chan films, but it is one of the most fascinating to view for its direction, production design, and cinematography.

Charlie Chan in Rio (Twentieth Century-Fox, 1941) 60m.

Producer: Sol M. Wurtzel, Director: Harry Lachman, Screenplay: Samuel G. Engel and Lester Ziffren.

CAST: Sidney Toler, Mary Beth Hughes, Cobina Wright, Ted North, Victor Jory, Harold Huber, Sen Yung, Richard Derr, Jacqueline Dalya, Kay Linaker, Truman Bradley, Hamilton MacFadden, Leslie Denison, Iris Wong, Eugene Borden, Ann Codee.

This chapter is not going to make any new friends for Charlie Chan and will probably lose many old ones. – Scho. Variety

PLOT/COMMENT: Charlie and son Jimmy are in Rio with Chief Souto (Harold Huber) of the Rio police to arrest nightclub singer Lola Dean (Jacqueline Dalya) for the Honolulu murder of Manuel Cardoso that occurred several years before. Not wanting to cause a scene at the nightclub, Charlie suggests that they arrest her at her home after the performance. Lola, not knowing of the impending arrest, invites some of her "friends" to an after-show engagement party where she and Clark Denton (Ted North) will announce their engagement. On her way home she stops at a hotel to meet with her Indian mystic/psychic Alfredo Marana (Victor Jory). Marana induces a semi-comatose state during which Lola confesses that she committed the Cardoso murder. Emotionally shaken by her meeting with Marana, Lola decides that she and Clark should elope later that night.

When Charlie, Jimmy, and Chief Souto arrive at Lola's house to make the arrest, her secretary Helen Ashby (Kay Linaker) asks maid Lili Wong (Iris Wong) to see if Lola is finished dressing. Lili's cries from the bedroom herald the discovery of Lola's dead body. She has been stabbed. Charlie and Souto begin their murder investigation and soon discover that most of the guests have some reason for not shedding tears over Lola's death. Drunken Joan Reynolds (Mary Beth Hughes) can't remember much of the evening, but she knows that she despises Lola for having an affair, she believes, with her husband Ken (Richard Derr). It is soon learned that mystic Marana is the brother of the murdered Cardozo and that Helen Ashby was earlier married to the murdered man. Paul Wagner (Truman Bradley), Lola's ex-husband who is still carrying a torch for her, sent her an orchid earlier in the evening which has been found on the floor next to her body. Rice, Lola's butler, is discovered to have the jewels from Lola's safe and appears to be a likely suspect until suddenly the lights go out, a shot rings out, and Rice is discovered dead on the floor. Grace Ellis (Cobina Wright), stuck with wimpy boyfriend Bill Kellogg (Hamilton MacFadden), has always had eyes for Clarke Denton, Lola's fiancé, and was jealous that Clarke and Lola were going to elope.

So Charlie is in detective heaven with a murder and a house full of suspects. When he discovers Lola's brooch on the floor next to the body, he notices that the pin is broken and that there are scratches on the floor suggesting that the murderer picked up a piece of the broken pin in his/her shoe.. Later, when he finds the same type of scratches under a chair in the dining room, Charlie asks all the guests to sit at the table in the same places they had earlier in the evening but after the murder. With this piece of detective work and a couple of other clues, Charlie soon wraps up the case.

Charlie Chan in Rio is a partial remake of *Black Camel*, a 1931 Chan episode with Warner Oland and directed by Hamilton MacFadden, who has the role of Bill Kellogg in this version. *Black Camel* has a better written, tighter script with characters that are perhaps more interesting, but technical improvements in filmmaking during the intervening years give this version a polish and modern "feel" that the former is lacking. The first half of *Charlie Chan in Rio* with its nightclub scenes, Brazilian samba dance number, and Lola's song gets the film off to a fast start. In fact, up to the murder of Lola, the film moves along at a rapid clip only to slow to a crawl during much of the investigation portion. I am delighted to report that Harold Huber as the "Delgado" or chief of police plays the role straight and does not chew up the scenery as in his previous Chan appearances, thus indicating that it may have been bad direction or bad writing that drove him to his earlier manic characterizations.

Interestingly, the film winds up with Charlie telling Jimmy that he has just received a letter from Mama in Honolulu stating that Jimmy has received his draft notice for World War II. Victor Sen Yung also received his draft notice around this time and only made one more Chan episode, *Castle in the Desert*, prior to going into the service. He wouldn't make another film until after the war when he would resume his role of Jimmy in the Toler Monogram Pictures' Chan series.

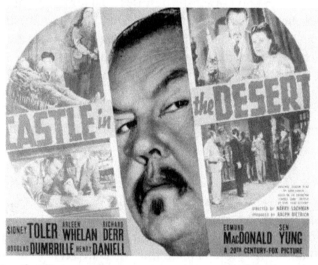

Castle in the Desert (Twentieth Century-Fox, 1942) 62m.

Producer: Ralph Dietrich, Director: Harry Lachman, Screenplay: John Larkin.

CAST: Sidney Toler, Arleen Whelan, Richard Derr, Douglass Dumbrille, Henry Daniell, Edmund MacDonald, Sen Yung, Lenita Lane, Ethel Griffies, Milton Parsons, Steve Geray, Lucien Littlefield, Oliver Blake, George Chandler, Paul Kruger, Eric Wilton.

It's the typical medieval castle setting, with walking armor, sinister suspects, a torture dungeon, and all the trappings. – Walt. Variety

PLOT/COMMENT: An isolated medieval castle in the Mojave Desert owned by descendants of the infamous Borgia family is the setting for this final Twentieth Century-Fox Charlie Chan mystery. Manderley Castle, with no electricity or phone, is occupied by a reclusive author named Paul Manderley (Douglass Dumbrille) and his wife Lucrezia "Lucy" Manderley (Lenita Lane). The plot gets underway when genealogist Professor Gleason (Lucien Littlefield) arrives at the castle to talk with the Manderleys and within minutes is poisoned by a cocktail drink. Because Paul Manderley could lose his twenty-million-dollar-estate inheritance if there is any type of scandal associated with his or his wife's name, his lawyer, Walter Hartford (Edmund MacDonald), talks Lucy's physician Doctor Retling (Steve Geray) into removing the body to the Mojave Wells Hotel, thirty-five miles away, and then claiming that the death occurred at the hotel. Doctor Retling reluctantly agrees.

Shortly after these events take place, Charlie receives a letter (supposedly) from Mrs. Manderley asking him to come to the castle because she fears for her life. A sculptor named Watson King (Henry Daniell) joins Charlie on the last leg of the journey to the castle. King is coming to the castle at Mrs. Manderley's behest to sculpt a bust of her; later King tells Charlie that he is with a detective agency in Los Angles and was formerly with Scotland Yard. He says that Mrs. Manderley has asked him to come, much in the manner that Charlie was asked. Soon Jimmy Chan, on leave after Army boot camp, makes his appearance at the castle with an eccentric old lady from Mojave Wells, Madame Saturnia (Ethel Griffies), a psychic who bills herself as "Prophet of the Desert." A house security guard catches a prowler on the grounds and brings him to Charlie and Manderley. His name is Arthur Fletcher (Milton Parsons), a private detective representing the family of Professor Gleason, who is conducting an investigation into the death of Gleason. A short time later at dinner Fletcher drinks some wine and promptly expires at the dinner table. (Charlie has had the good sense to have Mrs. Manderley sample his glass of wine before he imbibes.)

And there are others, too many others—red herrings all—who glide in and out of the plot as Charlie conducts his investigation. Presently Charlie comes to the conclusion that neither Gleason nor Fletcher have died; they have been given Tagara weed, the substance that Juliet took in the Shakespearean play to appear dead. It seems the whole situation has been a setup by Lawyer Hartford and Doctor Retling to get power of attorney from Manderley, who they would claim is not of sound mind. It looks as if Charlie has the whole situation under control when lawyer Hartford is struck dead by a medieval arrow that pierces his heart. Now Charlie has a real murder to solve.

The production is consumed by a moody, forbidding atmosphere that permeates every scene of the film—from the scraggly Joshua trees silhouetted against the gray sky during the lonely desert journey to the castle, to the shadowy below-ground dungeon of the castle with its grotesque artifacts from the medieval era, to the castle itself with candle-lit rooms, oversized dark-wood furniture, gloomy hallways, and drab hangings on the walls. In short, it's not a welcoming place for strangers but a great place to stage a murder mystery. Director Harry Lachman, as he did in *Dead Men Tell* but not as often, utilizes extreme close-ups of faces to catch ominous predictions of Madame Saturnia (the wonderful Ethel Griffies in a delightful performance), frightened facial expressions, or "knowing" looks that heighten the drama of the moment.

As indicated above, there seems to be an overabundance of suspects in this Chan episode, characters who have little to do other than to occasionally act suspicious. Richard Derr, as a professor of medieval history and "head of the European History Department at Manderley College," has almost nothing to do in the film except look handsome in his summer suit; there's not even a love interest to distract him. Arleen Whelan, as the lawyer's attractive wife, gets a brief moment to be bitchy and then resides in the background while other characters deal with the important stuff. This final Chan film for Fox is a neat little mystery that gets the job done very well, but it's a bit slow at times and not quite up to the level of many of the earlier films in the series.

———•———

VICTOR SEN YUNG (1915-1980) replaced Keye Luke in the Charlie Chan Film series as Number Two Son Jimmy when Sidney Toler took over the role of the Oriental detective. I had the opportunity to interview Victor Sen Yung in Miami, Florida, two years before he died in 1980. [The excerpt of the interview included here is from my 2010 book *Opened Time Capsules: My Vintage Conversations with Show Business Personalities*.] I was in Miami on business when I saw that he was appearing at a nearby department store where he was demonstrating wok cooking utensils and selling his book, *Victor Sen Yung's Great Wok Cookbook*. When I approached him later that morning about an interview, he very graciously agreed to meet with me early that afternoon.

Victor Sen Yung became Number Two Son Jimmy with the
start of the Sidney Toler Chan films and appeared in all of
the Fox films except *City of Darkness*.

We talked in the department store adjacent to where he had just
completed his presentation for about twenty or thirty housewives.
I started the conversation with the Charlie Chan film series.

David: Many film fans remember you played Number Two Son
Jimmy Chan in quite a number of the Charlie Chan films, and
they know you as Hop Sing on *Bonanza*. But let me go back and
ask you a few questions about your early days in acting. You were
very young at the time of the Chan films; did you have any acting
experience before that?

Victor: No, I didn't do any acting until I got into the Charlie Chan
series except for one thing: I worked as an extra in *The Good Earth*
with Paul Muni and Luise Rainer. I was one of the farmers on the
farm that helped fight the fires and kill the pests that came. But I
got into the Chan series just by accident.

After I graduated from college—I went to the University of
Southern California—things were tough. I had a job selling flame
proofing and moth proofing, so I made an appointment to go out
to the studio to talk to them about that. I didn't know they were
looking for a boy to do the part of the son in the Charlie Chan se-

ries. While I was there, they saw me and asked me to do a screen test, and that's how I got the part and got started.

David: Keye Luke was the number one son before you. Do you know why he left the series?

Victor: Well, there were two reports. One of them was that he was going to be featured in [a film entitled] *The Son of Chan Carries On* and that his agent held out for too much money, and they decided to go with another Charlie Chan and another son. The other story—and the one that I think is probably more likely—is that he was negotiating for a part in the Dr. Kildare series with Lionel Barrymore. He got into that series shortly after I got in the Charlie Chan series, and he worked at MGM for quite a few years as Dr. Lee in the Dr. Kildare series.

David: *Charlie Chan in Honolulu.*

Victor: That was the first one with Eddie Collins, Robert Barrat…

David: And that was the first film with Sidney Toler playing Chan.

Victor: I started with Sidney Toler in the Charlie Chan series. Then when I came out of the service, I went back into the series and worked with him. He passed away [in 1947] and then they signed Roland Winters to do the part of Charlie Chan and I did six pictures with Roland Winters. [Actually it was five. Victor wasn't in the last Winters film.] Then they discontinued the series.

David: I noticed that you weren't in the Chan pictures during World War II, and I wondered if that was because you were in the service.

Victor: I went in as a private and wound up in the first motion picture unit in Culver City, helping them make training films for the Army Air Force, but I was very dissatisfied and I kept requesting a transfer so I could get to China. Finally, I ended up in New York in the *Winged Victory* show. Oh, that was a great cast: Eddie O'Brien, Lee J. Cobb, just a great group of talent.

I was still unhappy, so while I was in New York I applied for OCS [Officer's Candidate School], and I was accepted by the board at Mitchell Field. Just when we went out to California to do the show [*Winged Victory*], I got my orders to go to OCS, so I wound up at Kelly Field, and then later went on up to Harvard Graduate School of Business Administration, and I wound up as a staff control officer down at Memphis, Tennessee.

David: Back to the Chan series. None of the actors who played Charlie Chan were Asian.

Victor: I think there was a main reason for that. In those days the star system was still very much a practice in the studios, and if they could build up anybody in the way of a name, they could use them in other parts and to do other shows. Also, I think they tried to maintain the appearance that Warner Oland first established as Charlie Chan, sort of stocky with the mustache and the hat, you know. I had no objection to that.

Toler was very helpful to me. Because it was about the first chance I had to do anything in the way of a speaking part in a motion picture, he guided me and taught me a lot. When I started under contract to Fox, I went to a dramatic school and started to learn as much as I could about the business. Toler taught me a lot about comedy and about timing, especially. He was a great comedian.

David: It's hard to think of him as a comedian. On screen we see him as Charlie Chan, the famous Honolulu detective, and he's very serious, wary, and brimming over with Chinese aphorisms. Some of those, however, were very funny. ["Silence is golden, except in police station." "Confucius say, 'Hasty decision is like ancient egg—look good from outside.'"]

Victor: He was full of the devil, very jovial, great sense of humor. After we started the series, he bought a golf driving range right across the street from the studio. We used to have a lot of fun out there just hitting golf balls and chatting, you know.

David: Sidney Toler, our Charlie Chan, hitting golf balls!

Victor: Right! [*Laugh*] The reason for it [the driving range] was not so much the golf range itself. It was because it was near the studio, and it also had a little sandwich stand and a patio. It was kind of a gathering place for all the young actors. This was what he enjoyed, mingling with the younger people.

David: The series was produced by Twentieth Century-Fox for a number of years and then it went to Monogram Pictures.

Victor: Yeah, that was during the war, while I was in the service. You see, during the time I was in the series, we worked three years and then the war broke out in Europe and then broke out in Asia. During that time Twentieth Century-Fox lost their foreign market, so as a result they discontinued the series because they couldn't recoup the cost of production by just American exhibition alone.

David: So Monogram, a smaller studio, took over the series and added the character played by Mantan Moreland.

Victor: Birmingham Brown, the chauffeur.

David: Everybody remembers Birmingham, the Black chauffeur in the Chan films. He was just tremendously popular; I believe he died only a few years back. What kind of a man was he on the set?

Victor: *[Chuckle]* Mantan was just like what you saw on the screen. He was a great dancer, a hoofer, and tap dancer. He was always kidding around, always had a fast quip. A lot of people mistook him for Rochester, you know, Eddie Anderson [from the *Jack Benny Program*]. He laughed it off most of the time, but a lot of times he insisted that, after all, he did have an identity of his own.

David: He certainly did. How long did it generally take to produce one of the Charlie Chan films?

Victor: Well, when we were shooting at Twentieth Century-Fox, it took between twenty-five and thirty-eight days, depending on the production schedule. At Monogram it was almost like television, seven days, six days. They were quick, fast.

David: I know. Roland Winters has made the comment that they really ground those out fast, those last ones at Monogram. There was a gap of some years from the time the Charlie Chan series ended until we next became very aware of you on the *Bonanza* television series. Did you keep busy during those years?

Victor: Oh, yes. I concentrated on character work. There were a lot of shows that I did, features: *The Left Hand of God* (1955), *Blood Alley* (1955), *The Hunters* (1958). There were many roles where nobody recognized me. Like the part that I did on *Bonanza*, Hop Sing; it's difficult for a person to recognize me because [reverting to the pidgin-English Chinese he used as Hop Sing] I speak so differently and with the hat on [breaking off the dialect] I look like somebody else.

After they cancelled the *Bonanza* series, I wrote this cookbook, *The Great Wok Cook Book*, and from that I got into the development of a wok, and that's what I'm doing now. It has been very, very rewarding in many respects, and it is just beginning. I've only been at it now on the road tour and selling like this for about a year and a half.

David: During your talk you mentioned the *Kung Fu* series (1972-1975). Did you appear in many episodes of that series?

Victor: Yes, I did about eighteen of those shows over a period of about three years, but every show I worked in I played a different character. It was fun, and working with David Carradine, was sort of…an experience, I would say. He had his own private life and all, but he was a great guy. I didn't know him as a child, but I remember his father quite well, John Carradine. He was under contract to Twentieth Century-Fox when I was there, when he was in *The Grapes of Wrath*. I used to see him on occasion and we would chat a bit.

I was just starting in then, working in the Charlie Chan series, and I'd look at these guys [under contract then at Twentieth Century-Fox]: John Carradine, Tyrone Power, and Don Ameche. I'd look at them with awe and thinking if I could only do what they are doing and do it well. I just learned so much by watching them and finally going to USC and taking the courses in cinematography and motion picture production and film editing—just to learn the business, learn the trade. It's just like anything else; as you get along, you continue to learn, which makes life interesting.

David: Very nice talking with you, Victor Sen Yung.

Victor: Thank you, Dave. I really enjoyed it.

When Victor Sen Yung died on January 9, 1980, authorities at first described his death as under "mysterious circumstances," but later determined that it was accidental. He had been working in his apartment making clay ware and curing it in his kitchen oven. He died from carbon monoxide poisoning due to a gas leak in the stove. Victor Sen Yung was survived by one child (from his marriage that had ended in divorce) and two grandchildren. Pernell Roberts, his friend from the *Bonanza* years, gave the eulogy at the funeral. It was reported that Victor Sen Yung was virtually penniless at his death.

The Sidney Toler Films for Monogram Pictures

Charlie Chan in the Secret Service (Monogram Pictures, 1944) 64m.

Producers: Philip N. Krasne and James S. Burkett, Director: Phil Rosen, Screenplay: George Callahan.

CAST: Sidney Toler, Mantan Moreland, Arthur Loft, Gwen Kenyon, Sarah Edwards, George Lewis, Marianne Quon, Benson Fong, Muni Seroff, Barry Bernard, Gene Stutenroth, Eddie Chandler, Lelah Tyler, John Elliott, Davison Clark.

> *There's a stage play quality to it, in that most of the scenes take place in three or four rooms. As with other films in the Chan series, the production design here is minimal and cheap looking. The emphasis is on the whodunit puzzle, but that's what counts most for murder mystery fans.* –Lechuguilla

PLOT/COMMENT: We are in Washington, D. C., during World War II, where Inventor George Melton is working in his upstairs lab at home on a secret torpedo device that will eliminate the enemy U-Boat menace. Because of the importance of the project, Secret Service agents are assigned to protect him at all times. Melton informs the two agents guarding him that friends are coming to a cocktail party that afternoon, and he does not wish their presence while he is with trusted friends.

Melton goes downstairs and is about to put his lab coat in a closet before greeting his friends. When he touches the overhead cord to turn the closet light on, he suddenly falls to the floor dead. Moments later when one of the cocktail party guests discovers Mr. Melton on the floor, she screams, thus bringing all of the guests to where his body lies. The Secret Service team checks the body, reports him dead, and then discovers that the secret plans for the torpedo, which were on Melton's person, are now missing. A call to Secret Service headquarters alerts Charlie Chan, special Secret Service agent, to what has happened, and he quickly comes to the Melton mansion to start an investigation.

Charlie suspects that the murder and robbery may be the work of a master spy named Manlich. He begins an interrogation of the Melton guests who seem a strange lot for the inventor to have over for afternoon cocktails, but never mind. The guests include wheelchair-bound Mr. Paul Arranto (George J. Lewis) and his sister Inez (Gwen Kenyon) who plan to leave for

California the next day; Peter Laska (Muni Seroff), Arranto's swarthy assistant, who has been in his employ for four years; the bland and blond David Blake (Barry Bernard), who works with the Department of Political Economy in Washington; Luis Philipe Vega (Gene Stutenroth), a war refugee now a traveling salesman for Herrick Brothers, an exporting company; a ditsy, middle-aged lady named Mrs. Winters (Lelah Tyler) who has brought a small likeness of the Statue of Liberty as a gift for Inez Arranto and, otherwise, seems to have no reason in the world for being at the cocktail party. Her chauffeur is Birmingham Brown (Mantan Moreland) who doesn't seem to be taken seriously as a suspect by anyone; and, finally, Mrs. Hargue (Sarah Edwards), Melton's mysterious and spooky housekeeper. In addition to having the assistance of Inspector Jones (Arthur Loft) of the Secret Service and several other agents, Charlie has the dubious assistance of his daughter Iris (Marianne Quon) and Number Three Son Tommy (Benson Fong) who are visiting their pop in Washington and hope to do some sightseeing—but, naturally, a murder investigation is more interesting for members of the Chan clan.

Before long Charlie has been shot at three times (assailants of the master detective seem to have terrible aim), has discovered that Paul Arranto can walk as well as anyone, and that salesman Luis Philipe Vega is really Phillip Von Vegon, a celebrated author and electrical engineer and up for "most likely murder suspect" until he is shot dead in front of everybody by a person unknown—but not for long. In the end Charlie identifies the guilty party and it is, of course, the master spy Manlich.

The viewer immediately misses the higher-class production values, writing, and direction of the Twentieth Century-Fox episodes as this much-lower-budgeted Monogram Pictures episode gets underway. For those viewers who complained of the slowness of some of the earlier Chan films, this episode will be a long, tedious slog. Unimaginative director Phil Rosen resorts to the hack technique of hitting each suspect with a quick close-up, their eyes guiltily flicking side to side, as any slightly incriminating evidence pops up along the way. Most shocking directorial goof of all is when the camera cuts to all of the suspects in a group after Luis Vega has been shot and we see the wheelchair-bound Arranto *standing*—this is *before* it is revealed that he is not crippled. Oh, well. Even Charlie's white suit is ill-fitting, and his hat looks as if somebody has been sitting on it.

The actors brought to the Monogram lot for this film are as familiar to "B" movie fans as the more "A" list actors from the Fox films were—just a couple of pay grades lower but serviceable actors nonetheless. Arthur Loft, Sarah Edwards, George J. Lewis, and Gene Stutenroth, among others, fall into this category. Mantan Moreland, making his debut in the Chan series, is a delightful comic actor when given the opportunity but is left without much to do in this episode. Youngsters Marianne Quon and Benson Fong, as two of Charlie's many kids, should have had a few more acting lessons before getting in front of a movie camera.

It probably isn't quite fair to judge the Monogram episodes which were produced for about seventy-five thousand dollars to the Fox pictures which came in for about two hundred thousand. Nevertheless, it is hard to ignore the frequent off-subject drivel of the writing and sloppiness of the direction. All in all, not a promising start for the Monogram films.

Mantan Moreland joined the cast of the Sidney Toler films when the Chan series moved to Monogram Pictures in 1944. Mantan is seen here with Victor Sen Yung during a tense moment in *The Trap*.

African-American comic actor **MANTAN MORELAND** (1902-1973) was brought into the Charlie Chan series with the move to Monogram Pictures in 1944. It was felt that Mantan would add comedy to the mysteries as the series took on more appeal for younger audiences. Mantan Moreland was born on September 3, 1902 (some say 1903), in the town of Monroe in Northeastern Louisiana to mother Marcella Brodnax and father Frank Moreland and given the birth name of Jesse James Brodnax. According to the book *Mantan the Funnyman, the Life and Times of Mantan Moreland* by Michael H. Price, Mantan's grandmother Mandy gave the boy his nickname of Mantan. According to Mantan's daughter Marcella, granny would sing him a song she made up about "Mantan the Funny Man." The name also may have been created as a variation on Mandy's own name.

Always high spirited with the extroverted demeanor of a comic, Mantan ran away to join the Hagenbeck-Wallace Circus when he was barely in his teens. Then he moved on to vaudeville, medicine shows, and touring on what was then called the "chitlin' circuit." All of this gave the young Mantan stage experience to sharpen his comic skills and eventually led him to New York where he was cast in *Lew Leslie's Blackbirds of 1928*—and other shows followed.

In the early 1930s Mantan migrated to Hollywood and soon got a foothold in films, appearing in such films as Herb Jeffries' black musical-western *Harlem on the Prairie* (1937) and, later, *Two-Gun Man from Harlem* (1938) with Jeffries. Monogram Pictures, one of the "poverty row" studios of the depression era, recognized Mantan's comic abilities and his appeal to all audiences, not just black ones, and signed him to a long-term contract.

Mantan was first assigned by Monogram Pictures to appear with Frankie Darro in a series of popular action films (*You're Out of Luck* and *The Gang's All Here* in 1941 and others) where the black actor honed his popular screen identity as a frightened, jittery, eye-bulging comic who was forever attempting to avoid ghostly, scary, or dangerous situations in which he constantly found himself.

Mantan's featured role of Birmingham Brown, chauffeur for Charlie Chan, became his most famous role in films and lasted from *Charlie Chan in the Secret Service* in 1944 until *Sky Dragon* in 1949, some fifteen films. By the time the Chan series had run its course, changes in racial attitudes were becoming apparent, and the civil rights movement was beginning to take hold in the country. Mantan's stock character in films and his type of comedy that had been once looked upon as hilarious was now seen as demeaning and offensive to African-Americans as well as to white Americans. Suddenly Mantan Moreland and several other popular black performers of the era, such as Stepin Fetchit and Willie Best, were ostracized, and their comedy styles were deemed inappropriate in the new order of things.

Many years were to pass before audiences would look back on the comedy of Mantan's films and appreciate the comic skill that the actor had brought to his characters. In the meantime he had to pick up whatever acting opportunities came along—and there weren't that many.

By the 1960s and despite declining health, Mantan was able to resurrect his career somewhat and take small guest roles in such TV series as *Julia*, *The Bill Cosby Show*, and *Adam-12*. Movie director Carl Reiner used him in his comedy *Enter Laughing* (1967), and he had a small role in *Watermelon Man* (1970) with Godfrey Cambridge. On September 23, 1973, Mantan died of a cerebral hemorrhage (some obits said heart attack) in Los Angeles. He was buried in Valhalla Memorial Park Cemetery in North Hollywood, California.

Charlie Chan in the Chinese Cat (Monogram Pictures, 1944) 65 m.

Producers: Philip N. Krasne and James S. Burkett, Director: Phil Rosen, Screenplay: George Callahan.

CAST: Sidney Toler, Joan Woodbury, Mantan Moreland, Ian Keith, Sam Flint, Cy Kendall, Weldon Heyburn, Anthony Warde, John Davidson, I. Stanford Jolley, Betty Blythe, Jack Norton, Luke Chan, Fred Aldrich, George Chandler, Terry Frost.

Changing times have led us to look upon [Mantan] Moreland's brand of comedy as demeaning to African-Americans, but he was an expert actor and comic and taken within the context of what was possible for a black actor in the 1940s, his work has tremendous charm and innocence. – gftbiloxi

PLOT/COMMENT: As the film begins we are in the study of Thomas Manning (Sam Flint). He is sitting in semi-darkness at his desk, studying the chessboard that is in front of him. We see a gloved hand turn the knob of the door leading into the study and a figure enter stealthily. The figure with the gloved hand points a pistol at Manning who looks up just in time to see his assailant fire. As Manning crumples to the floor, he grasps several chess men from the board, leaving only a lonely bishop standing. Alerted by the shot, Leah Manning (Joan Woodbury), stepdaughter to Manning, tries the door to the study but finds it locked. As Leah's mother (Betty Blythe) comes down the stairs from her room, she tells Leah they can get into the study from her room through a secret panel. (Don't all homes have them?) They find the body of husband/stepfather Manning and contact the police.

Following a six-month investigation by the police under the leadership of Detective Lieutenant Harvey Dennis (Weldon Heyburn), the police throw up their hands and state they cannot put the case together. The room where the murder was committed was locked from the inside, there was no weapon found, and there is no one with a credible motive—with the possible exception of wealthy socialite Mrs. Manning, since it was commonly thought that Manning married her for her money. Now a book has been published, *Murder by Madame*, by noted criminologist Dr. Paul Recknik (Ian Keith) who points to Mrs. Manning as the likely guilty party. In desperation daughter Leah contacts Charlie Chan and asks him to conduct his own investigation into the matter. Prodded by son Tommy (Benson Fong), he reluctantly agrees.

As the investigation progresses, we meet a plethora of suspects. Charlie receives a call from a man named Kurt Karzoff (John Davidson) who asks Charlie to meet him because he has evidence on the case. When Charlie and Tommy arrive for the rendezvous, they find him dead, strangled. George Webster Deacon (Cy Kendall) is Manning's junior partner in a realty company, a man who desperately seeks to have Charlie drop the case, he says, because of the bad publicity associated with it—and eventually he also is murdered by strangulation. The bodies are piling up! We are aware that first Leah and then Charlie are being tailed by a thug named Gannet (Stan Jolley) who reports to Catlen (Anthony Warde) and a couple of other suspects who have an office/hideout at a mysterious funhouse.

Some small figurines found hidden in loaves of bread where the murder of Karzoff took place lead Charlie to the artist who created them, Wu Song (Luke Chan). The artist is known to devise a hidden compartment in each of his creations; in the figurines Charlie brings to Wu Song it is discovered that each one contains a diamond in the secret compartment. Charlie suspects that the diamonds are part of the Calinor collection that was stolen a year before in Chicago. It turns out that Wu Song also created a Chinese cat figurine that is missing from the desk of the dead Manning. When Charlie locates the missing Chinese cat, he announces that he has the case solved.

This second Monogram episode is so much better than the first that it is hard to believe that the same production team put it together. The script is tight, action-full, and funny when it should be funny. The direction provides many atmospheric, fog-shrouded, eerie, mysterious scenes that give the film a flavor that the previous one was sorely lacking. Gifted comic Mantan Moreland is given some humorous lines and scenes that earn genuine laughs, especially in the later carnival funhouse scenes—moments that are played for laughs but also push the mystery aspects along.

Some critics have commented on the seemingly strained relationship between Charlie and Number Three Son Tommy in this film. Charlie is constantly putting the boy down with a series of scathing comments along the lines of "I fear you are weak limb to which no family tree may point with pride." At the funhouse Charlie sees three zombie-like figures on display and says to Tommy, "See one with no head. He remind me of you." These sorts of comments are ongoing throughout the film. Then, in the final minutes, Charlie and Tommy are in the hands of the bad guys who want to know where the diamond is. After Charlie refuses to tell, they proceed to beat up on Tommy unmercifully, but still Charlie does not talk. Fortunately, events change and the torture is stopped, but it appears as if Charlie would have let them kill the boy without giving up the information they seek. Scriptwriter George Callahan, it would appear, needed to lighten up a bit on the curt comments that he gave to Charlie about Number Three Son Tommy. Otherwise, the boy was going to have a complex!

Charlie Chan in Black Magic (Monogram Pictures, 1944) 67m. (AKA *Meeting at Midnight*)

Producer: Philip N. Krasne and James S. Burkett, Director: Phil Rosen, Screenplay: George Callahan.

CAST: Sidney Toler, Mantan Moreland, Frances Chan, Joseph Crehan, Helen Beverley, Jacqueline de Wit, Geraldine Wall, Ralph Peters, Frank Jaquet, Edward Earle, Claudia Dell, Harry Depp, Charles Jordan, Richard Gordon.

We've seen it before – the séance, the lights out, the gunshot, and the resolution exposed by Charlie. The frozen blood bullet is an interesting twist, but don't even try to understand the ballistics involved. –classicsoncall

PLOT/COMMENT: Birmingham Brown (Mantan Moreland) arrives at the Bonner house to begin his new job as butler just in time to be present for a murder. It seems that Mr. and Mrs. Bonner (Richard Gordon and Jacqueline de Wit) conduct séances to put persons in touch with their dearly departed beloved. In this case there are seven people holding hands around a table as the séance progresses, and Charles Edwards (Harry Depp) is seeking the spirit of the late Mrs. Edwards. Suddenly, during the séance a mysterious voice asks, "What happened in London the night of October 5, 1935?" With that the lights go out, there is a scream, and when the lights come up William Bonner is slumped over dead. When the police arrive to investigate, they discover that one of the persons at the séance is Frances Chan (Frances Chan), Charlie's daughter. Charlie is sent for and soon, reluctantly, agrees to help with the case since the police insist that Frances is one of the suspects—really just a ruse by Police Sergeant Matthews (Joseph Crehan) to get Charlie to take the case.

Charlie's investigation turns mysterious when he learns that a police search of the suspects and the house immediately after the murder did not turn up a gun. In addition, the police autopsy of the victim reveals no bullet in the body and no exit wound. The suspects turn out to be a diverse group, each with a possible ax to grind with the victim, William Bonner. Harriet Green (Geraldine Wall) was apparently having an affair with Bonner that was going nowhere. Mrs. Bonner knew of the affair and made threats against her husband if he refused to cease the affair. Paul Hamlin (Frank Jaquet) is on a lecture tour and Charlie learns that Mr. Bonner tried to blackmail him—over what is not revealed. Charles Edwards has a company that manufactures magician's supplies, some of which would likely be useful for the séances but otherwise seem to have no tie to the deceased. Charlie soon learns that Nancy Wood (Helen Beverley) is really Norma Duncan whose father Charles Duncan committed suicide a year ago after attending séances with the Bonners, séances during which Norma believes her father divulged business information that brought his company down and led to his suicide. Norma has been attending the séances in hopes of learning enough to, as she tells Charlie, "put them in prison." The last of the suspects are Tom and Vera Starkey (Charles Jordan and Claudia Dell) who work behind the scenes during the phony séances to bring the "spirits" to life.

Before Charlie can solve the case, Mrs. Bonner, obviously in a hypnotic state, goes to the seventh floor of a building and jumps off. Charlie now has two murders to solve. The murderer, apparently feeling that our master detective is getting too close for comfort, induces the same hypnotic state on Charlie and almost causes him to also make a leap from a tall building, the antidote to the hypnosis taking effect just in time. When Charlie gets a report back from Scotland Yard regarding the meaning of the murder séance question, "What happened in London the night of October 5, 1935," he is ready to gather all of the suspects back at the Bonner house for a final séance that will reveal the murderer.

This third entry in the Monogram series is much better than *in the Secret Service* but not quite up to the level of *The Chinese Cat*. For those viewers who have experienced previous séances in Chan films—Fox's *Charlie Chan at Treasure Island*, for instance—this film does not have the finesse or the more elaborate physical production values of the Fox entry, but Monogram's shadowy room with black curtains, lighted crystal ball, and moving wall panels works adequately for a murder setting. One gets the feeling after seeing several of the Monogram Chan pictures that the studio had only one modular house interior that was used over and over again by simply shifting the modular pieces slightly. When you enter a Monogram house, you have the vague feeling that you have been there before.

In this episode Charlie has the assistance of a daughter on the case. Unfortunately, Frances Chan, who plays the similarly named offspring, is not much of an actress, albeit she smiles nicely throughout. Charlie treats his daughter with much more kindness than he does his sons, who constantly receive his harsh verbal abuse—see *The Chinese Cat* for evidence. But Charlie calls Frances his "junior member with brains."

Mantan Moreland continues to be very funny in his Birmingham Brown characterization, which, of course, some may find demeaning by today's standards. But as one viewer has commented, "Moreland was a natural comic presence and he should be viewed as such." I couldn't agree more!

The Jade Mask (Monogram Pictures, 1945) 66m.

Producer: James S. Burkett, Director: Phil Rosen, Screenplay: George Callahan.

CAST: Sidney Toler, Mantan Moreland, Edwin Luke, Hardie Albright, Frank Reicher, Janet Warren, Cyril Delevanti, Alan Bridge, Ralph Lewis, Dorothy Granger, Edith Evanson, Joe Whitehead, Henry Hall, Jack Ingram, Danny Desmond, Lester Dorr.

This Monogram Chan outing has a nice atmosphere and some witty dialogue but a pretty way-out plot. No. 4 son Edward weighs in as Chunky Chan and likewise takes a decided backseat to the deductive powers of his esteemed father Charlie. –Gary170459

PLOT/COMMENT: The film has a wonderfully spooky opening scene with a shadowy figure in black slouch hat and overcoat lurking around the fog-shrouded closed gates of the Harper mansion. The locale then changes to inside the mansion where inventor Mr. Harper (Frank Reicher) and his assistant Walter Meeker (Hardie Albright) are in gas masks working feverishly in a gas-chamber laboratory on a secret formula that hardens wood to the toughness and durability of metal, a process the government has an interest in. Later that night murder enters the house, bodies disappear, dead men seem to walk, a ventriloquist's dummy shoots poisoned darts from his mouth, and a secret vault is discovered that can only be opened by a dead man's voice print. It all sounds like a case for the inimitable Chinese detective, Charlie Chan.

Dr. Harper, alone in his lab, is murdered by a poisoned dart that is shot into his open mouth and later escapes the notice of the coroner when he at first pronounces the death of natural causes. Charlie is called into the case because of the government's interest in Harper's work and the need to secure the secret formula before it falls into enemy hands. Charlie is dismayed to discover that everyone residing in the house with Harper can hardly disguise their pleasure at his demise. Meeker, the lab assistant, hated him openly for the way he was treated by the callous inventor. Harper's sister Louise (Edith Evanson) has been reduced to being his housekeeper in the mansion. Meek and young Jean Kent (Janet Warren) served Harper as a house maid. Roth, the butler, had been with Harper for fifteen years and, as Meeker states, must have hated Harper the most since he had spent the longest time with him. Stella Graham (Dorothy Granger) has been Harper's assistant on his experiments with puppets, ventriloquism, and toy robots for children. It is learned that she formerly was a strong woman in vaudeville. Michael Strong (Lester Dorr), a mute, was Harper's chauffeur and handyman. Late in the investigation another suspect arrives, Lloyd Archer (Jack Ingram), who is Harper's bitter stepson who wants to get back the house and gas formula that were, he says, stolen from his real father by Harper.

Charlie has the assistance of the hayseed Sheriff Mack (Alan Bridge), who is delighted to hand over most of the case to Charlie. As he says, "Seems to me when folks asked me to run for sheriff I missed a fine chance to keep quiet." Also along to "help" Charlie are Number Four Son Eddie (Edwin Luke, Keye's bother)—"Call me Edward; Eddie is so juvenile!"—and chauffeur Birmingham Brown (Mantan Moreland). The bodies pile up—a total of five—as Charlie sifts through the clues for the murderer.

This better-than-average episode in the Monogram series is what is frequently called an "old dark house mystery" with the participants rarely leaving the house and grounds for the duration of the story. Fortunately, the production staff provided an atmospheric setting with sliding panels, secret passages, the before-mentioned gas-chamber laboratory, and murky, fog-shrouded grounds around the house.

Edwin Luke makes his only appearance as a Chan son in this episode, and he offers his brother Keye Luke no competition in the acting department. Charlie, as is his custom with sons, berates the poor boy at every chance he gets: "Every time you open your mouth, you put in more feet than centipede." "He reach oversized decision with undersize brain." "My boy, if silence is golden, you are bankrupt." And so it goes. Alan Bridge as the hick sheriff is a delight and holds his own as a comic foil for the sometimes acerbic Chan. Mantan Moreland's humorous lines do not have the comic snap of the previous episode, but his race with Sheriff Mack's car at the finale is a hoot. All in all, *The Jade Mask* offers a diverting hour and six minutes of mystery fun.

The Scarlet Clue (Monogram Pictures, 1945) 65m.

Producer: James S. Burkett, Director: Phil Rosen, Screenplay: George Callahan.

CAST: Sidney Toler, Mantan Moreland, Virginia Brissac, Ben Carter, Benson Fong, Robert E. Homans, Jack Norton, Janet Shaw, Helen Devereaux, Victoria Faust, I. Stanford Jolley, Emmett Vogan.

Methodical Charlie Chan feature. Little suspense. No intrigue. But I still find it cool to watch. –Michael O'Keefe

PLOT/COMMENT: This opus features a wispy, feather-light plot that concerns an enemy espionage leader and cohorts who are after government records of radar experiments and copies of secret radar patents. Once that premise is explained, our attention becomes focused on who the bad guys and gals are and how to identify and catch them and the whole radar thing becomes relatively insignificant—pretty much like a Hitchcock MacGuffin.

As the story begins, Charlie is tailing a suspect named Rausch (Charles Wagenheim) who he hopes will lead him to the "Manager," as the top espionage agent is called. Even close underlings do not know the name of the Manager who only communicates to them via a teletype machine. Anyway, Rausch is the first of four victims who breathe their last while Charlie is conducting his investigation. A heel print left in blood at the site of the first murder provides the scarlet clue of the title.

A stolen car used by the murderer leads Charlie and his two assistants, son Tommy and Birmingham Brown, to the Cosmo Radio Center, which is a radio station and experimental television studio. As luck would have it, the Hamilton Research Lab is located on the same floor as Cosmo and is a government lab for conducting radar research and experiments. It is from the radio studio that Charlie draws his suspects, although, other than the physical proximity to the radar lab, there doesn't seem to be much obvious connection—but we mustn't second guess Charlie on these things. Charlie first questions Diane Hall (Helen Devereaux), a radio actress whose car was stolen and then returned to the studio by the murderer. Her best friend is Gloria Bayne (Janet Shaw), another radio actress who is something of a gold-digger and who attempts to blackmail the station manager Ralph Brett (I. Stanford Jolley) when she finds matches in the stolen car that she had given to him. During her next radio broadcast she is mysteriously poisoned and dies as she takes a couple of puffs from a cigarette. Two down!

It soon develops that Ralph Brett is really Rolfe Braut—get the Nazi hint—and has shoes with heels that match the one at the first murder site. Brett/Braut calls the Manager because he fears Charlie is on to him as one of the espionage agents. Before you can say "Heil, Hitler," the Manager has dropped him down an elevator shaft to his death. Victim number three! Another suspect is radio actor Willie Rand (Jack Norton) who tries to remember something that Gloria told him that might be helpful to Charlie in solving the case. While performing in a television test, Willie suddenly becomes dizzy, lights a cigarette, remembers the clue he had for Charlie, and instantly dies in the same manner as Gloria. Victim number four!

Other suspects include radio show sponsor/director Mrs. Marsh (Virginia Brissac)—referred to as a "battle-ax" by one of her actors, and she certainly is; announcer Wilbur Chester (Reid Kilpatrick) who, it is discovered, has the trap door device for the elevator in his office; cleaning lady Hulda Swenson (Victoria Faust); and hammy Shakespearean actor Horace Karlos (Leonard Mudie). Charlie trudges on with his investigation until the Manager falls, literally, victim to the trap door in the elevator. Body five!

Increasingly, the Chan episodes at Monogram were turning into platforms for the plentiful comic skills of Mantan Moreland and were less concerned with the business of Charlie Chan solving murders. Certainly comedy in a murder mystery was commonplace in detective films, especially those of the thirties and forties, but in these later Chan pictures the tail, as we sometimes say, was wagging the dog. Also, the comedy in these Chan films was animated and quick-witted while the solving of murders became more and more ponderous as Sidney Toler aged in the role. In this film Mantan Moreland and his nightclub partner Ben Carter have two scenes totally extraneous to the plot where they carry on a spirited dialog, each interrupting the other and finishing each other's sentences, a wonderfully hilarious turn, but it has nothing to do with the murder mystery plot.

The Scarlet Clue does have some intriguing bits within the scripting. The radar lab has a temperature/climate tunnel used for experiments—one section heated and the other compartment freezing cold, replicating a snowstorm. Twice during the film the tunnel is used interestingly, once for the comic antics of Tommy and Birmingham and then to reveal the hiding place of a body. The poison method used to kill two of the victims is also clever, if unlikely. Studio microphones are rigged with small capsules containing a gas. A short-wave radio beam is then sent from some part of the building, exploding the gas capsules in the mike. If the victim lights a cigarette immediately after inhaling the gas, the combination of gas and nicotine becomes the poison. (This takes careful planning, of course.) Lastly, the trap door in the elevator, which kills one person early on, creates the only real suspense in the film when Charlie, Tommy, and Birmingham enter the elevator later, and we know the Manager is at the switch. (One has to wonder about the planning it would take to construct a trap door in a public elevator without anyone noticing it.)

The denouement of the mystery is disappointing. When the Manager lies dead at the bottom of the elevator shaft, we discover, of course, which one of the suspects is the Manager. The disappointment is that Charlie provides no explanation regarding clues that led him to the Manager. In fact, we are left with *nothing* that suggests/states why this person is the guilty party.

BENSON FONG (1916-1987) became Number Three Son Tommy Chan at the start of the Monogram Charlie Chan series with Sidney Toler. He took over for Victor Sen Yung who went into the military during World War Two. Benson was born in Sacramento, California, the son of a wealthy mercantile family. He had no intention of going into show business; his plan was

Benson Fong, Number Three Son Tommy, is seen here with Marianne Quon, Number One Daughter Iris Chan, in *Charlie Chan in the Secret Service*.

to enter into the business world after a period of time studying in China.

Sometime in the mid-1930s a Hollywood talent agent encouraged him to consider working in films, so Benson saw the opportunity to supplement his income doing occasional small parts in films. Interestingly, his first appearance was as an extra in *Charlie Chan at the Opera*—but don't blink or you will miss him.

Then the Tommy Chan role became available at Monogram Pictures and Benson Fong, young Chinese actor, was ready for his close-up. Benson appeared in six of the Chan features, starting with *Charlie Chan in the Secret Service* in1944 and running through *Dark Alibi* in 1946. Benson was very competent in the role of Tommy, but most critics and the public felt that Victor Sen Yung made a better son for Charlie and that Keye Luke made an even better one. During Benson's tenure as Tommy, Edwin Luke, Keye's brother, was brought in to play Number Four Son Eddie in one film, *The Jade Mask*. His stiff, wooden acting made Benson look great in comparison. Benson Fong left the Chan series when Victor Sen Yung was released from the military and resumed his role of Jimmy Chan for the last three Sidney Toler films.

In 1946 with eleven thousand dollars he had saved up, Benson Fong opened his first Chinese restaurant called Ah Fong's on Hollywood's Vine Street. The restaurant became very popular, and eventually he added four more Ah Fong restaurants in the Los Angeles area.

While serving up Chinese cuisine in his restaurants, Benson continued acting in films and many television series over the years. A highlight of his later career was the movie version of Rodgers and Hammerstein's Broadway hit *Flower Drum Song* in which he played a leading role and also sang. Benson Fong died of a stroke in 1985. He was survived by his wife Gloria, five children, and three grandchildren.

The Shanghai Cobra (Monogram Pictures, 1945) 64m.

Producer: James S. Burkett, Director: Phil Karlson, Screenplay: George Callahan and George Wallace Sayre from a story by George Callahan.

CAST: Sidney Toler, Mantan Moreland, Benson Fong, James Cardwell, Joan Barclay, Addison Richards, Arthur Loft, Janet Warren, Gene Stutenroth, Joe Devlin, James Flavin, Roy Gordon, Walter Fenner, George Chandler, Cyril Delevanti, Stephen Gregory.

None of the Monogram Chan movies in the 1940s were "classics," but they all were entertaining and offered something different. This movie is typical: boring for some viewers, fascinating for others, lulls that shouldn't be there, but a good mix of humor, suspense, and mystery. – Michael O'Keefe

PLOT/COMMENT: Three employees of the Sixth National Bank have been murdered mysteriously by cobra venom. When it is discovered that Charlie Chan had a similar murder case in Shanghai back in 1937, he is summoned by Police Inspector Harry Davis (Walter Fenner). Charlie recalls the events of the case in Shanghai to Davis, where a suspect by the name of Jan Van Horn was arrested for the murder after being badly burned on the face and hands during the Japanese bombing of Shanghai. Protesting his innocence, Van Horn escaped before trial and was never seen again. The only time Charlie saw Van Horn was at the time of his arrest when his face was swathed in bandages from the burns. In addition,

possible plastic surgery during the intervening years would have changed his features even more. The *modus operandi* for the previous and present murders is so unique, however, that Charlie feels the same man must have some connection with the current murders.

As a government agent working the case, Charlie has two concerns: to help Inspector Davis with the murder investigation of the bank employees and to keep an eye on the bank where they worked. The bank's vault stores valuable radium which it distributes to hospitals and laboratories in the area as needed. The government would not want the radium falling into the wrong hands, especially during wartime.

Charlie discovers that a private detective named Ned Stewart (James Cardwell) has been following Paula Webb (Joan Barclay), the secretary for the bank president, Walter Fletcher (Roy Gordon). Stewart tells Charlie he was employed by a man he has never met named R. Rogers (no, not the cowboy) who paid him to follow Paula and protect her if necessary. (In the process the detective has become infatuated with the young lady—a little bit like Scotty in *Vertigo*, only without as much intrigue.) Stewart, following her one night, saw Paula meet with the third bank victim, Samuel Black (Stephen Gregory), in Joe's Coffee Shop, just before he died of cobra venom on the rain-drenched street.

Charlie soon realizes that all of the recent murders have taken place near Joe's Coffee Shop where many of the bank employees eat. A feature at Joe's is a fancy jukebox that is rigged with a television camera. A disc-jockey girl in an office several blocks away can see and talk with the customer and play the song requested. At first there seems to be no connection between Joe's Shop and the murders, but later events prove otherwise.

Police Detective Larkin (Cyril Delevanti), who has been placed in the bank by Charlie to work undercover as a guard, phones Charlie and asks him and Inspector Davis to come to the bank immediately. When they reach the bank, Larkin is missing, though it is known that he used no exits of the bank. Charlie then asks for the plans of the bank and discovers that there is a service and sewage tunnel underneath. An investigation of the tunnel reveals the dead body of the police detective, murdered by cobra venom, and evidence—a hand dug tunnel leading up to the vault—that an attempt is about to be made to steal the bank's radium. Charlie alerts the police so they can thwart the robbery, which they do, and, afterwards, Charlie brings the suspects together in the bank president's office to expose the cobra murderer.

There seems to be a fresh, creative breeze and a heightened energy in this episode, the first one directed by Phil Karlson, who would go on to direct such *film noir* pictures as *Kansas City Confidential* (1952), *99 River Street* (1953), and *Phoenix City Story* (1956)—a quality that he injects to a fair degree in *Shanghai Cobra*, especially in the early scenes. The opening rain-soaked night scene with the shimmering black streets, the shiny, wet raincoat worn by Paula, and the trench-coated detective with snapped-down fedora tailing her though the shadowy darkness creates a *noir* atmosphere of menacing gloom that gets the plot off to an alluring start. Another example of Karlson's *noir* edge is the moody, stark lighting in the police interrogation room as Charlie and the police question Detective Stewart in the bright glare of a desk light as they shift about in the room's outlying shadows, moving slowly in a subtly intimidating pattern. By the time the film hits the midway point Karlson has pretty much slipped back into the B-series mystery mode with the crafty aesthetics set aside.

Nevertheless, watching the film you get the feeling that the presence of the new director (or something) has infused the cast with renewed fervor. Charlie seems more engaged in the plot action as he conducts his investigation, even says his lines with more vigor. Benson Fong, never much of an actor, also seems to get into the spirit of the mystery, and his interaction with Mantan Moreland has more sparkle and punch to it. Unfortunately, Mantan is not given as much to work with in this script, but, on the positive side, the comedy does not swamp the mystery aspects this time as it did in the previous episode.

Then, too, there are some clever, if improbable, elements in the plot that add interest. The jukebox with the TV camera turns out to be an efficient dispenser of cobra venom, as does a specially rigged cigarette lighter that provides a venomous surprise. The bank vault set is more impressive than one would expect from "poverty-row" Monogram. And talk about production values, the underground bank tunnel even has spurting water pipes when struck by gunfire during a shootout. You get the point: the whole film has a better look and feel to it when compared to the other Monogram Chan pictures up to this time.

The Red Dragon (Monogram Pictures, 1945) 64m.

Producer: James S. Burkett, Director: Phil Rosen, Screenplay: George Callahan.

CAST: Sidney Toler, Fortunio Bonanova, Benson Fong, Willie Best, Carol Hughes, Barton Yarborough, Don Costello, George Meeker, Marjorie Hoshelle, Mildred Boyd, Barbara Jean Wong, Robert Emmett Keane, Donald Dexter Taylor, Lucino Villegas, Charles Trowbridge, Richard Lopez, Augie Gomez, Toni Raimando.

This is a very stiff, almost painful to watch, Chan film. –classicsoncall

PLOT/COMMENT: Charlie Chan—accompanied by Number Three Son Tommy and Chattanooga (Willie Best), Birmingham's cousin—is called to Mexico City to help with the investigation of the murder of Walter Dorn (Donald Dexter

Taylor), the secretary for Alfred Wyans (Robert Emmett Keane), whose research notes and formula for a new and previously unknown ninety-fifth element could, in Charlie's words, "create an atomic bomb with such titanic force that it could wipe out entire country." In addition to assisting Police Inspector Luis Carvero (Fortunio Bonanova) with the murder investigation, Charlie is to make sure that Wyans' notes and formula do not fall into enemy hands.

There are puzzling aspects to the murder. Dorn was shot while changing the ribbon on his typewriter, and a second bullet hole was found in the wall, but only one shot was heard. Inspector Carvero was on the scene immediately, as were Wyans' guests at a luncheon in a nearby room, but no gun was found. In addition, neither bullet had rifling marks from being fired from a gun. Tommy is intrigued by the fact that Dorn has a bottle of Red Dragon ink on his desk, a rare Chinese ink that one would not expect to find there.

Charlie and Inspector Carvero interrogate the suspects who were at the luncheon, a mixed bag of people with multiple reasons for wanting to get their hands on Wyans' papers and formula, seemingly the motive for the murder. Prior to his arrival in Mexico City, Charlie has gotten the lowdown on all of the suspects except one. There is Charles Masack (Don Costello) who claims to be an importer, but Charlie says the government knows that he is mainly "an importer of propaganda for defeated Nazis." Edmund Slade (George Meeker) says that he sells farm machinery, but Charlie knows he has "record as gunrunner. It is also known that you escape from one country because you suspected of murder." Joseph Bradish (Barton Yarborough) says he is an oil salesman, but Charlie says the government knows he "has a record as international smuggler." The Countess Irena Masak (Marjorie Hoshelle), an entertainer at the Capitol Nightclub, is married to a man who, Charlie says, "is secret agent to several countries." While Charlie has no information on Marguerite Fontain, who says that she is a United States citizen living in Mexico City since her father died, Inspector Carvero admits to him that he and the lady are lovers; later it is discovered that she has ties to Czechoslovakia where the papers and formula were originally stolen from the Allies.

During the ongoing investigation there are two more murder victims, Alfred Wyans and Countess Irena, both victims of the same *modus operandi* as the first murder: one shot heard, two bullets found, no rifling marks on the bullets, and no gun found. But more bad news: nobody knows where Wyans has hidden the papers and formula. Mysteries abound! But not for long because Charlie finds the killing, two-bullet mechanism in his pocket—just before it is to be used on him.

Charlie now knows how the murders were committed: the mechanism is slipped onto the victim's person unnoticed and then activated off scene. The murderer pushes a button which sends out a radio electric impulse that explodes the two bullets, aimed in opposite directions so that one is sure to kill the person. Charlie learns later that the sending device is in the form of a room thermostat. The murderer simply sticks the device to the wall unnoticed until it can be retrieved later. With this information, Charlie is ready to name the murderer and locate the missing pages and formula.

This is the weakest Chan mystery yet with a slack, slapdash script that is juvenile in content and execution. The murder device may have its intriguing aspects but certainly is not something that can be taken seriously. It also seems more than a little farfetched that Wyans would hide the papers and formula information on typewriter ribbon, using the space between where the keys hit and printing it in Red Dragon ink— hence the title of the film.

Director Phil Rosen's pacing is pedestrian with Toler and the other actors seemingly as bored with the material at hand as the viewer quickly becomes. Toler even seems to stumble and fumble with a couple of lines that should have been reshot. Perhaps his best scene in the film is when he performs an enthusiastic rumba with Barbara Jean Wong in a nightclub setting. Benson Fong, who has gotten more comfortable as an actor, is buddies with Willie Best in this episode. Unfortunately, Best, as Chattanooga, does not have the charm or talent to pull off the pseudo-Birmingham character with anywhere near the skill and comic timing of Mantan Moreland. In addition, their comic scenes together are overly juvenile in nature—for example, becoming inordinately frightened by an obvious dummy figure in a trunk or comically jumping into or behind cloth laundry bins to avoid getting shot during a shootout scene. Certainly these films wanted and needed kid appeal, but this endeavor has led to absurdity. In the final analysis, this red dragon doesn't breathe much fire.

Dark Alibi (Monogram Pictures, 1946) 61m.

Producer: James S. Burkett, Director: Phil Karlson, Screenplay: George Callahan.

CAST: Sidney Toler, Benson Fong, Mantan Moreland, Teala Loring, George Holmes, Ben Carter, Joyce Compton, John Eldredge, Russell

Hicks, Tim Ryan, Janet Shaw, Edward Earle, Ray Walker, Milton Parsons, Edna Holland, Anthony Warde, George Eldredge, Meyer Grace, William Ruhl, Frank Marlowe.

> *Unrealistic mystery that [is] held aloft by gimmicks... Much ado here about nothing.* –pbalos

PLOT/COMMENT: Fingerprints don't lie! Well, at least most of the time. In this Chan episode scenarist George Callahan sets up a situation where his Chinese detective has to prove that fingerprints left at a bank robbery by a known, previously-convicted felon are phony and that he shouldn't have been convicted of this crime or the murder of a bank guard who came upon the scene. The accused in question is Thomas Harley (Edward Earle) who is sentenced to die within the week unless Charlie, working to assist Harley's daughter June (Teala Loring), can find proof to save him. Most of the suspects who may have been involved in the case reside in the Foss Family Hotel run by Mrs. Foss (Edna Holland), a crusty, grumpy, middle-aged lady who sometimes takes in ex-convicts in hopes of rehabilitating them. Her borders include Emily Evans (Joyce Compton), a brassy, blonde showgirl who performed in a touring show in cities where two previous banks were robbed with the same *modus operandi*; Miss. Petrie (Janet Shaw) works as a typist but wears expensive clothes, and later we learn that she is secretly married to Jimmy Slade (Anthony Warde) who is in state prison for forgery and works in the fingerprint file room. Most interesting! Continuing the list of borders, there is a fast-talking salesman by the name of Danvers (Ray Walker) who just happens to sell teargas bombs and burglar alarm equipment to banks—yes, he recently was plying his trade in all three banks that were robbed. Finally, there's a creepy fellow by the name of Johnson (Milton Parsons), a public accountant who soon turns up dead in a suit of armor at a theatrical warehouse—a sort of retreat area for all those involved in these nefarious endeavors— so he can be checked off the list.

Knowing that he cannot hope to free Harley unless he can prove that fingerprints can be forged, Charlie has a crime lab technician running tests to find a way to do such a forgery.

In the meantime, Charlie's investigation takes him to the state prison where Warden Cameron (Russell Hicks) and prison guard Hugh Kenzie (George Holmes), who is sweet on June Harley, provide information on prisoner Jimmy Slade who, as stated before, works in the fingerprint file room. With the investigation narrowing in on him, Slade panics, somehow gets his hands on a gun, and tries to break out of the prison while Charlie is there. During a lull in the violent shootout that ensues, Slade exclaims in front of the warden, guard Kenzie, and Charlie, "You're not gonna make me take the rap for this!" With that he fires his gun, which unbeknownst to him has a plugged barrel. The gun explodes in his face, killing him. Charlie ponders what Slade might have meant in his final statement. Soon the Lab technician has the solution for the fingerprint forgery, Charlie identifies the boss behind the clever bank robbery operation, and John Harley is set free.

In my plot summary the reader will notice that I have not mentioned that son Tommy and Birmingham Brown were trailing along with Charlie on most of his investigation. This was not an oversight on my part, since their involvement had nothing to do with the mystery plot. They were along for comedy relief—only more relief was provided than was probably needed or desired by most viewers. To put it another way: the comedy tail was wagging the mystery dog. More and more this became the norm in the Monogram Chan films. In a repeat engagement, Mantan Moreland's nightclub partner Ben Carter was back for an encore of their comedy routine (see *The Scarlet Clue*) where they banter back and forth with neither finishing a sentence. The routine is very funny, but three variations of it in one sixty-one-minute film is a bit much. Even Charlie joins in on the last routine they do.

Director Phil Karlson keeps the plot moving along at a pretty good clip, but not fast enough to hide the illogic and silliness of George Callahan's script. Why, for example, would anyone go to the trouble of hiding a dead body in a standing suit of armor? Once the bad guys had safely robbed a bank wearing gloves, what was their motivation for putting someone else's fingerprints at the scene? Even obsessive/compulsives would probably not go to such lengths, and no "revenge" motivation is ever mentioned. The bottom line: Monogram Chan films were targeted more and more to the Saturday matinee kiddie trade and, what *Variety* frequently called, "undiscriminating" adults. How's that for a putdown of all us Chan fans!

Shadows over China-town (Monogram Pictures, 1946) 64m.

Producer: James S. Burkett, Director: Terry O. Morse, Screenplay: Raymond L. Schrock.

CAST: Sidney Toler, Mantan Moreland, Victor Sen Yung, Tanis Chandler,

John Gallaudet, Paul Bryar, Bruce Kellogg, Al Bridge, Mary Gordon, Dorothy Granger, Jack Norton, George Eldredge, Tyra Vaughn, Lyle Latell, Mira McKinney, Gladys Blake, Jack Mower, John Hamilton, Harry Depp, Charles Jordan.

I don't recall such gruesome deaths in the earlier Chans, although here they are only spoken of. – kga58

PLOT/COMMENT: When the commencing commences (as Birmingham might say), Charlie, Number Two Son Jimmy (Victor Sen Yung, back from military service), and Birmingham Brown are on a bus headed to San Francisco—why chauffeur Birmingham is not driving Charlie's car and they are taking an uncomfortable bus is never made clear. Also unclear (and remaining so) is why someone takes a shot at Charlie while they are waiting for the bus to be fixed at a rest stop along the way. Fortunately, his birthday watch in his breast pocket stops the bullet—only in the movies would a person be so fortunate. Anyway, Charlie is on his way to San Francisco where there has been a brutal torso killing. As Jimmy explains to Birmingham, that's where the arms, legs, and head are cut off—charming stuff for all the moppets in the audience to conjure. Charlie also gets involved in a missing person's case involving Mrs. Conover (Mary Gordon, Mrs. Hudson from the Sherlock Holmes film series) who is searching for her granddaughter, Mary Conover (Tanis Chandler), who is missing and feared the victim of the "torso" killer. It develops that the missing Mary and the torso killing are related, but Mary is not the victim.

Soon it becomes apparent that the Bay City Escort Bureau is connected to the torso victim and the disappearance of Mary. (Now we get to explain to the kiddies in the audience what an "escort service" is, and, no, according to this movie, it was not a cover for any illicit sexual acts, as we might suspect today.) Shortly there are two people murdered, not counting the torso victim: Kate Johnson (Mira McKinney), on the bus with Charlie at the beginning and later found stabbed in Mary's apartment; and Mike Rogan (Paul Bryar), originally a phony bus driver who mugged the real one (since the real bus driver is never seen on camera, this seems to be a moot point) and is really a thuggish employee at the escort bureau who gets shot by the head man late in the goings-on. Among the suspects are a handsome AWOL Marine named John Thompson (Bruce Kellogg) who is sweet on the missing, later found, Mary; Jeff Hay (John Gallaudet) who early on claims to be a private detective but really is the head of the escort bureau; and, lastly, a man named Cosgrove (Jack Norton), a pickpocket who turns up when anything nefarious occurs. Using the found Mary as a decoy to flush out the torso killer, Charlie soon wraps up the case in fine fashion.

The subject matter in this Chan film may have been more "adult" with the gruesomeness of a torso murder and the questionable activities of an escort service, but the handling of the plot and the "comic fillers" are juvenile in execution. For example, are we to believe that a murderer's bullet would hit Charlie's pocket watch thus saving the detective's life? Can we believe that Jack Norton, doing his stock drunk act, could remove all the bullets in the bad guy's gun while simply bumping into him? And, imagine this: he leaves one bullet in the gun so that the bad guy can, moments later, shoot him. Then, as he is lying wounded on the floor, he tells Charlie that the gun is now empty. Come on! There are also unlikely coincidences, such as the torso murder just happening to be linked to the disappearance of Mary, whose grandmother just happens to run into Charlie seeking assistance in finding Mary. Then Charlie is having tea in a restaurant and discovers that his waitress is—guess who—the missing Mary. None of this can be taken seriously by the viewer.

And as for the comedy scenes, Victor Sen Yung and Mantan Moreland, responsible for the comic relief in between murders, do not at this point have the rapport that Benson Fong and Moreland developed gradually in Fong's six Chan films as Tommy Chan. Benson Fong was weak in the acting department for his first couple of films but then developed as a nice foil for Mantan's comedy high jinks—just in time to be replaced by Sen Yung. In this film Mantan has one extended comic scene in a curio shop where he encounters human-like inanimate native figures, mirrors that distort his appearance, and other comic setups. He is, as usual, a delight—my only caveat is that the scene had absolutely nothing to do with the main mystery plot.

As I have mentioned, after Moreland's tenure in the Chan films and as civil rights became a dominant issue in the fifties and sixties, his performances as a frightened black man were felt to be racist by many people—and maybe they were. But I never felt that way when I saw the films in movie theatres as a youngster, and I always admired his comic ability. I agree with another patron of the films who wrote that Mantan Moreland's performance as a frightened man was not really any different from Lou Costello's performance as a frightened man in such films as *Abbot and Costello Meet the Mummy, Meet Frankenstein,* etc. They were both extremely talented performers with excellent comic timing who made an indelible mark with their performances in scores of motion pictures.

Dangerous Money (Monogram Pictures, 1946) 64m.

Producer: James S. Burkett, Director: Terry Morse, Screenplay: Miriam Kissinger.

CAST: Sidney Toler, Gloria Warren, Victor Sen Young, Richard Vallin, Joseph Crehan, Willie Best, John Harmon, Bruce Edwards, Joseph Allen, Dick Elliott, Amira Moustafa, Tristram Coffin, Alan Douglas, Selmer Jackson, Dudley Dickerson, Rito Punay, Elaine Lange, Emmett Vogan, Leslie Denison, Kit Carson, Gerardo Sei Groves, Don McCracken, Mavis Russell.

Story wise, this is yet another disposable Chan story, industrialized moviemaking. – tedg

PLOT/COMMENT: Charlie, son Jimmy, and second assistant Chattanooga Brown (Willie Best) are onboard the *SS Newcastle* on their way

to Sidney, Australia, with a stop in Samoa. As the story opens, Charlie meets on the fog-shrouded deck of the ship with Scott Pearson (Tristram Coffin) who identifies himself to Charlie as a United States Treasury Agent. He tells Charlie that there have been two attempts on his life already and that he wants Charlie to know about the case that he is on. He's been assigned to investigate the sudden appearance of "hot money" and artworks stolen from Philippine banks during the war with Japan and now showing up on the islands. A few minutes later in the show salon of the ship, Pearson is stabbed to death with a knife thrown into his back.

Working with the ship's captain (Joseph Crehan), Charlie begins his investigation into the murder. He learns from Pearson's portfolio that the headman's name is Lane, but he is probably working his evil deeds using a pseudonym. Charlie's list of suspects is long and diverse: Tao Erickson (Richard Vallin) claims to be a trader, and he and his wife Laura (Amira Moustafa) own a restaurant in Samoa. Harold Mayfair (Bruce Edwards) is the assistant of Professor Martin (Emmett Vogan), who has an ichthyologic (fish) museum in Samoa. Mayfair seems to spend a lot of time ogling the beautiful wife of Professor Martin, Cynthia (Elaine Lange). Freddie Kirk (John Harmon) has a knife throwing act in the ship's salon and seems to be in cahoots with P. T. Burke (Dick Elliott), a cotton goods salesman who is blackmailing beautiful, young Rona Simmonds (Gloria Warren), supposedly a British tourist (but no accent) whose visa papers have apparently been forged by ship's Purser, George Brace (Joe Allen), who is in love with Rona. Finally, there are two missionaries, Reverend Whipple (Leslie Denison) and his "wife" (Alan Douglas).

During Charlie's investigation two of his suspects are dispatched with knives in their backs: Salesman P. T. Burke and knife-throwing showman Freddie Kirk. With his list of suspects lowered by two and time running out, Charlie knows he must bring the head man and any confederates to justice before the *SS Newcastle* gets to Australia.

Dangerous Money is often cited as the worst of the Chan films. Ken Hanke in his fine book *Charlie Chan at the Movies* states that "this is the nadir of the series, the bottom of the barrel, the lower depths, as bad as it gets." While I cannot offer a strong defense or claim any accolades for the film, I would suggest that the previous entry in the series, *Shadows over Chinatown*, tops *Dangerous Money* in the nadir department. This film at least has a somewhat better, more logical, and believable script even though the "hot money" premise is hard to make understandable and interesting. Production values are much better in this film, especially in the settings—the believable on-deck amenities of the *Newcastle*, the night-club-like salon on the ship, the island-flavored décor of the restaurant in Samoa, and the ichthyologic museum (although it's seen mostly in semidarkness). The first five minutes of the film, at night on the foggy deck of the ship with Charlie and Pearson setting up the plot circumstances, are very moody and atmospheric and get the story off on a mysterious footing. I can offer little defense for the childish inanities of son Jimmy and Chattanooga, which we are forced to endure during too many of the sixty-four-minutes running time.

Comments have been made too about Sidney Toler's waning health and that his performance in this film seems tired and phlegmatic. I do not see this in his performance. In fact, he even dances a waltz briefly in one scene, and in his exchanges with Jimmy and Chattanooga he appears feisty as ever. One could argue that the viewer is pretty much left in the dark regarding clues that lead Charlie to the denouement. In fact, this film, I believe, is the only Chan episode where almost all of the suspects are guilty of some involvement in the caper. If only Charlie would take us into his confidence more, we might also have a chance to figure out the guilty parties.

The Trap (Monogram Pictures, 1946) 68m.

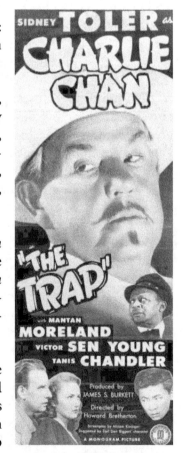

Producer: James S. Burkett, Director: Howard Bretherton, Screenplay: Miriam Kissinger.

CAST: Sidney Toler, Mantan Moreland, Victor Sen Young, Tanis Chandler, Larry Blake, Kirk Alyn, Rita Quigley, Anne Nagel, Helen Gerald, Howard Negley, Lois Austin, Barbara Jean Wong, Minerva Urecal, Margaret Brayton, Bettie Best, Jan Bryant, Walden Boyle.

Be warned, this one is not for serious Chan lovers but for people who like Plan Nine from Outer Space. *But you have to watch it once to appreciate how much better other lowly-rated Chan films are in comparison with this movie. – dpalmer-2*

PLOT/COMMENT: "Maestro" Cole King (Howard Negley), his showgirls and their assistants, and press agent Rick Daniels (Larry Blake) arrive at 62 Malibu Drive on Malibu Beach for a month's vacation only to have two of the showgirls precipitously murdered in the beach house: an underage showgirl named Lois (Jan Bryant) who is strangled while attempting to steal some letters that contain incriminating evidence against Marcia (Anne Nagel), King's current paramour, who is hated by all the other girls in the company and soon becomes the second victim. The assistant to Marcia, San Toy (Barbara Jean Wong), is first suspected of the murders because the cords used to strangle the victims suggested a Chinese *modus operandi* to one of the none-too-swift showgirls. (Anyway, the plot needed a reason for the Chinese assistant to seek the assistance of a Chinese detective.) Fortunately, San Toy happens to know Jimmy Chan and calls him because, as she says, "He is the world's greatest detective." Unfortunately, Birmingham gets the call and, confused by the frightened shrieks of the showgirls in the background, thinks that Jimmy has been murdered. Birmingham and Charlie rush to the address he has been given, 26 Malibu Drive (even though the number "62" is clearly visible next to the front door when the performers first arrived at the start of the film). Nevertheless, Charlie and Birmingham find the house and discover that it is really two showgirls who have been murdered; presently, Jimmy gets the message from a note Birmingham left and follows them to the murder site.

Charlie soon deduces that many members of the troupe had reasons to want the incriminating letters and to kill Marcia (pronounced "Marsha" by everyone in the cast except actor Howard Negley who for no discernable reason pronounces her name "Mar-see-a.") To keep the surviving showgirls from all morphing together into one imperceptible personality, screenwriter Miriam Kissinger gives two of them annoying characteristics—Adelaide Brandt (Tanis Chandler) has an absurd phony French accent (although it is supposed to be genuine) that makes portions of her dialogue unintelligible, and Clementine (Rita Quigley) is a compulsive, hysterical screamer who, unfortunately, never becomes one of the victims—and leaving the other two, Ruby and Madge (Helen Gerald and Margaret Brayton), resolutely insipid and indistinguishable. Additional suspects include Mrs. Thorn, the bland wardrobe mistress for the troupe, and physical culture therapist George Brandt (Walden Boyle), secretly married to Adelaide. The redoubtable Minerva Urecal is humorously ominous and arch as the housekeeper Miss Weebles. She is fond of curtly muttering to the show people, "Liquor is the root of all evil; crime the stem and branches." Finally, in the cast, Kirk Alyn, just a couple of years away from becoming the first live-action (sort of) Superman of the screen, struts around as motorcycle highway patrolman Sergeant Reynolds looking supercilious and stiff in his uniform and sporting a ridiculous mustache that looks as phony as Tanis Chandler's French accent sounds.

There are no clues to the murderer in this feeble last Charlie Chan episode with Sidney Toler. The plot just runs its course and the murderer is revealed after a listless car chase—Charlie and Birmingham in pursuit of the slayer—in which the murderer's car careens over an embankment and down a ravine. Charlie rushes to the crash scene in time to hear a confession just prior to the killer's demise.

The film is a sad farewell performance for the very talented Sidney Toler. In poor health during production of *The Trap*, he died two and a half months after the film was released. He seems dazed, even confused, at times in his performance. There are several moments when the camera cuts awkwardly to him, alone, and he recites a line, supposedly to the other person(s) in the scene, in an apparent attempt to piece together shots where there were difficulties. The character of Charlie Chan does not appear on screen until fifteen minutes into the action, and later in the film he "goes for a walk" with San Toy and is missing from the action for an extended period.

Howard Bretherton, known for his direction of western films, was brought in to direct this Charlie Chan episode and seems utterly lost in the detective film milieu. His direction is lacking in pace, atmosphere, and guidance for the actors, some of them young and novices in the film medium. Even Mantan Moreland is unable to brighten up the proceedings with his usual comic hijinks and is left to ad lib too frequently, "Good gracious, me" and then call out "Mr. Chan!" Long stretches of time are expended by characters lurking around looking suspicious but leaving the plot stalled— as we in the audience are rapidly losing any interest in "who done it."

The Roland Winters Films

Roland Winters (1904-1989) became the third actor to portray the venerable detective in what would become the final Chan movie series. His assumption of the role came with the death of Sidney Toler in 1947 from cancer. In the ensuing months Monogram Pictures selected Winters to continue the series with a commitment for six episodes and with the possibility of several more episodes being produced abroad utilizing funds tied up in England. When the funds were devalued, the additional films were cancelled, and no more Monogram episodes were produced.

Roland Winters had already had a varied show-business career prior to the Chan series. He was the restless son of Felix Winternitz, a world-famous violinist and composer during the late 19th century who later became a teacher at the New England Conservatory of Music in Boston, Massachusetts. By the time young Roland reached his mid-teen years, he shipped out as a deckhand on a cargo vessel headed for Central America and later the West Indies. Somewhere along the line he discovered a love for the theatre and decided he wanted to become an actor. By 1924 he was doing well enough to make it to Broadway in a featured role in *The Firebrand,* a comedy by Edwin Justus Mayer (which also had such fledgling actors as Edward G. Robinson, Joseph Schildkraut, and Frank Morgan in the cast).

Roland Winters took over the role of Charlie Chan upon the death of Sidney Toler and made six more films in the series.

But regular acting gigs were a sometime thing, so Winters had to look elsewhere for opportunities to make a buck as a performer—and discovered radio. In 1931, returning to his family's home base in Boston, he took on the task of announcing the Braves and Red Sox baseball games for station WNAC, where he stayed for six years. After then moving to New York, he was soon working regularly in a variety of radio roles including that of Clarence K. Muggins in the serialized comedy-drama *Lorenzo Jones*; Russell Bartlett on the now-forgotten sitcom *My Best Girls,* and as a comic foil for Milton Berle in the comedian's late thirties radio comedy, *The Milton Berle Show.* Roland's most memorable role on radio was probably that of the longtime announcer on *The Goodwill Hour* where he would open the program with "You have a friend and advisor in John J. Anthony, and thousands are happier and more successful today because of John J. Anthony."

Surprisingly, Winters did not pursue Hollywood films, or at least was not successful in this endeavor, until 1946 when he had the uncredited role of Van Duyval in the Twentieth Century-Fox film *13 Rue Madeleine* starring James Cagney. (It should be noted, however, that he did have a fleeting moment in one of the most memorable films ever made, *Citizen Kane,* where he had the uncredited role of a newsman in the Trenton Town Hall scene.) It was after these two inauspicious roles that he was recommended to Monogram Pictures for the Charlie Chan role.

Fearing being too identified with the Chan role after six features, Roland was not overly disappointed when the series ended in 1949. Now recognized as a capable and dependable character actor, he moved easily into featured roles in such films as *Abbott and Costello Meet the Killer, Boris Karloff* (1949); *The West Point Story* (1950); *A Lion Is in the Streets* (1953); and later two Elvis Presley movies: *Blue Hawaii* (1961) and *Follow That Dream* (1962), just to name a few.

During these same years he was becoming a favorite of television producers and directors. He is probably still best remembered for his performance as J. R. Boone, Sr. in the *Meet Millie* television series of 1953-1954, but throughout the 1950s, '60s, and '70s he made appearances on most of the major network television series and moved back and forth between TV and films all during these years. By the mid-1970s Roland began cutting back on the roles he accepted. His last acting job before total retirement was that of Senator Thaddeus Jones in the TV movie *A Conflict of Interest* (1982), directed by Jose Ferrer and also starring Edward Binns and Barnard Hughes. Roland Winters died of a stroke in 1989.

Roland Winters' tenure as Charlie Chan was much briefer than that of his two predecessors in the role, and he is generally thought of as the least effective portrayer of the role when matched with Oland and Toler. Certainly, the overall production quality of Winters' six Monogram efforts cannot compare with the sheen of the much bigger-budgeted Fox features with better writers, directors, and actors to draw upon. I believe it is a fair assessment to say that the Winters features were comparable with the Monogram Toler films—leaving the final assessment a personal preference for one actor's performance in the role over that of the others.

The Chinese Ring (Monogram Pictures, 1947) 68m.

Producer: James S. Burkett, Director: William Beaudine, Screenplay: W. Scott Darling.

CAST: Roland Winters, Warren Douglas, Mantan Moreland, Louise Currie, Victor Sen Young, Philip Ahn, Byron Foulger, Thayer Roberts, Jean Wong, Chabing, George Spaulding, Paul Bryar, Thornton Edwards, Lee Tung Foo, Spencer Chan, Thayer Cheek, Kenneth Chuck, Charmienne Harker, Jack Mower, Richard Wang.

Watchable, but the nap monster will probably get you. – Steve Brown

PLOT/COMMENT: The first Chan picture with Roland Winters is a lethargic affair with little-to-no action until the final moments, and Charlie Chan, as played by Roland Winters, is a somewhat bland character. The plot begins when Princess Mei Ling (Jean Wong) arrives at Chan's home in San Francisco and almost immediately is murdered by a shadowy figure that shoots her with a poisonous dart propelled by an all-but-silent rifle. Before expiring she scrawls the words "Captain K" on a note pad. Chan eventually learns that the princess is in America to purchase planes for China and brought with her one million dollars for that purpose. As they used to say, to find the murderer, follow the money trail. *The Chinese Ring*, it should be noted, is a remake of the Boris Karloff film *Mr. Wong in Chinatown* (1939).

Chan's closing words to the lady reporter (Louise Currie) would cause consternation in the present day: "Woman not made for heavy thinking but should always decorate scene like blossoms of plum." There are some other disconcerting elements in this initial Chan entry with Winters that take some getting used to. Didn't the scriptwriter peruse any of the preceding Chan films to get the history of the character? Number Two son Jimmy (Victor Sen Young, no longer billed as Yung) of the Toler films is now Number Two son Tommy who used to be Number Three son Tommy (Benson Fong). And Charlie, who used to be a Honolulu Police

Detective and then a Honolulu Police Detective on loan to the United States Secret Service, has apparently lost both of those positions and has left the rest of his family back at the Bowl House in Hawaii and now lives in San Francisco working as a private detective. Where is Earl Derr Biggers when you need him?

Docks of New Orleans (Monogram Pictures, 1948) 64m.

Producer: James S. Burkett, Director: Derwin Abrahams, Screenplay: W. Scott Darling.

CAST: Roland Winters, Virginia Dale, Mantan Moreland, John Gallaudet, Victor Sen Young, Carol Forman, Douglas Fowley, Harry Hayden, Howard Negley, Stanley Andrews, Emmett Vogan, Boyd Irwin, Rory Mallinson, George J. Lewis, Paul Conrad, Haywood Jones, Dian Fauntelle.

Everyone seems suspect, clues are boundless but don't seem to fit into any particular pattern or too many patterns, take your pick.
– Jim Knoppow

PLOT/COMMENT: In *Docks of New Orleans* we are concerned with the LaFontanne Chemical Company co-owned by Simon LaFontanne (Boyd Irwin) and two new partners, Von Scherbe (Stanley Andrews)

and Henri Castanaro (Emmett Vogan). LaFontanne's niece, Rene (Virginia Dale), has a smaller share in the company. LaFontanne's two new partners are of questionable merit, but an agreement has been struck to send a shipment of the new poison gas that has been formulated to South America—to who in South America is never quite clear. Soon we discover that there are three foreign agents, Andre Pereauz (Harry Hayden), Nito Aguirre (Carol Forman), and their henchie Grock (Douglas Fowley), who want the formula for the poison gas so they can sell it to the highest bidding foreign government—obviously not a government that would be friendly to the United States. Another complication in the plot is that Oscar Swenstrom (Harry Hayden), the inventor of the gas formula, has been forced out of the company by LaFontanne and his two partners and coerced into selling his formula for a measly five hundred dollars—and he's none too happy about it. So unhappy, in fact, that he attempts to kill LaFontanne but is stopped before he can fire his gun.

Charlie, who just happens to be in New Orleans with son Tommy and Chauffeur Birmingham, is brought into the situation when LaFontanne receives a threatening letter and asks the famous detective to investigate. When Charlie arrives at LaFontanne's office the next day, he discovers LaFontanne dead. He is at first thought to be the victim of a heart attack, but a later autopsy reveals that the death was caused by a poison gas. Charlie discovers a broken radio tube in LaFontanne's office and suspects that the tube has something to do with the mysterious death. Before Charlie can get to the bottom of things, the other two partners, Von Scherbe and Castanaro, die in a similar manner.

Charlie finally stumbles upon the *modus operandi* for the murders when, much to his annoyance, Tommy and Birmingham break into a rendition of "Chop Suey Boogie" on the piano and violin. One of the high notes on Tommy's screeching violin causes the radio tube Charlie is holding to explode. Charlie soon learns that each of the murder victims had a radio turned on at the time of his murder, and each had received a threatening letter that caused him to stay inside close to where there just happened to be a radio. Then Charlie discovers that the wife of one of the suspects is an operatic singer who has a radio show each day. Yes, you guessed it! When her singing voice hits the death note, the radio tube with the poison gas bursts, thus killing the person in the room. Case solved!

The one interesting aspect of this film *is* the method used to commit the murders; otherwise, it's a pretty dismal, slow-moving sixty-four minutes with a lot of characters to keep straight. Once the method is revealed at about the forty-five-minute mark, the identity of the murderer and the resolution of the film are telegraphed to the audience with still a lot of time left to fill.

Roland Winters, regrettably, brings little energy to the role of Chan, and his slowness in delivering his lines sometimes militates against the meaning of what he is saying. His delivery of several Chan aphorisms is so sluggish that the actors playing opposite him actually seem impatient for him to get to the point. Victor Sen Young and Mantan Moreland have surprisingly little to do in this episode and could actually have been cut from the whole film with little loss, their one bright and meaningful moment being when they play "Chop Suey Boogie," thus revealing the means for the murders.

The Shanghai Chest (Monogram Pictures, 1948) 61 m.

Producer: James S. Burkett, Director: William Beaudine, Screenplay: W. Scott Darling and Sam Newman from Newman's original story, Additional dialogue: Tim Ryan.

CAST: Roland Winters, Mantan Moreland, Tim Ryan, Victor Sen Young, Deannie Best, Tristram Coffin, John Alvin, Russell Hicks, Pierre Watkin, Philip Van Zandt, Milton Parsons, Olaf Hytten, Erville Alderson, George Eldredge, William Ruhl, John Shay, Charles Sullivan.

The mystery is clever enough to hold up until the final revelation of who done it, with many humorous and atmospheric scenes leading up to the finale. –miraymond

PLOT/COMMENT: In a very atmospheric opening we see a mysterious figure in a long black coat and black fedora stealthily enter the home study of Judge Wesley Armstrong (Pierre Watkin) through a French door as the judge is examining some papers at his desk. An upraised hand with a dagger is revealed just prior to its being plunged into the back of the unsuspecting judge, killing him. As the black figure retreats into the shadows, Vic Armstrong (John Alvin), the judge's nephew, arrives at the locked front door. Getting no response, he goes around to the unlocked French door and enters as the phone rings. He answers the phone, not noticing the judge's body on the floor. Phyllis Powers (Deannie Best), the judge's secretary, recognizes Vic's voice just before he is knocked unconscious by the dark figure. When Vic awakens, he discovers the judge's body, and (get this) removes the knife from the judge's back, thus putting his fingerprints on the weapon. (Every

When Victor Sen Yung (now Young) continued in the Charlie Chan series with Roland Winters, instead of being Number Two Son Jimmy he was now Number Two Son Tommy. Mysteries abound!

ten-year-old in the audience knows that's a no-no.) And, of course, Lt. Mike Ruark (Tim Ryan) and Officer Pat Finley (George Eldredge) of the San Francisco police department arrive at this moment, responding to Phyllis's call of concern, and find Vic standing over the judge's body with the murder weapon in his hand. Case closed, as far as Lt. Mike Ruark is concerned.

It takes the follow-up murder of District Attorney Bronson (Russell Hicks) to bring Charlie into the case at the behest of Lt. Mike, as Charlie affectionately calls him. Lt. Mike and Charlie are baffled by the fingerprints of criminal Tony Pindello—who was executed six months prior to the two murders—that are found at the site of both murders and a later murder of a jury member, all of whom had been involved in the case that resulted in the conviction of Pindello. When Charlie asks that the body of Pindello be exhumed, it is discovered that the coffin with the body is missing from the gravesite. Later, Charlie encounters undertaker Grail

(Milton Parsons, everyone's favorite undertaker in films) who has reluctantly had the task of reburying the meandering body of Pindello and now must answer to Charlie and Lt. Mike.

Suspects in the case include the judge's lawyer Ed Seward (Tris Coffin) who, interestingly, had been the lawyer for the executed man at the trial six months before; Walter Somerville (Erville Alderson), Judge Armstrong's clerk of court, who is found going through the judge's papers by Charlie and Lt. Mike; Pindello's brother Joseph, who was recently released from jail; and dumb Vic, of course, who didn't have sense enough to leave the knife in the judge's back—but we know he didn't do it because we saw what *really* happened in the opening reel. But, never fear, our Oriental detective has matters well in hand. When he gets all of the suspects together in one room for the denouement, one can be confident that the guilty person will crack and be taken into custody by Lt. Mike.

The Shanghai Chest is a considerable improvement over the first two entries in the Roland Winters cycle of Chan films. Winters is a more "take-charge" Chan in this film, and while he is the least Asian-looking of all the Chan actors—way too tall and he only squints to suggest Oriental eyes—he now brings command to the role that makes him more acceptable as the venerable detective. Victor Sen Young as son Tommy and Mantan Moreland as Birmingham have somewhat less to do in this episode, but their contributions are the usual mix of getting in the way of the investigation and then providing a face-saving action near the end that makes Charlie forgive their earlier ineptitude—all performed in a gently humorous manner.

Director William Beaudine brings a sure hand to the direction of the film. His atmospheric opening sets the tone for ensuing scenes, and the use of flashbacks and montages during the early investigation process works effectively to keep the action flowing instead of relegating it to talking heads. It is a bit surprising that the screenwriters utilized the same fake fingerprint gimmick that was used just a couple of years previously in Sidney Toler's episode entitled *Dark Alibi*. If you saw the previous film, you had it all figured out before Charlie got around to showing us—although the explanation using Birmingham was handled better here.

The Shanghai chest of the title appears for approximately fifteen seconds late in the film and has absolutely no importance within the plot. It makes a nifty title, but one could hope for a stronger link to the goings-on in the film.

The Golden Eye (Monogram Pictures, 1948) 69m.

Producer: James S. Burkett, Director: William Beaudine, Screenplay: W. Scott Darling.

CAST: Roland Winters, Wanda McKay, Mantan Moreland, Victor Sen Young, Bruce Kellogg, Tim Ryan, Evelyn Brent, Ralph Dunn, Lois Austin, Forrest Taylor, Lee "Lasses" White, Edmund Cobb, John Merton, Lee Tung Foo, George Spaulding.

The Golden Eye *is an average Charlie Chan mystery, made somewhat more interesting with the comedic bits by Mantan Moreland and the quite effective interplay of Tim Ryan's drunken character O'Brien.* –classicsoncall

PLOT/COMMENT: Our scene opens on a dark and foggy night in San Francisco as Arizona goldmine owner Mr. Manning (Forrest Taylor) visits Wong Fai Curios in Chinatown in hopes of locating Charlie Chan. He tells Wong Fai (Lee Tung Foo) that he fears his life is in danger and, sure enough, a sinister gunman who has been following Manning, takes a shot at him through the curio shop's window, only missing the frightened Manning when the bullet is deflected by the window glass. Charlie is located and brought to the curio shop by Manning's daughter Evelyn (Wanda McKay). Since the threats to Manning seem to be connected to his goldmine in Arizona, it is soon decided that Charlie will go "on vacation" to the Lazy Y Dude Ranch located near Manning's Golden Eye mine in Arizona.

When Charlie, along with son Tommy and chauffeur Birmingham, reaches the dude ranch, he discovers that his old friend Lt. Mike Ruark (Tim Ryan) of the San Francisco Police Department has been assigned by the government to investigate activities at the mine. It seems that after many years of low yield, the goldmine has suddenly turned into one of the richest mines in the country. The amount of gold flowing in to San Francisco is too good to be true, and the government wants to know what's up. Lt. Mike is doing his investigation secretly while pretending to be a drunken, obnoxious guest at the dude ranch. Charlie also learns upon his arrival that Manning has had an "accident," falling down a mineshaft and suffering a badly bruised head and shoulders with a possible skull fracture and is under a doctor's care.

Several suspects come under scrutiny by Charlie and Lt. Mike: Jim Driscoll (Ralph Dunn), the superintendent of the mine (who Lt. Mike learns

has a criminal record) and his wife Margaret (Lois Austin); Talbot Bartlett (Bruce Kellogg), the local assayer who knows Charlie from Honolulu and who was a school friend of Tommy *and* Bartlett has eyes for Manning's beautiful daughter Evelyn. A marriage to her would put him very close to a fortune in gold when the elderly Manning is dead. The last suspect is Nurse Sister Teresa (Evelyn Brent), a nun who has come to attend the bedridden, comatose Manning. Charlie discovers that she is probably a bogus nun when he notices the high heels she is wearing under her habit.

Charlie and Lt. Mike finally determine that the gold is being smuggled from Mexico to the Arizona mine because it is worth much more in the United States—thirty-five dollars an ounce compared to only seven in Mexico. After several treks through the mine, the death of Manning and an old prospector named Pete (Lee "Lasses" White), and a surprising number of shootouts—both in and out of the mine—Charlie and his helpers bring the bad guys and gals to justice. An interesting aspect of the film is that all of the suspects are guilty to one degree or another.

This is one of the more interesting Roland Winters entries in the Chan series. Director William Beaudine is right at home in the horse opera milieu, having directed a slew of B-westerns during his long career. The western setting also gives Tommy and Birmingham a chance to put on some western togs and become comic cowboys for a short time, and they make the most of it. Brief use of the Monogram Ranch western street and old mission (for the Manning Ranch) in Newhall, California, provide the appropriate backdrop for plot development as Charlie and his cohorts go about their crime investigation. (The Monogram Ranch was the setting for literally hundreds of western films over the years and was later purchased by Gene Autry who renamed it Melody Ranch and continued to lease it for films and television episodes well into the 1960s.) Longtime cowboy sidekick Lee "Lasses" White had just wrapped up his side-kicking duties at Monogram with singing cowboy Jimmy Wakely prior to taking on the role of prospector Pete in this Chan episode.

The plot may not gallop along, but it does mosey at a leisurely trot, which is an improvement over many of these later entries in the series. W. Scott Darling, the screenwriter, took a fair amount of criticism as a "hack screenwriter" for his writing endeavors in the Chan series and other Monogram low-budget films over the years, so it's nice to be able to give him some praise—even if it is faint. There is a disturbing, mood-shattering ending to the film when Mantan Moreland as Birmingham steps out of the action of the concluding scene and speaks directly to the audience, praising the sleuthing abilities of his boss and giggling, as the other actors in the scene stand at awkward attention behind him.

The Feathered Serpent (Monogram Pictures, 1948) 61m.

Producer: James S. Burkett, Director: William Beaudine, Screenplay: Oliver Drake.

CAST: Roland Winters, Mantan Moreland, Keye Luke, Victor Sen Yung, Carol Forman, Robert Livingston, Nils Asther, Beverly Jons, Martin Garralaga, George J. Lewis, Leslie Denison, Erville Alderson, Fred Cordova, Juan Duval, Frank Leyva, Jay Silverheels, Charles Stevens.

I like the outdoor atmosphere and the wind howling at night. It's like Charlie Chan goes camping. –Phantom Moonhead

PLOT/COMMENT: Charlie, Number One Son Lee, Number Two Son Tommy, and chauffeur Birmingham are on vacation in Mexico when they encounter an ill, exhausted man in a field next to the road they are traveling. When they take the man into the nearest town, San Pablo, to be treated by a doctor, they discover that he is Professor Scott (Erville Alderson), half of a two-man expedition that has been searching for the ancient Aztec Temple of the Sun. Charlie and his entourage also learn that a second expedition is leaving the next day to search for the missing archaeologists—now reduced to one. Among the members of this expedition are archeologists John Stanley (Robert Livingston) and Professor Paul Evans (Nils Asther); Sonia Cabot (Carol Forman), who is engaged to the missing Professor Henry Farnsworth (Leslie Denison); and Joan Farnsworth (Beverly Jons), the sister of Henry. Not only do they hope to

find the missing archeologist, but they too are seeking the ancient Aztec Temple of the Sun where, secondarily, there is supposedly a great fortune in jewels—not that any of these high-minded archeologists would be interested in filthy lucre.

Later that night the sick and delirious Professor Scott awakens and indicates that he and Farnsworth found the temple and were made prisoners by people unknown and forced to do hard labor. As the members of the new expedition and Charlie listen, he begins to tell the location of the Temple. Suddenly the lights go out, and moments later Scott is found dead on the floor with an Aztec knife in his back. Charlie, examining the angle of the wound, states that it was thrust into the unwitting Scott by someone in the darkened room. Since the missing Farnsworth turns out to be a friend of Charlie's (wouldn't you know?), he decides to join the expedition.

The next day they start the expedition, using the location where Charlie found the unconscious Scott the preceding day as a starting place. It is soon revealed that John Stanley is the leader of a gang that has located the Temple but not the area where the jewels are hidden. The secret location is indicated by the hieroglyphics on the walls of the temple which only the captive Professor Farnsworth can interpret. Late that night at the encampment, the body of Sonia is discovered outside her tent with Professor Evans standing over her. The knife used to kill her is identified as belonging to Evans, causing Charlie to comment that sometimes "incriminating evidence a little too obvious."

The next day when Lee and Tommy discover some hieroglyphics of a feathered serpent, Charlie deduces that the serpent undoubtedly marks the entrance to the Temple, and shortly they locate it with the villains inside. Upon entering the Temple and with Charlie gazing on bemusedly, Lee and Tommy engage in a frenetic fistfight with assorted bad guys just prior to Captain Juan Gonzalez (George J. Lewis) of the San Pablo police arriving with deputies to round up the rest of the gang and escort them away.

The Feathered Serpent has had much abuse heaped upon it over the years, and I was pleasantly surprised to discover upon reviewing it after many years, that the film certainly has its faults but is not without charm. It plays more like a relatively fast-paced adventure film (or a western, since it is a rewrite of Oliver Drake's Three Mesquiteer film *Riders of the Whistling Skull* [1937] where Robert Livingston was one of the heroes, not the villain) than it does a murder mystery. The mystery "whodunit" angle is almost totally missing because we discover early on that Stanley is the main villain of the piece. (It is of little importance or relevance when we learn in the closing scene that Sonia, working in cahoots with Stanley, killed Scott and then Stanley killed Sonia. Got that?) Part of the film's sentimental/nostalgic charm for viewers is that this is the only Chan film where actors Keye Luke and Victor Sen Yung appear together as sons one and two of Charlie Chan. (It's a bit disconcerting to realize that son Keye Luke was actually older than dad Roland Winters in real life.) The film spends a lot more time out of doors than is usual for a Chan mystery. Most of the outdoor footage was shot at Monogram Ranch in Newhall, California.

There is also much more humor in the film than one usually expects in a Chan mystery. Some of the scenes, such as the fight scene with Lee and Tommy taking on the bad guys late in the story, are played "over the top" in a somewhat comic manner more suggestive of the way the Bowery Boys, also of Monogram Pictures, might have routed the villains. There is even some ironic humor in the fact that Jay Silverheels (shortly to become the good and loyal iconic Indian Tonto in *The Lone Ranger* TV series) has a bit part which calls for him to attempt the assassination of iconic detective Charlie Chan. Who knew what evil lurked in Tonto's past?

Sky Dragon (Monogram Pictures, 1949) 64m.

Producer: James S. Burkett, Director: Lesley Selander, Screenplay: Oliver Drake and Clint Johnston, Original story: Clint Johnston.

CAST: Roland Winters, Keye Luke, Mantan Moreland, Noel Neill, Tim Ryan, Iris Adrian, Elena Verdugo, Milburn Stone, Lyle Talbot, Paul Maxey, Joel Marston, John Eldredge, Eddie Parks, Louise Franklin, Lyle Latell, George Eldredge, Steve Pendleton, Lee Phelps, Emmett Vogan.

While Charlie moves through his investigation, dropping Oriental witticisms here and there, three more corpses add to the mystery, while cutting down the numbers of suspects to sift through. –Les Adams

PLOT/COMMENT: Charlie and son Lee are on a flight headed for San Francisco when they and the other passengers and crew on the plane are drugged into unconsciousness by the coffee that was served to them. When they awaken, it is discovered that two hundred and fifty thousand dollars belonging to the Apex Insurance and Bonding Company and under guard by two detectives on the plane, John Anderson (Paul Maxy) and Ed Davidson (Lyle Latell), has been stolen with no trace of the money on the plane. In addition, Davidson's body is found stabbed to death next to the compartment where the money was being stored.

Charlie asks the pilot, Captain Tim Norton (Milburn Stone), to call ahead to Lieutenant Mike Ruark, Charlie's friend with the San Francisco Police Department, and have him meet the plane when it lands. In the meantime, Charlie begins his investigation of the theft and murder. Everyone on the plane is a suspect, of course, including Captain Tim (as Charlie calls him) and his copilot Don Blake (Joel Marston), because if they had not conveniently re-awakened the plane would have eventually crashed. But then it is discovered that Detective Anderson and passenger Andy Barrett (Lyle Talbot) also have a pilot's license, and it is later learned that Barrett has a police record for a confidence scheme he ran a while back that bilked an airlines out of sixty thousand dollars which was never recovered. Wanda LaFern (Iris Adrian), a hard-edged dance hall girl in San Francisco, is traveling with Barrett, and the two of them are surprised to see plane hostess Marie Burke (Elena Verdugo), who we discover later used

to be known by the name of Connie Jackson and was married to Barrett (and was probably mixed up in Barrett's earlier confidence scheme and the missing sixty thousand).

Lieutenant Mike (Tim Ryan) and his men meet the plane, as does the head of the Apex Insurance and Bonding Company, William E. French (John Eldredge), who wants to know what's happened to his quarter of a million dollars that's missing from the plane. As the investigation is moved forward by Charlie and Lieutenant Mike, two of the suspects are murdered, but finally Charlie masterminds the denouement by bringing all of the remaining suspects back to the airplane, the setting of the original crime for, as Charlie puts it, "a little scene in manner of Chinese drama." Charlie's little "drama" on the plane, including another death, causes the real culprits to reveal themselves and be arrested by Lieutenant Ruark.

The first twenty minutes of the film, including the exposition introducing the main characters, the drugging of the people on the plane and its immediate aftermath, and the initial questioning of all on board at police headquarters, are handled extremely well by director Lesley Selander and nicely set up the mystery aspects of the plot for the audience. But then the script begins to meander aimlessly as the red-herring situations come into play that seem to be more in number than usual in this episode. The concluding "Chinese drama," as Charlie calls it, again lifts the interest level of the film for an exciting climax. If only the middle portion had not drifted into tediousness.

The interplay between Charlie and Lee is handled nicely, with less comic horseplay by the son, probably because Keye Luke was a little too old for such shenanigans. In fact, Lee addresses Charlie not as "Pop" for the first time but uses the more adult and dignified "Dad" when speaking to his father. Lee and Birmingham do get into some brief comic high jinks during the slower middle portion of the film, but Mantan Moreland as Birmingham is also given some delightfully humorous moments on screen as he tries to win the affections of Wanda's cute maid Lena (Louise Franklin). The film is also enhanced by the presence of appealing and familiar character actors, in some cases actors who would go on to fame in future roles. For example, Noel Neill, playing an airline hostess, would soon become Lois Lane in the popular *Superman* TV series, and a few years later Milburn Stone would take on the role of venerable Doc Adams in the long-running *Gunsmoke* television series.

The title of this final series episode has little meaning, *Sky Dragon* seemingly referring to the airplane in an Oriental manner—a stretch considering that it is never referred to in the dialogue.

Charlie Chan and the Curse of the Dragon Queen with Peter Ustinov

Charlie Chan and the Curse of the Dragon Queen (American Cinema, 1981) 97m.

Executive Producers: Alan Belkin, Michael Leone, Producer: Jerry Sherlock, Director: Clive Donner, Screenplay: David Axelrod, Stan Burns, from a story by Jerry Sherlock.

CAST: Peter Ustinov, Lee Grant, Angie Dickinson, Richard Hatch, Brian Keith, Roddy McDowall, Rachel Roberts, Michelle Pfeiffer, Paul Ryan, Johnny Sekka, Bennett Ohta, David Hirokane, Karlene Crockett, Michael Fairman, James Ray.

When all is said and done, the end result is rather like The Good Earth *meets* The Pink Panther. –gftbiloxi

Peter Ustinov as Charlie Chan.

PLOT/COMMENT: This is not, in the true sense, a Charlie Chan film. It is a parody, a spoof, a satire on the Charlie Chan mythos, and is included and discussed here only as an oddity in the Chan canon of films. The murder plot, what there is of it, consists of a series of "Bizarre Murders," as the newspapers keep headlining them, taking place in San Francisco that are baffling Police Chief Baxter (Brian Keith) who has called in retired detective Charlie Chan to help with the investigation. Complicating their efforts is Charlie's grandson Lee Chan, Jr. (Richard Hatch), who wishes to become a detective like his "grandpop."

It soon becomes apparent that Charlie's old nemesis, the Dragon Queen (Angie Dickinson), who put a curse on the Chan clan to the third generation, has a hand in the murders, but there are other suspects, too. They include the wealthy widowed Mrs. Lupowitz (Lee Grant), whose husband was murdered by the Dragon Queen a few years before and who also happens to be Lee, Jr.'s grandmother on his maternal side (this makes Lee, Jr. half Jewish and half Chinese!); Gillespie (Roddy McDowall), the butler in the Lupowitz household, who is confined to a motorized wheelchair; Mrs. Dangers (Rachel Roberts), the housekeeper; and Stefan (Johnny Sekka), the Lupowitz chauffeur who has a strange set of scars on each cheek.

Richard Hatch plays Charlie's Number One Grandson—half Jewish and half Chinese—in this satire on the Charlie Chan mythos.

But the murders are of relatively little importance in the film, as is Charlie Chan. The primary thrust of the plot concerns Lee, Jr. and consists of a series of "set pieces" (some would say vignettes) to demonstrate the bumbling, dim-witted (comic?) behavior of grandson Lee, Jr. who is really the main character in the story; everyone else plays off his role. There is the breakfast set piece where he tries feebly to cut a bagel in half, nearly severing his genitals but finally only cutting off his tie. Next comes the walking-to-his-office set piece where, through his bumbling ineptness, he causes the entire street to end up in a shambles. Later there is the carriage-chase-after-the-Dragon-Queen-with-horses-a-gallop set piece with Charlie and Lee, Jr.'s fiancée (Michelle Pfeiffer) riding in the carriage driven by his clumsy grandson. The chase soon includes a large posse from the local riding academy with a police cruiser trailing behind. The list of set pieces continues seemingly ad infinitum but finally climaxes in another chase involving all the major participants in the plot (even butler Gillespie in a souped-up electric wheelchair rolling through the streets of San Francisco) to an old movie theatre in Chinatown where the Dragon Queen is holding Lee, Jr. and his fiancée hostage. In true Charlie Chan fashion all of the suspects are rounded up backstage at the movie theatre, and Charlie gets to declare "You are the murderer!" to the least likely suspect.

George S. Kaufman, the great playwright, theater director, and wit, once famously said, "Satire is what closes on Saturday night." By that pithy statement he meant that satire is a risky business, and it takes unusual skill to pull it off. In the film medium Mel Brooks has probably faced the risk and beaten the odds more than most directors with, for example, successful satirical jabs at the western and horror film genres in *Blazing Saddles* and *Young Frankenstein*. But even the great Brooks has come up short occasionally in his spoofing endeavors—*Space Balls*, anyone?

The detective genre had already been lampooned successfully four years before in 1976 with Neil Simon's *Murder by Death*, which also had an all-star cast and top production values. The diabolical plot had Truman Capote calling in a slew of famous detectives (such as Charlie Chan, Sam Spade, and Miss Marple) to solve his mysterious whodunit. So there was really very little new ground to cover with *Charlie Chan and the Curse of the Dragon Queen*; it had been pretty much done already—and, sadly, much better.

Director Clive Donner, probably best known for the 1965 hit comedy *What's New, Pussycat,* directs his *Dragon Queen* in a frantic, stressed-out, would-be-comic style that has most of his actors delivering their lines in an over-the-top, frenetic manner. Lee Grant, as the Widow Lupowitz and working desperately to reach the acting altitude called for by director Donner, chews up the scenery with a voraciousness seldom seen on film. Fine character actor Brian Keith takes his right-on-the-mark hyper performance as film producer H. H. Cobb in Peter Bogdanovich's *Nickelodeon* from 1976 and kicks it up way too many more notches for the fire-breathing, profane, Police Chief Baxter. Richard Hatch, badly miscast and never having had any previous acting experience working in pratfall physical comedy, seems totally lost but gamely does his best, stumbling and bumbling along in the picture. For his role of Lee Chan, Jr. to really work, a master in this style of performing is required—someone like a young Peter Sellers, for example. (Are there any of those around?) Richard Hatch has said that Timothy Dalton was also up for the role. Lucky Timothy!

In an apparent homage by the scriptwriters to several classic films of the past, we have Rachel Roberts as spooky housekeeper Mrs. Dangers; see, of course, mysterious housekeeper Mrs. Danvers (Judith Anderson) in Alfred Hitchcock's *Rebecca* as the more-sinister model for the role. Backstage in the old movie theater in Chinatown, Charlie and his cohorts chase after the fleeing murderer who goes through a funhouse door and hits a slide down to a lower level, much as Orson Welles did in another San Francisco funhouse in the *film noir* classic *The Lady from Shanghai*. The final chase scene with everyone after the murderer takes place in the movie theater where there is a Charlie Chan murder mystery on the screen (with Ustinov inexplicably playing Charlie) and continues in back and in front of the movie screen with the confused audience watching and occasionally applauding the goings-on. All of this might remind one of the closing scene from another Hitchcock film, *The 39 Steps.* And there are other examples, but you get the idea. In not an homage but probably just an attempt to be cute, Richard Hatch, as Lee Chan, Jr. in a nightclub scene, orders a "Captain Apollo on the rocks." Apollo, of course, was the role he played much more successfully in TV's *Battlestar Galactica.*

As an aside, in 1979 I brought Richard Hatch to Sarasota, Florida, as a "guest artist" when I was director of a visual and performing arts school. The program was federally funded, and I had funds to bring in professional actors to meet and work with the students. Richard had recently come off the *Battlestar Galactica* TV series and, of course, was a popular choice with the students. I remember that he had just gotten word from his manager that he would be playing the role of Lee Chan, Jr. in a new Charlie Chan film and how excited he was to be working with the great Peter Ustinov as Charlie Chan in a big-budget major motion picture— really his first, since he had been primarily a television actor, and this was seemingly a big break for Richard. If the film had worked, it likely would have changed his whole career as a leading man in motion pictures. But, as they say, "That's show business!" Richard returned to television and has worked pretty successfully through the years not only as an actor but also as a writer, producer, and director. And, oh yes, *Charlie Chan and the Curse of the Dragon Queen* was a flop at the box office and received mostly negatively reviews from the critics.

The Radio Case Files
of Charlie Chan

CHARLIE CHAN ON RADIO was a mish-mash of formats and time slots, and the program never reached beyond ordinariness during the years of its hit-and-miss existence on the airwaves, sporadically from December of 1932 through 1950, and only about forty-two recorded episodes are known to exist today. Not even all of the actors who played Charlie in the radio series' many incarnations have been identified, but it is known that the popular character actor of the movies Walter Connolly (1887-1940), who was not really known much for radio work, was the first Charlie in the short-lived (six months) series of the early 1930s. The mid-1940s series had another well-known character actor, Ed Begley (1901-1970), essaying the role of the Oriental sleuth with popular young radio actor Leon Janney (1917-1980) playing his Number One Son. (Janney had already earned his detective badge as *Chick Carter, Boy Detective* in an earlier radio series.) Begley worked extensively in radio over the years, appearing in most major series and doing even more police work as Lieutenant MacKenzie on *The Fat Man* radio series shortly after leaving the Chan series. Santos Ortega (1899-1976), another popular radio actor who had already played detective Nero Wolfe and Police Commissioner Weston in *The Shadow* on radio, covered the Chan role for the 1947-48 season (again with Janney as his son) before moving on to other detective roles such as Peter Salem in *The Affairs of Peter Salem*. The final identified actor to play the venerable Chan was William Reese, whose name was credited at the end of one episode of the Australian series produced in 1950. Nothing else seems to be known about this actor.

Unlike the Charlie Chan film series where Charlie's task each time was solving a puzzling murder, the radio programs veered back and forth between murder mysteries and basic cops-and-robbers adventures. This lack of focus in the various radio series perhaps diminished the character on radio and made him just another cop/detective—albeit one who talked a little "funny" compared to most of the others.

The fact that there are only forty-two recorded episodes that are known to have survived from the seven different series (and in two of those series no episodes have survived) makes it difficult to judge the overall quality of the various series. It is probably safe to say that Charlie Chan on radio was never very notable and that of all the formats where the character has appeared (novels, movies, comics, radio, TV, TV cartoons, etc.), his radio adventures would be on the lower end of the quality ladder.

Popular stage and film actor Walter Connolly was the first Charlie Chan on radio.

What follows is a brief description of each of the Charlie Chan radio series with a plot summary and short commentary about each of the surviving episodes.

Title: *Charlie Chan*

December 2, 1932 through May 26, 1933.
NBC Blue, Friday, 7:30 p.m., 30 minutes.
Sponsor: Standard Oil Company for Esso gasoline, motor oil, and
    other automotive products.
Charlie Chan: Walter Connolly.

This first radio incarnation of Charlie Chan was aired as the Friday program of *Five Star Theater*, which presented a different type of show each weeknight. It was on this series that three of Earl Derr Biggers' novels were presented in ongoing episodes. The novels were *The Black Camel, The Chinese Parrot,* and *Behind That Curtain.* No episodes of this series are known to exist.

Title: *Charlie Chan* and, later, *The Adventures of Charlie Chan*
   September 17, 1936 through April 22, 1938.
   Mutual Broadcasting System, weekdays, 5:15 p.m., 15 minutes.
   Sponsor: Sustaining.
   Charlie Chan: Unknown.

There were two sets of Charlie Chan radio adventures presented on the Mutual Broadcasting System between 1936 and 1938, both fifteen-minute episodes with a different, unidentified actor in each series. On these two series a Charlie Chan case would be serialized over a period of days or even weeks, as in *The Case of the Madame Landini Murder*. Some sources claim that Walter Connolly again played Charlie Chan, but James Widner in his online *Radio Detective Story Hour*, "The History of Charlie Chan on Radio," states that it "(n)ever has been determined who the actor was who played Chan in this series." My own observation is that the voice does not sound like Walter Connolly. The first set was entitled simply *Charlie Chan*, and the format was as follows:

Orchestral Music: Music interlude very much in style of that used on *The Shadow* and *The Green Hornet*.
   Announcer Introduction: "The most delightfully fascinating character from the realms of mystery: Earl Derr Biggers' Charlie Chan."
   Music interlude: Providing time for station commercial.
   Omniscient Narrator: Introducing that day's episode.
   Fifteen-minute episode
   Announcer and Charlie Chan: Closing comments related to episode, ending with a Chan aphorism.
   Closing music.

Extant cases from the first series:

The Case of the Steamship Lacronia Mystery
PLOT/COMMENT: There have been seven murders aboard the *S.S. Lycronia* on her last eight trips. These murders have occurred in cabin fifteen, and, in desperation, Captain Petersen, the vessel's commander, has asked Honolulu's famous detective Charlie Chan to sail from San Francisco to Honolulu aboard the ship in hopes that the island detective can solve the mystery. Charlie asks that he be given the murder cabin, number 15, and Mr. Butler, the passenger occupying cabin 13, shows Inspector Chan to his cabin. In the morning Butler is found murdered, and it devel-

ops that someone had changed the numbers on the cabin doors. Inspector Chan had actually spent the night in cabin 13, while Butler had occupied the fatal cabin 15.

The only known existing episode from this serialized case is "Murder in Cabin Fifteen."

The Case of the Colonel Willoughby Murder

PLOT/COMMENT: Charlie Chan, a guest at Mr. Blake's home in San Francisco, finds himself involved in a baffling murder mystery. Colonel Willoughby, also a guest, while showing some motion pictures of China, is stabbed in the back in the darkened hallway outside the room where the pictures are being shown. The Colonel has been searching for his son, supposedly killed during World War I, and Honolulu's Detective Inspector Chan insists that the search for the whereabouts of the son has brought about the Colonel's death. The following day, the one man who might provide an explanation of the murder, Simmons the butler, is found at the front door shot through the heart. Gerald Willoughby, the murdered man's nephew, wires that he is flying from Chicago to San Francisco to be present during the investigation. Charlie Chan has the assistance of Inspector Duff of Scotland Yard and O'Brien of the San Francisco Police during his investigation of the case.

As far as is known, there are only four untitled fifteen-minute episodes extant in *The Case of the Colonel Willoughby Murder*.

The Case of the Madame Landini Murder

PLOT/COMMENT: Charlie Chan is invited to Pine View at Lake Tahoe by Dudley Ward to assist in tracing the millionaire's son who was born after Ward's separation from the famous opera singer Madame Landini. Landini refuses to talk about the son. Presently, with house guests visiting Pine View, a shot rings out and Madame Landini is found murdered. Ward and all of his house guests are suspects in the murder investigation. They include John Ryder, Mr. Romano, and Dr. Swan, all ex-husbands of Madame Landini and all with motives. Additional suspects include pretty Leslie Beaton who had an intense dislike of Madame Landini, her brother Hugh Beaton who was currently engaged to Landini, Captain Ireland, Landini's pilot, and a mysterious elderly Chinese servant named Ah Sing. Local Sheriff Don Holt and Inspector Chan begin their investigation into the murder.

The Case of the Madame Landini Murder is based on Earl Derr Biggers' last novel *Keeper of the Keys*. There were thirty-nine individual fifteen-minute daily episodes of the Landini case. The extant episodes start with episode seven and are entitled as follows:

07-39 "The Chinese Suspect"
08-39 "A Barking Dog"
09-39 "The Premature Corpse"
10-39 "Too Many Suspects"
11-39 "Too Many Lies"
12-39 "Jealousy"
13-39 "Blind Sight"
14-39 "Blackmail"
15-39 "A New Corpse"
16-39 "Fear in the Night"
17-39 "Who Killed Dr. Swan?"
18-39 "The Missing Key"
19-39 "A New Clue"
20-39 "Double Murder Weapon"
21-39 "The Heir"
22-39 "More Accusations"
23-39 "Chan Gets Tough"
24-39 "The Telegram"
25-39 "The Gun"
26-39 "The Play is the Thing"
27-39 "Ryder's Cover-up"
28-39 "Blind Man's Bluff"
29-39 "The Second Bullet"
30-39 "Conversation with Ah Sing"
31-39 "New Developments"
32-39 "Cecil's Story"
33-39 "Chan's Proclamation"
34-39 "Landini's Diary"
35-39 "Color Blind Killer"
36-39 "Eye Witness"
37-39 "A Test of Color"
38-39 "A Getaway"
39-39 "Murderous Revelation"

The following two case files are from the second set of Charlie Chan radio programs that were presented on the Mutual Broadcasting System between 1936 and 1938. This series was called *The Adventures of Charlie Chan*, and the format was basically the same as for the first set except that the show began with a Chinese gong sound and Oriental music. The announcer said: "*The Adventures of Charlie Chan*" and then the Oriental music continued in order to allow for station commercials. Then the announcer returned to introduce that day's episode. The second set was produced by a company called American Radio Features Syndication. It is not known for sure if this second series was presented as a continuation of the first Mutual series or if it was sold as a syndicated radio series to individual radio stations across the country. The two cases that survive from this series are *The Case of the Eye of Buddha* and *The Case of the Murder of Deacon Jessup*.

The Case of the Eye of Buddha

PLOT/COMMENT: Charlie Chan has gone from Honolulu to the island of Maui in pursuit of Morton Rand, head of a notorious international syndicate, who has stolen a magnificent ruby, The Eye of Buddha, from Timothy Eden, a millionaire jewel merchant in San Francisco. Rand is hiding on the cattle ranch of Malcolm Boyd, another leader of the gang. Because neither Rand nor Boyd knows Charlie Chan by sight, he believes himself comparatively safe in his disguise as Ah Kim, a Chinese cook. But Charlie is soon recognized by Whitey Burke, one of Rand's henchmen. Eventually, Charlie regains the upper hand, though Rand escapes. Charlie's Number One Son Lee Chan, back in Honolulu, is conducting his own investigation of the missing ruby while Charlie is returning from his sojourn in Maui.

Only two episodes of this case are believed extant. They are episodes seven, "Pursuit of Morton Rand," and eight, "Return to Honolulu."

The Case of the Murder of Deacon Jessup

PLOT/COMMENT: Inspector Charlie Chan, number one son Lee, and Sergeant Mulligan go to a small, disreputable hotel in response to a frantic telephone call from a man known to the Honolulu underworld as Deacon Jessup, a despicable man who has been involved in numerous crimes. When they arrive at the hotel, they find that Jessup has been stabbed to death. Leaving Sergeant Mulligan in charge, Charlie and Lee return to headquarters to make a report to Police Commissioner Williams. During Charlie's report Sergeant Mulligan arrives with the handcuffed Dennis Rand, an irate young man who came to the hotel asking for Jessup. Charlie interrogates Rand and learns that Jessup had called Rand shortly before his death. Charlie releases Rand after the questioning but asks Lee to follow him. The name Rand is familiar to Charlie and soon he recalls Morton Rand from the long-ago *Case of the Eye of Buddha* in which Rand had an infant son. Charlie believes that Dennis is the grown-up son. Lee phones Charlie at this point to report that he has followed Dennis Rand to a hotel where he has asked the desk clerk for Morton Rand's room. It appears that Chan's old nemesis is in Honolulu and is in some way involved in the murder of Deacon Jessup.

This episode, entitled "Chan Reports to the Commissioner," is the only one known to exist from *The Case of the Murder of Deacon Jessup*.

Title: *The Adventures of Charlie Chan*

> July 6 through September 28, 1944, Sponsored.
> October 4, 1944, through April 5, 1945, Sustaining.
> NBC, Thursday, 7:30 p.m., 30 minutes.
> Sponsor: Lever Brothers Company for Lifebuoy soap and
>   Rinso detergent.
> Charlie Chan: Ed Begley.

Only one episode from this series is known to exist and only as an episode extracted from the series and presented as an episode of *The Mystery Playhouse*. *The Mystery Playhouse* was a radio series consisting of previously aired network radio programs that was hosted by Peter Lorre and produced for the Armed Forces Radio Service to provide radio entertainment for our servicemen during and after World War II. One of the Ed Begley thirty-minute Charlie Chan episodes was included in the series. For this episode, "Charlie's Daughter Is Kidnapped," Howard Duff substitutes for Lorre as host and calls himself Sergeant X. (Anyone who was a regular radio listener at the time would immediately recognize Duff's voice as that of the character Sam Spade from radio's *The Adventures of Sam Spade*.) Duff introduces the episode in a dry, low-key manner that makes him sound as if he is bored with his responsibilities, which he probably was. The episode is a standard cops-and-robbers police drama with none of the mystery aspects commonly associated with Charlie Chan stories.

Charlie Chan's Daughter is Kidnapped

PLOT: Charlie's daughter Rose goes to a newsstand one evening to get a newspaper for Charlie and finds herself abducted by three bank robbers as they are making their escape in a borrowed taxicab. Charlie and Number One Son Tommy (yes, Tommy! This radio episode is from the

Leon Janney (left) played Number One Son to Ed Begley's
Charlie Chan on the weekday series that aired on ABC radio
stations during the summer and fall of 1945.

era when Benson Fong was playing Tommy Chan in the Sydney Toler
films, so that may account for the use of the name Tommy—but Tommy
was Number *Three* Son in the films) join Captain Flannery of the police
department in the investigation into the bank robbery and kidnapping.
The owner of the taxi used in the robbery says that his trouble-prone
brother borrowed the taxi and is probably part of the gang of robbers.
Soon a ransom note is sent to Charlie's home asking for ten thousand dollars in ransom for the return of Rose. With the help of the police and son
Tommy's firecrackers, Charlie locates and captures the gang. Tommy says
that his firecrackers were to be used to energize a crowd in Chinatown to
buy war bonds. The episode ends with Charlie saying he is going to buy
war bonds and that all Americans should do so to help our soldiers in the
fight to win World War II.

Title: *The Adventures of Charlie Chan* (aka *The Incomparable Charlie Chan)*

June 18 through November 30, 1945.
ABC, weekdays, 6:45 p.m. 15 minutes.
Sponsor: Sustaining.
Charlie Chan: Ed Begley.
Number One Son: Leon Janney.
Alfred Vester: Writer.
Chick Vincent: Producer.
Dorian St. George: Announcer.

The format for this serialized version of Charlie Chan was as follows:

Announcer introduction: "The incomparable Charlie Chan. (Chinese gong) The American Broadcasting Company presents the incomparable Charlie Chan—detective, philosopher, modern Chinese sage in a new and exciting series. Join the famous detective every day at this time, Monday through Friday, as he combines the wisdom of the East and the science of the West in a thrilling and dramatic chapter from *The Adventures of Charlie Chan."*

Organ music up and then fade under voice.

Charlie Chan introduces the episode: (example from "The Case of the Marching Ants") "Charlie Chan humbly gives you greeting and extends warm welcome. Sage has said nature sometimes reveals deepest truths in wildest jokes (music sting). Today apparent joke reveal truth about (music sting) murder. But first word from honorable announcer."

Announcer: (public service announcement) Plug for war bonds and patriotic support for WWII. Then: "And now back to Charlie Chan. (organ music) This week's adventure (music sting) 'The Case of the Marching Ants.'"

Organ music bridge into episode.

Announcer introduction to episode.

Fifteen-minute episode.

Announcer: "We will return to Charlie Chan in just a moment." (another Public service announcement) "And now, here is Charlie Chan."

Organ music up and under.

Charlie Chan: Closing comments on this day's episode as a teaser for tomorrow. Then, "Hope you will join self on same tomorrow. Until then, goodbye. Thank you."

Announcer: "Be sure to join us tomorrow at this same time for 'The Case of the Marching Ants.' There'll be more thrills, excitement, and comedy in *The Adventures of Charlie Chan*. *The Adventures of Charlie Chan* is based on the famous character created by Earl Derr Biggers. Charlie Chan is played by Ed Begley; Number One Son by Leon Janney. This series, written by Alfred Vester, is produced by Chick Vincent. Dorian St. George speaking. This is the American Broadcasting Company.

Episodes in existence from this series are as follows:

The Case of the Marching Ants

PLOT: Howard Roark, an eccentric student of necromancy and the occult, has called Charlie Chan and son to his home to explain a strange procession of marching ants. Charlie and Number One Son follow the ants to a large vine-covered oak tree behind which is the crypt where Roark conducts his mysterious researches. In the tree Lee discovers the dead body of lawyer Clarence Brighton, clothed in his pajamas. Soon two of Brighton's relatives, Everod and Clarence Brighton, call Chan and claim the other relative is the guilty party.

There is only this one episode extant for *The Case of the Marching Ants*.

The Case of the Man Who Moved Mountains

PLOT: Charlie Chan receives a call supposedly from Professor Arthur Moore who runs a roadside Hall of History with statues of famous people and famous events. Professor Moore, in an emotional state, claims that one of his statues is coming to life, and he wants Chan to investigate. Charlie's Number One Son says, "This guy must be crazy." Nevertheless, Charlie and son drive to the Hall of History where Professor Moore denies he ever called Charlie. While the professor is showing the venerable detective and son around the outdoor display, they suddenly notice the arm of one of the statues is moving. When they examine the statue, they discover that it is a dead man later identified as Charles Burnett. He has been shot. Charlie's investigation discloses that Burnett has been buying up mountain slag from worn-out goldmines and, apparently, manufacturing diamonds from this thought-to-be-useless material. Soon, Chan and his Number One Son have several suspects for the murder: Professor Moore, the owner of the Hall of History where Burnett's body was found; Marion Green, Burnett's secretary; Mr. Brock, a diamond dealer who claims he has never bought any diamonds from Burnett; and Martin Hayward, a trucker who moved the mountain slag for Burnett.

Only untitled episodes one and four of the five-part series of *The Case of the Man Who Moved Mountains* are known to be extant.

Santos Ortega, a popular radio actor of the time,
played Charlie Chan for the 1947-1948 radio series.

Title: *The Adventures of Charlie Chan*

August 18, 1947, through June 21, 1948.
Mutual Broadcasting System, Monday, 8:30 p.m., 30 minutes.
Sponsor: Pharmaco, Inc. for Feen-A-Mint laxative chewing gum
    and other health care products.
Charlie Chan: Santos Ortega.
Lee Chan: Rodney Jacobs and Leon Janney.

No recorded episodes are known to exist.

Title: *The Adventures of Charlie Chan*

1950, Australian Broadcasting Company.
Grace Gibson Radio Productions, 52 syndicated episodes,
    30 minutes.
Producer: Reg Johnston is credited as producer in most of the
    extant episodes, but Lawrence H. Cecil also served as producer
    for a time during the production of the fifty-two episodes.

Charlie Chan: There are at least two actors who play Charlie in the series but only one actor's name is known, William Reese, who is credited in one of the extant episodes; otherwise, there are no acting credits announced.

The episodes are, for the most part, standard cops-and-robbers crime dramas rather than the murder mysteries that make up the Chan canon in motion pictures and television. Even though the series is set in San Francisco, the Australian radio actors in the series never were able to lose their Aussie/English accents; even Number One Son Lee has such an accent. The only Oriental-style music used is in the opening and closing moments of the program; within each episode the bridge music for scenes is standard "canned" American-sounding orchestrations that could be purchased for this purpose.

The format for this last Chan radio series is as follows:

Introductory Music: (Oriental-type orchestral music is heard.)
Announcer: "The Incomparable Charlie Chan."
Music Interlude: (During which local commercials are presented.)
Announcer: "We proudly present the incomparable Charlie Chan in a new and exciting series of adventures combining the wisdom of the East and the science of the West in a dramatic chapter from *The Adventures of Charlie Chan.*"
Music up and under.
Charlie Chan: "Charlie Chan humbly bids you good evening and extends warm welcome. It is written, man who gives good counsel to others becomes fool when advising self. Tonight we meet people who advise self to escape murder. Person is Charlie Chan. Listen, please. Thank you."
Music up and under.
Announcer: "Tonight's adventure: The Case of the _____."
Omniscient Narrator: (He presents the introduction of the episode.)
Thirty-minute episode.
Music Interlude: (During the music commercial announcements are presented, and then the music is lowered as Charlie speaks.)
Charlie Chan: (He delivers comments regarding current or next episode, ending with Chinese aphorism.)
Music interlude: (During the music local commercials are presented.)
Announcer: "Be sure to join us next week at the same time for *The Adventures of Charlie Chan*, based on the famous character created by Earl Derr Biggers. This is a Grace Gibson production, produced by Reg Johnston."

Episodes known to be extant of the series are as follows:

The Case of the Romantic Engineer

PLOT/COMMENT: The Polo Café in San Francisco's underworld is a hangout for criminals. It is there that petty crook Emory Haggert meets with mining engineer "Doc" John Nash and plots a counterfeiting enterprise in which Haggert will do the "groundwork" making the fake, unfinished coins and supplying the paper for the bills and Nash will provide the artistic touch of the silver plating and printing press, and they will share 50/50 on the take. Charlie and son Lee become involved when Nash's wife fears that her husband, who supposedly is in Texas on a job, is really missing because his romantic letters to her, she has discovered, are taken from a novel she has found in the library. Charlie discovers that the money Nash has been sending her is counterfeit and is wrapped in a local San Francisco newspaper. Charlie and Lee work with the Secret Service to round up the counterfeiters.

This episode is a standard cops-and-counterfeiters tale with none of the murder mystery design that one expects of a Charlie Chan story. The production values of music and sound effects are typical of other radio productions of the era. One disconcerting aspect of the program is Number One Son Lee. The unidentified actor who plays the role possesses a radio voice that is somewhat high-pitched (at times even oddly feminine in timbre) and suggests that he is an early teenager. Even the nature of his dialogue suggests youthfulness, but the script calls for Charlie to send him out to do a man's work. While individual episodes vary from murder mysteries to cops-and-robbers affairs, each episode ends with Charlie enumerating (usually to son Lee) the clues or his mysterious *modus operandi* that led him to the murderer and/or bad guys.

The Curious Ride of the Sea Witch

PLOT/COMMENT: On a dark and foggy night in Honolulu a prison break occurs, and two men, Big Lou Gleason and Porky Bates, each serving a life sentence for murder, make their way to freedom in a row boat. On that same murky night, a luxury yacht named *Sea Witch* is forced to drop anchor in a nearby cove until the fog lifts. The yacht's owner, the extremely wealthy Mrs. Hanna Bromfield, opposes her daughter Bernice's impending marriage to a young man named Burton Henry. The three of them quarrel bitterly over the mother's objections that the boy is unworthy of her daughter who will someday inherit a fortune. That night Charlie Chan, son Lee, and the Honolulu police capture the two escaped prisoners who have made their way onto the *Sea Witch* but not before someone has shot Mrs. Bromfield while she was preparing for bed in her cabin. Burton Henry, the fiancé, claims that he saw Gleason shoot her through the porthole in her cabin, but both Gleason and Bates deny that they had anything to do with the murder and that they were only trying to take command of the ship so that they could complete their escape from Honolulu. Charlie and Lee search for clues to determine who is lying and who is telling the truth.

This episode utilizes the murder mystery format that Chan fans expect, but the murder occurs very late in the proceedings (the last ten minutes), and the suspects are few. The rather simplistic plot and its development make it quite obvious who the murderer is, but Charlie's disclosure of the clues makes the ending palatable.

The Case of the Talking Doll

PLOT/COMMENT: Charlie Chan is pursuing Knife Glencannon and Spider Brady, two thieves who have recently made off with the valuable Hopkins sapphires and are holed up in a San Francisco machine shop. While there Knife has made an acid bomb and placed it inside a doll that he plans to leave at Charlie Chan's house. It is his hope that the bomb will explode and perhaps kill Chan and his family. In a shootout at the machine shop, Spider is shot, but Knife, though wounded, escapes with the fatal doll. For a time it appears that Charlie's Number Five Daughter Patsy has been given the doll by someone who left it at the door. But then Charlie discovers that Patsy gave the doll to a passing junkman who then gave the doll to his daughter. Charlie, son Lee, and Lt. Regal rush to the home of the junkman. It turns out that the junkman's daughter left it with an "awful sick man" who lives a few houses away. She put the doll next to the man as he slept so that he would have company when he awakened. Before Charlie, Lee, and Lt. Regal can get to the house, the bomb goes off, killing the awful sick man, Knife Glencannon.

The murder mystery format is again forsworn and replaced utilizing a suspense/drama motif with an ironic denouement. Interestingly, the plot introduces Chan's Number Five Daughter Patsy, probably six or seven years old as depicted in the script. The car sound effect that is utilized in these episodes suggests a Model T or some other ancient jalopy. There are no smooth-running, high-octane cars such as The Green Hornet's Black Beauty.

The Case of the Escaped Musician

PLOT/COMMENT: Young, talented musician Ronnie Post has been tricked into being a lookout for thief Pete Walsh on the robbery of an office building. During the burglary a night watchman shoots at Ronnie, wounding him in the hand. When Charlie, son Lee, and the San Francisco police arrive, they find the watchman stabbed to death. Later, through a contact with Ronnie's mother, Charlie finds the boy who says that he did not kill the watchman and that he was led down the path to crime by Pete Walsh, who has escaped. Charlie then seemingly presents a plan for the boy to escape capture by the police, giving him specific instructions for making his escape. Charlie then calls Sergeant Brady of the police and has the boy's route broadcast over the radio, much to the dismay of son Lee who thinks that his dad is double-crossing the boy. In the denouement Charlie explains that he knew Pete would be looking for Ronnie to "shut him up," and by broadcasting his route, Pete would know where to find Ronnie—thus allowing Charlie and Lee to follow and catch Pete.

The flimsy plot relies heavily upon the stupidity of the bad guy, since the police would obviously be following Ronnie and would thus have a good chance of catching Pete—but then these radio melodramas were never meant to be very complicated. The fact that Ronnie is a musician is of no significance in the plot; he could just as easily have been a football player.

The Case of the Frightened Shroff

PLOT/COMMENT: "A shroff," Charlie Chan tells his Number One Son Lee, "is an Oriental word that means money changer, small banker, or bill collector." The question comes up when Charlie and Lee are visiting with the grieving mother of Jimmy Bates who was shot and killed in a gunfight with the police. While they are commiserating with Mrs. Bates, a messenger arrives at the house to collect on an IOU for fifty dollars that has what appears to be Jimmy's signature on it. Charlie recognizes this as a scam to fleece money from relatives of the recently deceased who feel a moral obligation to come forth with the money. Charlie's investigation leads him to a Russian shroff named Demetrius Greggor, an associate con-man named Dan Temple, an old forger named Inky, and a lady assistant, June Morris, who gathers names of deceased persons—and turns up dead before Charlie can talk with her. Now Charlie has a murder case to solve.

This is a routine episode in the radio series, maybe slightly more interesting because of the nature of the crime. Following the regular format for the program, there are several clues Charlie explains at the conclusion that make clear the puzzling tactics he used to determine which of the three suspects was the murderer.

The Case of the Telltale Hands

PLOT/COMMENT: Charlie and son Lee find themselves on a strange case where a house robber uses nitroglycerine to blow up home safes and then makes off with the loot. Each time the robbery takes place after the home piano has been tuned by a young blind girl named Judy Carroll. Charlie and Lee soon discover that the blind girl's father Rollo Carroll is the culprit and has murdered his henchman and left him at the scene of the last robbery, himself wounded in the head in the scuffle. Charlie finds nitro moisture on the dead man's neck and deduces that it is from the nitro used in the robbery and that the murderer must have nitro on his hands. Soon a pattern of people with terrible headaches emerges. Charlie and Lee follow the trail of headaches, each person with a severe headache having had contact with the murderer, until they corner him as he tries to escape in a motor launch on the San Francisco wharf. In the denouement Charlie explains to Lee that nitroglycerine is a highly potent poison, instantly absorbed through the skin and producing intense headaches and shock. The nitro is so strong that it can be passed merely by the touch of a hand.

This is the most bizarre episode yet in the series. The plot relies on huge coincidences and a very unlikely series of events that allow Charlie and Lee to follow a path of headaches through the city of San Francisco until they capture the murderer. In most of these episodes, the listener can detect an occasional Australian accent slipping into the dialogue supposedly taking place in San Francisco. In this episode it is even more prevalent and a bit amusing. Even Number One Son Lee has an Aussie accent intermittently.

The Case of the Fiery Santa Claus

PLOT/COMMENT: Fiery-haired Gary Holland enters Bolton's Department Story shortly before Christmas to buy four engraved silver lockets for four middle-aged, wealthy ladies he is wooing—all at the same time. Taking a moment to hit on the cute, young salesclerk before telling her the lockets are for four of his former teachers, Gary gives her the wording for the inscriptions (" From Gary with all my love") and the name for each locket: Martha, Betty, Dolores, and Maude. Before leaving Bolton's, the charming, handsome, red-haired Gary wheedles a date with the cute salesclerk. Upon Gary's leave-taking, Inspector Chan arrives, warns the girl about meeting the debonair redhead who's wanted in Seattle for defrauding older women, and asks for the names and addresses of the ladies who are to receive the lockets.

During all of this, Charlie's resourceful son Lee takes photographs of the unaware lady charmer as he leaves Bolton's.

Gary's luck is running out. Shortly after proposing marriage to Maude, she receives her Christmas locket only to discover that the inscription proclaims, "From Gary with all my love to Betty." Furious, Martha accosts Gary on the street corner where he is working as a sidewalk Santa in full holiday garb, white beard and all. Santa Gary abducts the matronly Martha in her car and drives to a remote area with cabins, planning to burn a cabin with Martha in it. Charlie and Lee, hot on their trail, arrive in time to whisk Martha out of the burning cabin, but Gary is incinerated in his highly-flammable fur-lined red suit and combustible beard. End of case!

This is one of the more interesting episodes in the series, although it has its bizarre and unlikely aspects—but so do most of these Chan adventures. For example: Would Gary really take a job as a sidewalk Santa? Would he really abscond with Martha and then try to murder her by burning down a cabin with her in it? Anyway, the listener can take some enjoyment from the episode even though many of the happenings are problematical.

The Case of the Man Who Murdered Santa Claus

PLOT/COMMENT: There's quite a back story to this Chan episode. It seems that in 1779 there was a book collector in England named Jennings Carton who came upon a priceless manuscript copy of Shakespeare's *Richard III*. Later it was stolen by a madman named Richard Wells who hid it in his mantelpiece. When Wells died, his will revealed the theft of the manuscript and its location in the mantelpiece, but by then all of his belongings had been sold, including the mantelpiece. Neither the mantelpiece nor the manuscript was ever found.

Now we jump to San Francisco in the present day just before Christmas. Charlie and son Lee are visiting wealthy Cyrus Granger who is preparing for the annual Christmas party given for the police orphanage fund. Presently, the talent agency Santa Claus arrives, and he and Granger go into the ballroom to plan the party while Charlie and Lee visit with Granger's niece, Nancy. Soon they notice a van leaving that was to deliver chairs for the party, but Sampson the butler says that no chairs were left. Charlie and Lee go to the ballroom which is now in total disarray and find Santa Claus stabbed to death on the floor and Granger missing. Closer examination reveals that it's really Granger dead in the Santa costume and the Santa actor missing—and also the mantelpiece over the fireplace. Charlie's investigation reveals the longtime search for the missing mantelpiece containing the Shakespeare manuscript and a rash of mantelpiece robberies that have taken place in England and America for many years.

The plot covers a lot of time and territory and only incidentally has any connection to Christmas and Santa Claus, but it is one of the better constructed plots in the series. The closing credits on the program indicate that Lawrence H. Cecil was now the director, where on several other episodes he was billed as producer. Most likely, the producer was also the director for these episodes.

The Case of the White Heel

PLOT/COMMENT: This episode is included just for the record since only the first half of the episode is known to exist. Charlie and son Lee are traveling by car on a fishing trip when they notice something in the road and stop. The item is a lady's white hat with fresh blood on it. A search of the area reveals the body of a young lady who has been stabbed. In her hand Charlie discovers the heel of a white shoe, not her own. A package next to the body contains an apron for the Golden Gate Cake and Coffee Shop with the initials PA on it. Charlie and Lee decide to forgo their fishing trip and investigate the murder by heading for the cake and coffee shop. Charlie discovers that the owner of the coffee shop, a Mr. Miller, was engaged to the girl they found beside the road, now identified as Peggy Atkins. Several other people figure in the investigation, including Peggy's old boyfriend Joe Murphy and Helen Woods, a worker at the coffee shop who didn't get along with Peggy. By the mid-episode commercial break, Charlie has another dead body on his hands, that of Helen Woods, Peggy's old nemesis. This time the victim has been stabbed with an ice pick.

Barring some old-time-radio archivist locating the concluding thirteen minutes of the episode, the murderer is safe from prosecution.

The Comic Strips, Comic Books, Better Little Books, and Games Case Files of Charlie Chan

Case Files of Charlie Chan

In 1938 Alfred Andriola (1912-1983) was selected by Earl Derr Biggers to create a *Charlie Chan* newspaper comic strip for the McNaught Newspaper syndicate. Andriola was born in New York, grew up in New Jersey, and studied at Cooper Union and Columbia University. He became an assistant to cartoonist Milton Caniff, famous for his *Terry and the Pirates* and later *Steve Canyon* strips, after sending Caniff a fan letter. Andriola is perhaps most famous for the comic strip *Kerry Drake* (starting in 1943) but also, certainly, for *Charlie Chan,* which was his first strip. For the Chan comic strip Andriola created a hard-fisted young man named Kirk Barrow as Charlie's sidekick. Kirk, maybe not surprisingly, bore a striking resemblance to Caniff's Terry Lee and Steve Canyon. The *Charlie Chan* comic strip by Andriola

The Afred Andriola Charlie Chan newspaper comic strip was reprinted in *Feature Comics* starting with issue 23 in August of 1939.

started on October 24, 1938, and ran until May of 1942. The cancellation was attributed to the December 1941 Japanese attack on Pearl Harbor—a misguided consequence since Charlie Chan was Chinese and China was not America's enemy in World War II.

Feature Comics, Publisher: Quality Comics, 68 pages, $.10 each issue.

The popularity of the Alfred Andriola newspaper comic strip of *Charlie Chan* resulted in *Feature Comics* picking up reprint rights starting with issue 23 in August 1939 and running for nine issues through April of 1940. The *Charlie Chan* strip joined such other popular characters in the comic as *Joe Palooka, Reynolds of the Mounted, Mickey Finn, Dixie Dugan,* and *Jane Arden.*

> #23 – August 1939, Story: "Introducing Charlie Chan," Writer: Alfred Andriola, Pencils: Alfred Andriola, Inks: Alfred Andriola. (All stories are Andriola newspaper comic strip reprints.)
> #24 – September 1939, Story: "The Mahati Diamond."
> #25 – October 1939, Story: "The Hedrin Gold Mine Mystery: Part 1."
> #26 – November 1939, Story: "The Hedrin Gold Mine Mystery: Part 2."
> #27 – December 1939, Story: No title available.
> #28 – January 1940, Story: "The Kidnapping of Donna Grant: Part 1."
> #29 – February 1940, Story: "The Kidnapping of Donna Grant: Part 2."
> #30 – March 1940, Story: "The Dr. Croft Ruby Mystery: Part 1."
> #31 – April 1940, Story: "The Dr. Croft Ruby Mystery: Part 2."

Big Shot Comics, Publisher: Columbia, 68 pages, $.10 each issue.

In May of 1940 several of the popular characters in *Feature Comics* moved to *Big Shot Comics*, including *Joe Palooka, Dixie Dugan, Charlie Chan,* and a few others. The Charlie Chan stories continued to be reprints of the Alfred Andriola newspaper strip. When the newspaper strip was cancelled in May of 1942, the strip in *Big Shot Comics* had already ended with the April issue. And that was the last that was seen of the *Charlie Chan* comic strip except for a one-issue publication of *Columbia, Gem of the Comics* in 1943, which contained a Charlie Chan story that was again a reprint of the Andriola newspaper strip.

> #1 – May 1940, Story: "The Murder of Norda Nol, l" Script: Alfred Andriola, Pencils: Alfred Andriola, Inks: Alfred Andriola. All stories are Andriola newspaper comic strip reprints.
> #2 – June 1940, Story: "Revelation."
> #3 – July 1940, Story: "Search for a Weapon."
> #4 – August 1940, Story: "The Mute."

#5 – September 1940, Story: "The Bad Doctor."
#6 – October 1940, Story: "The Kidnapping of David Frome, Part 1."
#7 – November 1940, Story: "The Kidnapping of David Frome, Part 2."
#8 – December 1940, Story: "The Kidnapping of David Frome, Part 3."
#9 – January 1941, Story: "The Macaw Mystery, Part 1."
#10 – February 1941, Story: "The Macaw Mystery, Part 2."
#11 – 16, March 1941 through August 1941, Story: No titles available.
#17 – September 1941, Story: "The Frame-Up."
#18 – October 1941, Story: No title available.
#19 – November 1941, Story: "The Carnival Killer."
#20 – 22 December 1941 – February 1942, Story: No titles available.
There was no publication of the comic in March 1942.
#23 – April 1942, Story: No title available.

Columbia, Gem of the Comics, Publisher: Columbia, 68 pages, $.10. There was only one issue published.

#1 – 1943, Story: No title or credits available. The strip is another reprint one of the Alfred Andriola *Charlie Chan* newspaper comic strips.

Charlie Chan, Publisher: *Prize Comics* (Crestwood Publications), 52 pages, $.10 each issue.

Joe Simon (1913-) and Jack Kirby (1917-1994) were very successful comic book artists, writers, editors, and publishers. Together they co-created *Captain America* in 1941, one of the great superheroes of comicdom that started in *Timely Comics* which later evolved into *Marvel Comics*. In 1948 they created *Prize Comics'* *Charlie Chan* which ran for five issues.

#1 – June-July 1948, Stories: "The Hit and Run Murder Case," "You Are Guilty of Many Crimes," "The Land of the Leopard Men." Creators: Joe Simon and Jack Kirby, Pencils: Carmine Infantino, Inks: Carmine Infantino, Joe Simon. All subsequent credits are the same except as noted.
#2 – September 1948, Stories: "Number One Trouble," "The Vanishing Jewel Salesman," "Murder on the Midway."

#3 – October—November 1948, Stories: "The Secret of the Smuggled Silk," "The Mystery of the Phantom Killer," "Chan, You Cannot Defeat a Phantom."

#4 – December 1948—January 1949, Stories: "The Burial-at-Sea Mystery," "The Model Murder Case," "The Case of the Missing Planet."

#5 – February—March 1949, Stories: "The Antique Burglar," "Murder on Ice," "The Dude Ranch Hold-Up." Pencils: Dick Briefer, Inks: Dick Briefer.

Charlie Chan, Publisher: Charlton, 36 pages, $.10 each issue.

Joe Simon and Jack Kirby seemed to pick up where they left off with *Charlie Chan* at *Prize Comics*, starting with issue #6 six years later at Charlton, this time for a four-issue run.

#6 – June 1955, Stories: "See no Evil," "Pawns of Peril," "Pitfall," "Ride 'Em, Birmingham." Pencils: Jack Kirby, Inks: Joe Simon. All subsequent credits are the same except as noted. (The Number One Son in this comic series is named Jimmy. In the movie series Jimmy was the Number Two Son.)

#7 – August 1955, Stories: "Silent Witness," "The Talking Stone Face," "Trick Ending."

#8 – October 1955, Stories: "Clever Victim," "The Emerald Turtle," "The Lock without a Key."

#9 – March 1956, Stories: "Troublesome Time," "Fool's Gold," "The Penalty."

The New Adventures of Charlie Chan, Publisher: DC, 36 pages, $.10 each issue.

This six-issue series is, of course, based on the television series starring J. Carrol Naish and James Hong. As in the television series, each issue is set in a different exotic locale and Charlie is depicted as a master of judo.

#1 – May 1958, Stories: "Secret of Phantom Bells!" and "Charlie Chan's Invisible Clue!" Writer: John Broome, Pencils: Sid Greene, Inks: Joe Giella, Cover art: Sid Greene, Joe Giella, Editor: Julius Schwartz. All subsequent credits are the same except as noted.

#2 – July 1958, Stories: "Menace of the Giant Statues!" and "Riddle of the Runaway Mummy!" Cover art: Sid Greene.

#3 – September 1958, Stories: "The Two Lives of Charlie Chan" and "Secret of the Calypso Doll." Inkers: Sid Greene, Bernard Sachs.

#4 – November 1958, Stories: "Case of the Vanishing Man!" and "The Highwayman's Last Ride." Inker: Sid Greene, Cover art: Sid Greene.

#5 – January 1959, Stories: "The Monarch of Menace" and "Challenge of the Crimson Clown."

#6 – March 1959, Stories: "Trail across the Sky!" and "The Case of the Hillbilly Detective."

Charlie Chan, Publisher: Dell, 36 pages, $.15 each issue.

In what seems something of an afterthought, Dell revived the *Charlie Chan* comic for two issues in late 1965 and early1966 with Frank Springer (1929-2009) art. Early on in his career Springer had worked on the *Terry and the Pirates* comic strip after George Wunder had taken it over from originator Milton Caniff. By the 1960s Springer had become a penciler/inker for Dell Comics, working on many of their comics including *Ghost Stories, Tales of the Tomb, The Big Valley, Iron Horse,* and the two Charlie Chan issues.

> #1 – October—December 1965, Stories: "The Touch of Midas," "Escape to Danger," "Kayu Strikes Again." Pencils: Frank Springer, Inks: Frank Springer, Editing: Don Ameson.

#2 – March 1966, Story: "Claws of the Cat." All credits the same.

The Amazing Chan and the Chan Clan, Publisher: Gold Key/Western Publishing.

Comic strip and comic book artist Warren Tufts (1925-1982) is remembered today primarily for his creation of the syndicated western-adventure strips entitled *Casey Ruggles,* which ran from 1949 until 1954. By 1960 Tufts had left the comic strip field and had begun to work in comic books, primarily for Dell and Gold Key comics. His work can be found in such comic series as *The Pink Panther; Korak, Son of Tarzan; Wagon Train;* and *The Amazing Chan and the Chan Clan.* Tufts' hobby was building and flying private airplanes, which led to his death. He died in 1982 when the plane in which he was flying crashed in Placerville, California. *The Amazing Chan and the Chan Clan* only ran for four issues.

#1 – January 1973, Story: "The Hot Ice Cream Man," $.15.
#2 – August 1973, Story: "To Catch a Pitcher," $.20.
#3 – November 1973, Story: "Sticky Fingered, Mr. Chan," $.20.
#4 –February 1974, Story: "Eye of the idol," $.20.

Charlie Chan, Publisher: Pacific Comics Club, black & white interior, color cover, 8.5 x 11 inches, bound horizontally.

Volumes 1-3 –1979, Stories: Reprints of the original Alfred Andriola *Charlie Chan* newspaper comic strip first published from October 24, 1938, through May 1942.

Charlie Chan, Publisher: Malibu, black & white interior, 2-color cover.

#1-6 – March—August 1989, Stories: Reprints of the original Alfred Andriola *Charlie Chan* newspaper comic strip first published from October 24, 1938, through May 1942.

Earl Derr Biggers' Charlie Chan, Publisher: Pacific Comics Club, black & white, softbound 2-color cover, 6 x 9 inches, 48 pages, $9.50 each. The stories are again reprints of the original Alfred Andriola *Charlie Chan* newspaper comic strip.

2002 – Story: "The Return of Keeno," Dailies and Sundays
11/20/39—1/14/40.
2003 – Story: "Drama at the Crown Circus," Dailies and Sundays
1/15/40—3/20/40.

Charlie Chan Mystery Magazine, Publisher: Renown Publications.

Starting in late 1973 publisher Leo Margulies with editors Cylvia Kleinman and Thom Montgomery published four issues of *Charlie Chan Mystery Magazine*. Basically a successor to earlier pulp magazines, it followed in the steps of the popular *Mike Shayne Mystery Magazine* and *Alfred Hitchcock's Mystery Magazine*. Each issue contained a Charlie Chan novel ranging from fifty-six to seventy-five pages in length at a cover price of seventy-five cents per issue.

Volume One, Number 1 – November 1973, Story: "Walk Softly, Strangler." Contributors: Robert Hart Davis, Jim Duke, Robert W. Alexander, Andrew Bogen, Bill Pronzini, Pauline C. Smith, George Antonich, and Lawrence Treat.

Volume One, Number 2 – February 1974, Story: "The Silent Corpse." Contributors: Hal Ellison, John Lutz, James P. Cody, Henry Slesar, Lawrence Treat, M. G. Ogan, and Edward D. Hoch.

Volume One, Number 3 – May 1974, Story: "Temple of the Golden Hoard." Contributors: David Mazroff, John Lutz, James Holding, Syd Hoff, Jack Foxx, Evelyn Payne, and Herbert Harris.

Volume One, Number 4 – August 1974, Story: "The Pawns of Death." Contributors: Francis Clifford, M. G. Ogan, Al Nussbaum, Ronald Anthony Cross, Gary Brandner, Clarence Alva Powell, and Pauline C. Smith.

Charlie Chan **Better Little Books**, Publisher: Whitman Publishing Company.

Starting in 1939 the Whitman Publishing Company published three *Charlie Chan* Better Little Books based on the Alfred Andriola *Charlie Chan* newspaper comic strip. The Better Little Books were 3 5/8 x 4 1/2 x 1 ½ inches in size with a hard cover. In each of the books there is the credit: "Adapted from the work of Earl Derr Biggers."

BLB-1478 – 1939, Title: *Charlie Chan* (On the inside title page the title is given as *Inspector Chan of the Honolulu Police*.)

BLB-1459 – 1940, Title: *Charlie Chan Solves a New Mystery*.

BLB-1424 – 1942, Title: *Charlie Chan, Villainy on the High Seas.*
Cover Artist: John Coleman Burroughs.

Charlie Chan Games

For the record it is noted that in 1937 a board game was published with the title *The Great Charlie Chan Detective Mystery Game.* Two years later in 1939 a *Charlie Chan Card Game* was released.

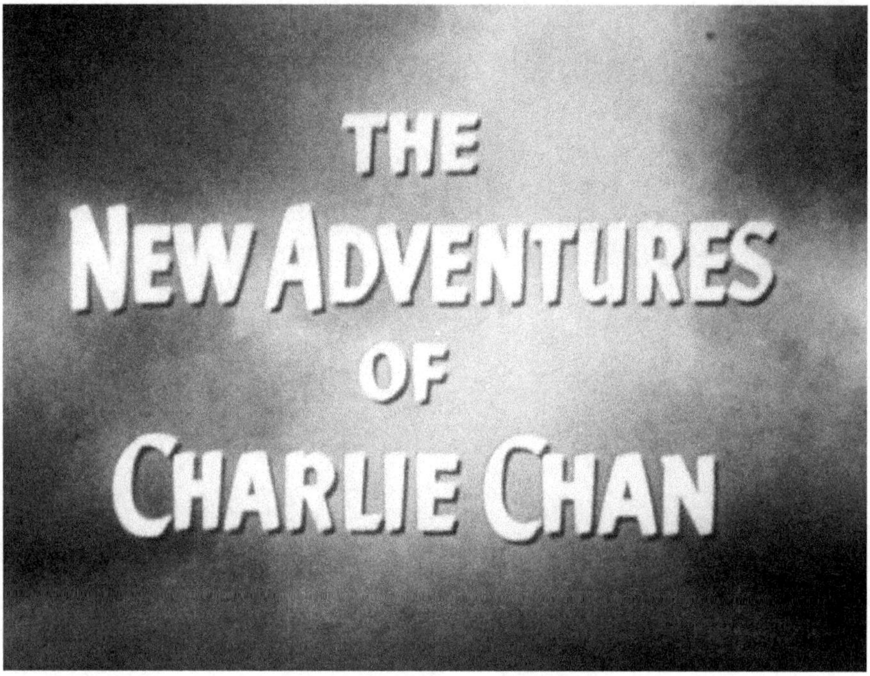
THE
NEW ADVENTURES
OF
CHARLIE CHAN

The Television Case Files
of Charlie Chan

The New Adventures of Charlie Chan starring J. Carrol Naish

The New Adventures of Charlie Chan was a syndicated, thirty-minute, black-and-white television series produced in 1957. There were thirty-nine episodes made during the run of the series with well-known American character actor J. Carrol Naish starring as Charlie Chan and the young, relatively inexperienced James Hong portraying Number One Son Barry. (Where the name Barry came from and why he was not named Lee as in the film series is anyone's guess.) The series was a joint venture of American producer Leon Fromkess's Television Programs of America (TPA) and English film mogul Sir Lew Grade's Incorporated Television

Company (ITC Entertainment). The first five episodes were filmed in the United States with all of the rest filmed in England and various parts of Europe.

J. Carrol Naish (1896-1973) was a very well-known stage, movie, radio, and television character actor by the time *The New Adventures of Charlie Chan* came about in 1957. New York born, he got his start in vaudeville as a member of Gus Edwards's troupe of kid performers. He made his adult stage debut with a touring company of *The Shanghai Gesture* in 1926 and that same year started his film career with an uncredited bit role in *What Price Glory*. Although born of an Irish heritage, his incredible ability to do foreign dialects and portray ethnic types gave him a wide range of characters to play in films and eventually earned him two Academy Award nominations: playing an Italian prisoner of war in the Humphrey Bogart film *Sahara* (1943) and a Mexican father in *A Medal for Benny* (1945). Naish reached the height of his popularity playing the role of Luigi Basko, a little Italian immigrant, in both the radio and television versions of *Life with Luigi* starting in 1948 and running through 1953.

So when Charlie Chan came along in 1957, Naish was well prepared to assume a Chinese guise and manner for the cameras. He concentrated mostly on television acting after the Chan series ended, continuing to portray a string of ethnic types. In the 1960-61 sitcom series *Guestward Ho* he played an Indian named Hawkeye for thirty-eight episodes. In 1964 on *Amos Burke, Secret Agent,* he played another Asian, Mr. Toto. On a *Green Acres* episode in 1967, he was an Indian, Chief Yellow Horse. And so it continued until the late 1960s when his health started to deteriorate. J. Carrol Naish died of emphysema on January 24, 1973, at the age of seventy-seven.

The New Adventures of Charlie Chan had a "modern" feel to it. Naish's Chan was much more active than the character had been in the film series. This Charlie was a master of Judo (much like Mr. Moto) and frequently got physical with his opponents. Son Barry, supposedly, was studying to be a criminologist while abroad with his "pop." Unfortunately, Barry, as written, was frequently an insufferable character that this writer found more annoying than any of the past Chan sons. Understand, this was mostly a problem caused by the writing for the character and not necessarily the fault of the actor—although James Hong's inexperience at that point in his career did not help matters. (I am confident that James Hong was/is well-aware of the deficiencies of the Barry role. Interestingly, in his long film and television résumé on his website, there is no mention of his involvement in the Charlie Chan series, and my efforts to contact him for an interview proved fruitless.)

Episodes in the series began with a short "teaser" of the plot followed by stirring orchestral music (almost of a fanfare type) and the image of a fog-shrouded street scene as the title of the show appeared in Chinese then dissolved into English. As the English title dissolved, Naish appeared as Charlie in a conservative dark suit, tie, and hat, slowly walking through the fog, arms behind his back, looking inscrutable. Then the words "Starring J. Carrol Naish as Charlie Chan" appeared on his left. Finally, the scene slowly faded to black, allowing for a first commercial. There was no opening credit for James Hong as Barry Chan.

The New Adventures of Charlie Chan – The Episodes

Episode One: "Your Money or Your Wife"

Executive Producer: Leon Fromkess, Producer: Sidney Marshall, Director: Charles F. Haas, Teleplay: Richard Grey and Brock Williams.

CAST: J. Carrol Naish, Lowell Gilmore, Virginia Gregg, Dayton Lummis, Liam Sullivan, Howard Culver.

PLOT/COMMENT: An expensive sports car races along a dusty mountain road until it is forced to a screeching halt. A man on crutches pulls himself from the car and painfully lumbers his way to where he sees a cable is stretched across the road, leaving nowhere to go except off a cliff—fade to opening credits.

Called to the beachfront home of the wealthy Mr. Kramer, Charlie is asked to investigate Kramer's fear that someone is out to murder him. Shortly thereafter, it is discovered that Kramer's wife Marcia has been kidnapped and a ransom note and audiotape are found in Kramer's car. On the tape Marcia says that her life is in jeopardy and that $50,000 should be delivered to a spot she designates. When Marcia's body is later found, Charlie has three suspects for the murder: Mr. Kramer himself; his secretary, Ella Parsons, who admits that she hates Marcia; and a handsome artist, Andre Patton, who is found with the body and is known to have been in on the kidnapping plot.

Charlie Chan functions as a private investigator in the series and is no longer connected to the Honolulu police as in the Oland and Toler films. Here Naish's Chan functions more in the mode of the 1947-49 Roland Winters films. He also is without the help of a numbered son; that was to come a bit later in the series. This first episode in the TV series is a typical twenty-six-minute, low-budget detective story designed for syndication to individual TV stations. The earlier (1951) *Boston Blackie* series made by ZIV with Kent Taylor starring would be a comparable syndication series. There is some good location work in the episode to open up the story, but the close-up photography preludes a need for much in the way of decorative indoor sets. The eye makeup designed to give Naish an Oriental look to his eyes is poorly done in this episode, making his eyes look strangely hooded. Other than that disturbing factor, it's an adequate start to the series.

Episode Two: "The Secret of the Sea"

Executive Producer: Leon Fromkiss, Producer: Sidney Marshall, Director: Charles F. Hass, Teleplay: Tony Barrett, Sidney Marshall, Brock Williams.

CAST: J. Carrol Naish, Harry Shannon, Jean Willes, Lane Bradford, Arthur Space, Stuart Randall, John Baradino, Philip Ahn, Victor Sen Yung (uncredited).

PLOT/COMMENT: The story begins in San Pedro, California, at the Harbor of Los Angeles. We see a very familiar person walking across the dock to a pay phone. It's Victor Sen Yung, Charlie's son Jimmy from the Sidney Toler films or Tommy from the Roland Winters films—take your choice. Only Sen Yung is a ship steward this time and *neither* son; he is the son of Mr. Kim (Philip Ahn). We discover later that the phone call is to an insurance company that covers the *Honolulu Star*, Victor's ship, regarding "something big" that is going to happen to the cargo ship which is sailing in the morning. Sen Yung steps out of the phone booth; an unseen gunman shoots three times—fade to opening credits.
And that's the end of Victor Sen Yung in the episode; he doesn't have a character name and doesn't even make it into the cast credits. Was he invited to do a cameo in the TV series or was he just an out-of-work actor looking for a job? It's a mystery without an answer. But moving right along, Charlie Chan is brought into the situation by Mr. Kim, Victor's father, who asks him to investigate his son's death. Charlie manages to hitch a ride on the ship and finds that Captain Conover (Harry Shannon) has also allowed his young wife, Doris (Jean Willes), to come along, too—perhaps to keep an eye on her because she seems to have eyes for

Victor Sen Yung makes a brief appearance in the second
episode of the TV series.

other men, in this case First Mate Johnny Flynn (Lane Bradford). Soon
the ship's engines stop abruptly, and it is discovered that the thrust block
has been jammed, making the ship dead in the water. About this same
time First Mate Flynn is killed by some falling tackle on the ship. The
radio operator Ed Barker (Arthur Space) sends a distress message which
is answered by the *El Gaviland* out of Acapulco, captained by Arturo
Rameirez (John Baradino), who just happens to be an old flame of Doris.
Is it a coincidence or a plan? The ship is tugged back to Los Angeles by
the *El Gaviland* whereupon Captain Rameirez puts in a $150,000 claim
for his salvage of the *Honolulu Star*. Chan has his hands full tracking
down the murderer of the two men, but finally subdues the killer with a
bit of unexpected Judo.

This second episode in the series is an improvement over the first,
possessing a stronger script and quickening action as the plot weaves to
its conclusion. The sets used for the ship look authentic and some of the
scenes were actually shot on a ship. The supporting cast is made up of
regulars that we have seen many times before and who know how to get
the job done. On a personal note, John Baradino (Captain Rameirez)
was a retired professional baseball player who played ball with my older
brother Bob on a farm team for the Cleveland Indians back in the mid-
1940s.

Episode 3: "The Lost Face"

Executive Producer: Leon Fromkess, Producer: Sidney Marshall, Director: Charles F. Hass, Teleplay: Richard Grey and Sidney Marshall from a story by Brock Williams.

CAST: J. Carrol Naish, Frank Gerstle, Rodney Bell, Dabbs Greer, Willis Bouchey, Austin Green.

PLOT/COMMENT: We see a lady vacuuming her living room in a San Fernando Valley, California, middle-class home. Then a man approaches the house and enters. Presently we hear a scream from the house, the man exits, and passes a little girl who is bouncing a ball on the sidewalk. The ball gets away from the little girl, the man retrieves it, and tosses it back to her as he leaves—fade to opening credits.

We learn later that the woman, blinded by the assailant who threw acid in her face, is the wife of Zac West (Dabbs Greer), a reporter who covers the Valley crime beat and who has been seeking evidence against a corrupt attorney named Dan Randolph (Willis Bouchey). Coincidentally, Charlie has just been appointed special investigator for a grand jury probing into the activities of Randolph who, according to Zac, is behind "all the filthy rackets in this town, including narcotics." Police Lieutenant Stutz (Frank Gerstle), with whom Charlie is working, also has a beef with attorney Randolph. A couple of years previously the Lieutenant's teenage brother was killed in a street fight by one of Randolph's men who had gotten the kid hooked on drugs to the point where he was a junkie. Charlie goes with Zac to a local coffee shop to console him on the blinding of his wife, and there he encounters Willie Brower (Austin Green), the Bible-quoting owner of the shop who seems to take a great interest in what has occurred and even asks Charlie to take an envelope of money to help out Zac on the hospital bills.

When Randolph thug Jack Hart (Rodney Bell) is identified by the little girl as the man who was at the West house, attorney Randolph quickly arrives and springs him from the police but not before Chan points out that the last three clients of Randolph who were released on writs were soon found shot to death. Chan warns Hart that he could get the same treatment. Later, when Charlie goes to Randolph's home to meet with him, he discovers the lawyer's body on the floor of his office, shot. Charlie Chan now has a murder to solve.

It is at this point the script goes awry: Charlie solves the mystery by tricking the most likely suspect into confessing. (Since the guilty party is never the *most* likely suspect in a mystery, the plotting is either brilliant or dumb. Take your choice.) Charlie then states that the dead attorney's accomplice has been the coffee shop owner who, he says, shot the three clients released on writs. Charlie offers absolutely no evidence against coffee shop owner Willie Brower except to tell Lieutenant Stutz that the gun that shot them is behind the counter. Case closed!

Episode 4: "Blind Man's Bluff"

Executive Producer: Leon Fromkess, Producer: Rudolph C. Flothow, Director: Leslie Goodwins, Teleplay: Richard Grey from a story by Paul Conlan.

CAST: J. Carrol Naish, James Hong, Jay Adler, Strother Martin, Carleton Young, Jeanne Bates, Robert Williams, Carlos Vera, Frank McLun, Robert Strong, Fred Shellac, Chris Christie.

PLOT/COMMENT: Crooked wholesale diamond merchant Manny Ross (Jay Adler) tells his henchman Tomar (Strother Martin) that he is to meet an incoming flight from Mexico City and take the seeing-eye dog from a blind man who will be on the flight—fade to opening credits.

It turns out that Charlie and son Barry are on that same flight arriving at Los Angeles International Airport. Before they can get their luggage and find a taxi, they become embroiled in the plot to dognap the canine. Eventually, Charlie learns that there are smuggled diamonds in the dog's collar—but not before there is one murder, a claim of rabies, and a little Mexican boy's pooch turns into an attack dog to save our Oriental sleuth.

This is the first episode in which James Hong as Charlie's son Barry makes an appearance. To discover after all these years that Charlie has a Number One Son by the name of Barry comes as something of a shock when for twenty-some years we thought he had a Number One Son by the name of Lee. Anyway, young James Hong's acting experience was still very limited at this time, and he comes across, I'm sorry to say, as a somewhat geeky, callow youth who seems to be lost in the company of the more experienced character actors who were recruited for this episode. It can be noted, however, that Strother Martin's histrionics when Charlie suggests that he probably has rabies from a dog bite go considerably over the top, culminating almost with foaming of the mouth. This is not one of the better episodes in the series, but it should be noted that as of this fourth episode, the makeup department has finally come up with eye makeup for J. Carrol Naish that gives him believable-looking Oriental eyes.

JAMES HONG (1929-) appeared much younger on screen than his late twenties when he was cast as Barry Chan in 1957, and his long career continues in 2011 as this is being written. Born in Minneapolis, Hong received his early education in Hong Kong, returned to the United States and studied engineering at the University of Southern California, and worked for a year or so as a road engineer for the County of Los Angeles. Starting with uncredited bit roles in such big-budget films as *Soldier of Fortune* (1955) with Clark Gable, *Love Is a Many-Splendored Thing* (1955) with William Holden, and *Blood Alley* (1955) with John Wayne, he also soon became a "voice" actor in films redubbing soundtracks of a number of Asian films, including *Godzilla, King of the Monsters* (1956). Small roles in television series (*Sky King, Four Star Playhouse, The Millionaire, Tombstone Territory*, and others) gave him experience prior to his assignment in *The New Adventures of Charlie Chan.*

Following the Chan series, James Hong worked in roles small and large in films and television series right up to the present, including such film hits as *Chinatown* (1974), *Blade Runner* (1982), *Kung Fu Panda* (2002) in which he did the voice of Mr. Ping, and *The Day the Earth Stood Still* (2008). In addition, through the years he expanded his credits to include writing, producing, and directing. Among his writing/directing credits are *The Vineyard* (1989) and *Singapore Sling* (1999), for which he also added producing. For the documentary *The Man with a Thousand Faces* (2008) he appeared on camera and was the executive producer and writer. In addition to the above-mentioned films and many others, James

James Hong played Number One Son Barry in *The New Adventures of Charlie Chan.*

Hong has acted in numerous television series, gained respect as an acting teacher, and in 1965 was one of the founding members of the East-West Players in Los Angeles, one of the first Asian-American theater companies. Now in his early eighties, James Hong continues to work in films and television and is a popular guest at film conventions all over the country.

Episode 5: "The Great Salvos"

Executive Producer: Leon Fromkess, Producer: Rudolph C. Flothow, Director: Jack Gage, Teleplay: Barry Shipman.

CAST: J. Carrol Naish, James Hong, Maria Palmer, Hans Conried, Gordon Rhodes, Gertrude Michael, Ralph Moody, Damian O'Flynn, William Tregoe, Pat Colby.

PLOT/COMMENT: We are in a home office in Washington, D.C. Through a crack in the door we see a gray-haired, distinguished man rise from his desk and cross to a wall safe with important-looking files. A gloved hand pushes the door open as the man begins to place the files in the safe. There is a blow to the head and the man falls to the floor, files scattered. One file, Project 5, is picked up by the gloved hand—fade to opening credits.

Project 5, it turns out, contains plans for combat jet engines, plans which must not fall into enemy hands. Charlie happens to be a friend of Douglas Fenton (Gordon Rhodes) who had the files taken from his safe and has no idea who could be involved in the affair. He and his wife Joyce (Gertrude Michael) invite Charlie and Barry to a nightclub owned by Dick Rand (William Tregoe) that evening just prior to Charlie's planned trip to Madrid. At the club they also meet Joyce's physician, Doctor Kruger (Ralph Moody), who has also been invited. While they are there a mind-reading act is performed by a Hungarian brother-and-sister team called "The Great Salvos," Reeno Salvo (Maria Palmer) and Carlo Salvo (Hans Conried). During the act Charlie's watch is handled by Carlo. Presently, Charlie receives a phone call at the club informing him that his trip has been cancelled, and later that night there are two attempts to mug Charlie, neither successful. Charlie suspects that maybe his watch is what the muggers are after because of something that Salvo might have placed in the case during the mind-reading act. He senses that maybe he was to be a "mule" delivering something valuable—like microfilm of Project

5—to an espionage ring in Madrid. The wise Chinaman sets a trap into which the espionage agents eventually fall.

This is a well-constructed, fast-paced episode with a solid cast of respected character actors. Hans Conried, drawing upon his skill as a dialectician, handles the role of the Hungarian with his usual skill and flamboyance. Ralph Moody in the smaller role of the doctor is sufficiently shifty to make him a viable suspect. Moody, a very busy older actor, was a regular on Jack Webb's radio and television *Dragnet* series. James Hong as Barry Chan is still struggling to get his acting legs, but acquits himself a bit better in this episode. This was the last of the five episodes made in Hollywood. The rest of the series was produced in England and Europe with British casts for the most part.

Episode 6: "The Counterfeiters"

Executive Producer: Leon Fromkess, Producer: Rudolph C. Flothow, Director: Leslie Arliss, Teleplay: Richard Grey.

CAST: J. Carrol Naish, James Hong, Marne Maitland, Patrick Holt, Peter Elliott, Mackenzie Wart, Peter Allenby, Guest star: John Loder.

PLOT/COMMENT: At the London offices of Gaylord & Carnot, Banknote Engravers & Publishers, the French finance representative, Edouard Brossolette (Mackenzie Ward) arrives to collect the plates for the 5,000-franc issue from Sir John (John Loder), Chairman of Gaylord & Carnot, only to be told that the plates were picked up earlier by a courier who presented official-looking diplomatic papers. Brossolette, shocked at what has occurred, exclaims, "If the plates are in the wrong hands, France could be flooded with counterfeit currency." Sir John picks up the phone, "Get me Scotland Yard at once"—fade to opening credits.

Charlie and son Barry meet with Sir John and Inspector Duff (Patrick Holt) of Scotland Yard and are briefed on events. They then fly immediately to Paris where they meet with Inspector Chauvet (Peter Elliott) of the Paris police. Chauvet believes that a master forger named Spanish Roy (Marne Maitland) may be behind the theft of the plates but tells Charlie that the French prefer to deal with internal problems themselves. Nevertheless, Charlie locates Spanish Roy who at first refuses to help Charlie even though he acknowledges his involvement in the theft. Later he relents and says that he got the plates for the French Secret Service for the benefit of France. Charlie convinces him that he has been duped and that the theft of the plates was for the benefit of a single individual. Soon Charlie meets with the megalomaniac who concocted the whole scheme as a test of abilities between himself and the formidable detective.

This first episode produced in England is a bit complicated with many twists and curves but is ultimately a fairly satisfying little mystery. Unlike the Chan movie series, the television episodes do not necessarily involve a murder but hinge on such matters as theft or international espionage. Guest star John Loder adds some acting weight to the proceedings that are otherwise populated with an all-male English cast that would be unfamiliar to American audiences.

Episode 7: "The Death of a Don"

Executive Producer: Leon Fromkess, Producer: Rudolph C. Flothow, Director: Don Chaffey, Teleplay: Maurice Tombragel from an original story by Brock Williams.

CAST: J. Carrol Naish, James Hong, Francis Matthews, John Bailey, William Franklyn, Leonard Sharp, Maurice Durant, Betty McDowall.

PLOT/COMMENT: While Barry Chan is studying criminology at Stratford University in England, his best friend is a music composition student named Derek Robinson (Francis Matthews). Barry observes an encounter Derek has with music professor Don Wellman (John Bailey) where the professor berates Derek with considerable sarcasm for the poor quality of his new composition. In the angry exchange which follows, Derek exclaims heatedly, "You're dead. You're washed up, dead; there's nothing in the future for people like you except death"—fade to opening credits.

Charlie pays Barry a visit at the university and learns that Barry's friend Derek has been expelled for his outburst at Professor Wellman. Charlie suggests an apology. The scene shifts to Wellman's visit to Janet Rushton (Betty McDowall) at the theatre where she is the lead dancer in a show entitled *In a Dancing Mood*. Wellman and Janet are married but have been separated for several years. During the visit Wellman asks her to return to him, but while open to the idea, she is uncertain. The theatre manager Jack Pearson (William Franklyn) is concerned about Wellman's entreaty to Janet because he is very "fond" of her, and without her in the show, it would have to close. During that night's performance, Professor Wellman's body is found outside the theatre by the doorman (Leonard Sharp) who sees Derek leaning over the body before he rushes into the night. Charlie offers to assist Inspector Rawlins (Maurice Durant) with the investigation where Derek is the number one suspect.

Despite the title which suggests an entirely different type of story, this episode is well developed and involves interesting characters. One might quibble a bit about the somewhat melodramatic and soap opera quality that creeps in when the plot becomes embroiled in the romantic triangle of Wellman, Janet, and Pearson, but, fortunately, it is well acted and for the most part does not slow down the plot.

Episode 8: "Charlie's Highland Fling"

Executive Producer: Leon Fromkess, Producer: Rudolph C. Flothow, Director: Leslie Arliss, Teleplay: Fred Schiller.

CAST: J. Carrol Naish, James Hong, Percy Marmont, Conrad Phillips, Ian Fleming, Ballard Berkeley, Jack Lambert, Sheila Cowan, Hugh Moxey.

PLOT/COMMENT: A sports car races along a lonely country road during the early dawn hours. We see a rifle appear in close-up, aiming at the just-passed vehicle. A shot rings out and the car crashes—fade to opening credits.

Charlie and Barry are in Scotland on vacation and visiting an old friend, Sir Malcolm Gregg (Percy Marmont), at his vast, palatial estate when word arrives that Lady Gregg has been killed by someone who shot her as she was returning home from London. Charlie and Sir Malcolm's lawyer and business manager Christopher Wingate (Ian Fleming) try to console him over his loss, as does the butler Runnals (Ballard Berkeley). Soon Sir Malcolm's grown son Donald (Conrad Phillips) arrives and learns of his stepmother's death. It is presently learned that Duncan (Jack Lambert), whom Lady Gregg had had arrested as a salmon poacher, escaped from jail that morning. Charlie, working with the local police official, Inspector Forsyth (Hugh Moxey), soon discovers that each member of the murder puzzle had motive and opportunity to kill Lady Gregg—even the proverbial butler.

Scripter Fred Schiller packs a lot of information and characterization into the twenty-six minutes of plot time he is allowed. Actor Ian Fleming, the shady lawyer for the Gregg estate, is not to be confused with the creator of James Bond. This Ian Fleming is a character actor who was born in Melbourne, Australia. This is one of the stronger episodes in the series.

Episode 9: "The Patient in Room 21"

Executive Producer: Leon Fromkess, Producer: Rudolph C. Flothow, Associate Producer: Herman Blaser, Director: Don Chaffey, Teleplay: Robert Leslie Bellem, Paul Erickson.

CAST: J. Carrol Naish, James Hong, Peter Dyneley, Henry B. Longhurst, Honor Blackman, Raymond Francis, Leslie Perrins, Nancy Graham.

PLOT/COMMENT: We are in Ottawa, Canada, in 1947. Doctor Paul Liggat (Peter Dyneley) stands before a judge (Leslie Perins) for sentencing in a mercy killing case. Liggat is sentenced to five years imprisonment, but the judge adds, "In view of your spotless character and the humane motive which prompted the crime, the sentence is suspended on condition that you never again practice medicine or surgery in Canada"—fade to opening credits.

We jump ten years in time and find Charlie Chan and son Barry at Mercy Hospital in London where the Chief Surgeon, Dr. George Morely (Henry B. Longhurst), wishes to confer with Charlie regarding an anonymous letter he has received about Doctor Michael Winsted, a prominent surgeon on the hospital staff. The letter, which Charlie notes is written on paper with the hospital watermark, claims that Dr. Winsted is the Dr. Liggat who was convicted of a "euthanasia murder" ten years before in Canada. Morely is concerned that if the letter is accurate that it could cause a scandal at the hospital and asks Charlie to investigate.

Sir Edward Pomercy (Raymond Francis), chairman of the hospital board of directors, says the investigation is unnecessary and that Morely is pushing it because he fears that Dr. Winsted will be appointed to his job of chief surgeon. Charley calls the police chief in Ottawa and learns that the victim's private nurse from ten years before, Anne Gerald (Nancy Graham), is willing to come to London to state whether Winsted is really Liggat. Shortly after arriving in London, she is murdered at the hospital. Charlie's suspects include all of the above and Elizabeth Vernon (Honor Blackman), Dr. Winsted's chief nurse who is in love with him.

Charlie's work is cut out for him!

The script is interesting and not as convoluted as many mystery stories are in order to keep the viewer guessing and "off balance" regarding the identification of the guilty party. The acting by the all-British cast is, as usual, excellent. Honor Blackman, in the less than challenging role of Nurse Vernon, was pretty much unknown at the time the episode was filmed; nevertheless, she displays the husky, sexy voice and figure that would a few years later entice James Bond into trouble in *Goldfinger* (1964), where she was Pussy Galore.

For his makeup as Charlie Chan, J. Carrol Naish only wore an application to make his eyes appear Asian; otherwise, he created the role with his voice and demeanor.

Episode 10: "The Rajput Ruby"

Executive Producer: Leon Fromkess, Producer: Rudolph C. Flothow, Director: Don Chaffey, Teleplay by John K. Butler from an original story by Brock Williams.

CAST: J. Carrol Naish, James Hong, Michael Rittermann, Jill Melford, Bill Nagy, Maurice Kaufmann, Harold Young, Charles Morgan, Arnold Marle, Dodnal Donnelly.

PLOT/COMMENT: We are on a conducted public tour of the Tower of London when the beautiful female companion to a Maharajah suddenly screams and exclaims, "My necklace, the ruby; it's gone!"—fade to opening credits.

Charlie and son Barry are visited at their London hotel suite by the Maharajah (Michael Rittermann) and his American wife Ida Kelly (Jill Melford) who asks Charlie to investigate the theft of the very valuable necklace with the Rajput Ruby. Charlie soon learns who the possible suspects are: the private detective Joe Ratella (Bill Nagy) who was previously employed by the Maharajah, Ida's former lover (maybe still lover) American baseball player Lefty Ryan (Maurice Kaufmann), or Ida herself who may be being blackmailed. It doesn't strain Charlie too much to decipher "who done it."

This is a weak entry in the series that doesn't really call upon Charlie to use his deducting skills to locate the missing ruby necklace and the persons responsible. Mostly he just lets events play out and is on hand when the culprits mess up and reveal their game. Son Barry actually does most of the "heavy lifting" in this episode and helps to subdue one of the bad guys using his fists.

Episode 11: "The Final Curtain"

Executive Producer: Leon Fromkess, Producer: Rudolph C. Flothow, Director: Alvin Rakoff, Teleplay: Gene Wang.

CAST: J. Carrol Naish, James Hong, John Longden, Patricia Marmont, Mary Steele, David Oxley, Lynne Cole, Mike Malone, Rupert Davies.

PLOT/COMMENT: Aging actor Philip Royce (John Longden) is awakened from his drunken sleep by the arrival of Claire Harris (Patricia Marmont). She informs him that his daughter Barbara is seeing Johnny Douglas who "makes his living promoting rich girls." She asks Royce what he would do if this were true. "I'd kill him," he retorts. She tosses a gun onto the bed—fade to opening credits.

Charlie and son Barry are vacationing in London when they are visited by Philip Royce who asks Charlie to investigate Johnny Douglas (David Oxley) to see if he is attempting to swindle his estranged daughter Barbara (Mary Steele) out of her inheritance. Charlie learns that Royce's wife, now dead, was the daughter of a wealthy car manufacturer, and daughter Barbara has inherited millions from the estate. Presently we learn that Johnny and Claire are in cahoots on a con game to fleece Barbara out of her money, but Johnny has actually fallen for the heiress and wants to call off the con. Charlie receives a phone call from Royce in which he says that he is expecting a visit from Johnny. While on the phone there is a knock on Royce's door. Charlie hears Royce answer the door and then cry out Johnny's name just before a gunshot. Charlie and Inspector Duff (Rupert Davies) of Scotland Yard find the body of Royce in his room, but Charlie has trouble believing that Johnny committed the murder even though he heard Royce cry out his name.

This is an excellent episode in the series despite the fact that the teaser before the credits makes no sense. Why would Johnny's con partner Claire want to tell the girl's father about Johnny and provide a gun with which to kill him? At the time of the opening teaser Claire is in love with Johnny and does not yet know that Johnny is falling in love with the subject of the con, Barbara. Anyway, once past the teaser the story is well handled and particularly so from the time Royce is murdered. Nobody seems to have a motive for killing Royce, and yet there he is dead. Could it have been a clever suicide designed to incriminate Johnny? If so, where's the gun? The script by Gene Wang provides some intriguing plot twists that make for a fascinating episode.

Episode 12: "Death at High Tide"

Executive Producer: Leon Fromkess, Producer: Rudolph Flothow, Director: Leslie Arliss, Teleplay: Lee Erwin.

CAST: J. Carrol Naish, James Hong, Ivan Craig, Victor Beaumont, Peter Dyneley, Lisa Daniely, Thomas Gallagher, Henri Vidon, Leslie Weston.

PLOT/COMMENT: It is night at a war criminals' camp in Germany. A man in a trench coat hurriedly cuts the lower wires of a razor-topped fence. A dark figure signals to a guard as he crawls through the cut space in the fence. He and the trench-coated man move to a waiting car as the guard turns away—fade to opening credits.

In London Charlie and Barry meet with Frank Wells (Leslie Weston), head of the Wells Insurance Brokers Company. They are told that Nazi Karl Bretner (Victor Beaumont) has escaped from a war camp and that it is suspected that he plans to go after the ten million in gold bullion that went down with the SS *Patrick* during the war and was never located. Bretner was responsible for the sinking and would likely be able to find the lost gold which was insured by Wells's company. Wells sends Charlie and Barry to France where they meet Henrie Mazarac (Ivan Craig) and his wife Marie (Lisa Daniely) at their seaside inn. Henrie had earlier been hired by Wells to locate the gold but failed. Henrie informs Charlie that the only survivor from the lost ship, John Robey (Peter Dyneley), has become a friend and has assisted him in searching for the missing gold. Late that night Bretner and John Robey show up at the inn which Henrie and his wife run and at which Charlie and Barry are staying. It becomes apparent that the four of them are working together to find the gold for themselves. Soon Jacob Brun (Thomas Gallagher), the guard that allowed Bretner to escape, arrives, also seeking a share in the gold. The next day Bretner is found dead on the beach, clutching a gold bar. Now Charlie's task is to find a murderer and the gold bullion.

The episode is a fairly good entry in the series with only one problem worth mentioning. Barry, like all of the Chan offspring, is written to be an impetuous, can't-keep-his-mouth-shut, amateur detective. In the TV series, however, there seems to be an increasing habit of also writing him as a bit dense—or dumb! Some of Charlie's scripted putdowns—after Barry has been given a line that shows his ineptitude—turn out to be rather cruel, and they occur frequently. Add to this the fact that James Hong was a very inexperienced actor at this point with a slight speech impediment, and the problem is only exacerbated—at one point he mispronounces Bretner's name when talking to Charlie, and in Charlie's answering speech *he* pronounces the name correctly. In the rush to get a low-budget TV episode filmed, the director apparently ignored the flub and didn't do another take, leaving egg on James Hong's face.

Episode 13: "The Circle of Fear"

Executive Producer: Leon Fromkess, Producer: Rudolph C. Flothow, Director: Leslie Arliss, Teleplay: Tony Barrett.

CAST: J. Carrol Naish, James Hong, Leonard Sachs, Patricia Burke, Tom Macaulay, Arnold Marle, Nora Gordon, Keith Pyott, Michael Balfour, Ina Whittaker, Rupert Davies.

PLOT/COMMENT: A nervous, overwrought man moves from his work table to the phone and dials. "I can't do it; it's no use; I have to give it up," he tells his listener. "I can't cut the diamond, never mind why; it's impossible." The door next to the man opens and a blow is stuck to his head. A gloved hand reaches in and takes the diamond—fade to opening credits.

Charlie and Barry, as in the last episode, are at the Archway Hotel in London. Charlie is in town to speak to an international gathering of chiefs of police. While there he has a visitor who wishes him to investigate the strange disappearance of a huge diamond that was earlier discovered in a Nigerian diamond mine. The investigation leads Charlie to the diamond cutter's wife, Mrs. Van Boorman (Patricia Burke), and Doctor George

Laird (Leonard Sachs), who has been treating both her and her husband for a nervous condition. Presently, Mrs. Van Boorman's son Curt (not identified in cast), from a previous marriage and now a college student, comes on the scene and perhaps has a motive for stealing the missing diamond, as does an elderly house man employed by the Van Boormans. In addition, there is a shady bookmaker named Franz Webber (not identified in cast) who has been seen around the Van Boorman house and has a criminal past. Charlie also conducts an elaborate investigation into the medications that have been prescribed for the Van Boormans before he comes up with the culprit and a solution to the crime.

This is a weak episode in the series that cries out for a more focused and detailed scripting. The plot wanders through underwritten sequences with thinly-defined characters to where there are finally enough suspects to draw upon for a resolution. And the production values leave much to be desired—the living room set of the Van Boorman home, for example, and a couple of doctors' offices are skimpy and under "dressed" and suggest the low budget of the series.

Episode 14: "An Exhibit in Wax"

Executive Producer: Leon Fromkess, Producer: Rudolph C. Flothow, Associate Producer: Herman Blaser, Director: Alvin Rakoff, Teleplay: Sam Neuman from an original story by Lawrence Huntington.

CAST: J. Carrol Naish, Brian Nissen, Ronald Leigh-Hunt, Sidney Moncton, John Unicomb, Oliver Burt, Ralph Truman, Rosemary Frankau, Maitland Moss, Rupert Davies.

PLOT/COMMENT: Charlie is in London on a conducted tour of Madame Tussaud's World in Wax of famous murder cases when a distinguished-looking gentleman approaches the Edward Simpson wax figure and strikes the figure violently with a cane dislodging its head which rolls to the floor—fade to opening credits.

The wax figure attacker turns out to be Allen Roberts (Brian Nissen) who works for the Bank of England and offers no explanation for his actions. Charlie's curiosity is aroused, however, and he begins an investigation of the events surrounding the Simpson wife murder of thirty years before, which reveals that Simpson had a young son who was later adopted by people named Roberts—hence Allen Roberts is the son of the murderer. As the investigation expands, Charlie learns that young Roberts is being blackmailed by a person who threatens to reveal his identity as the son of the murderer—a fact that might look bad for Roberts at the bank.

Evidence begins to indicate that Edward Simpson was not guilty of his wife's murder and that the real murderer was someone very close to him.

One must pay close attention during this episode or the twists and turns of the plot and characters can get quite confusing. But that close attention will be rewarded with the enjoyment of an intriguing mystery—and one that the viewing amateur detective may be able to solve right along with the smart detective. Son Barry must have been having exams in his criminology classes because he fails to make an appearance in this episode.

Episode 15: "Backfire"

Executive Director: Leon Fromkess, Producer: Rudolph C. Flothow, Associate Producer: Herman Blaser, Director Don Chaffey, Teleplay: Richard Grey.

CAST: J. Carrol Naish, James Hong, Bruce Seton, William Franklyn, Virginia Keiley, Harold Scott, Amy Dalby, Rupert Davies.

PLOT/COMMENT: We are in Egypt near the site of the Sphinx. Two men enter an underground tomb, slide a heavy rock door open, and enter a hieroglyphics-lined inner room containing a mummy's sarcophagus. The man next to the sarcophagus turns to his partner and asks, "You're sure we haven't been followed, Seth?" "Quite sure, Sir Basil," he responds, casting his flashlight about the darkened room. "There's a heavy penalty for tomb desecration." In the cascading light we realize the two men are identical in appearance save for the beard on Seth. As Sir Basil turns to study the inscriptions, Seth strikes him hard on the head with his flashlight and then struggles to close the heavy rock door before Sir Basil can recover. "Twelve years since you're in England," Seth calls through the door. "No friends, no relations. I think like you, I look like you, and now I *am* you." "You'll never get away with it," Sir Basil cries out. "One thing that will hang you is my wife," he exclaims as he begins to laugh hysterically—fade to opening credits.

At the British Museum in London Charlie and Barry meet with a man who claims to be Sir Basil Dawson (Bruce Seton) and who asks Charlie to help him locate his missing wife. He tells Charlie that she left him twelve years ago and that he now wishes to remarry. "If Monica is dead, I want proof," he tells Charlie. "If she is alive, I want a divorce." Charlie reluctantly accepts the assignment and soon talks with Monica's mother (Amy Dalby) who is in a nursing home. She tells Charlie that she has disowned her selfish and unfaithful daughter. Next, Charlie interviews the young cousin of Sir Basil, Richard Dawson (William Franklyn), the black sheep in the family, who claims that the picture Charlie shows him is not Sir Basil.

Barry, trying to be helpful on the case, puts an ad in the "unclaimed money" column of the paper, seeking the whereabouts of the lady. Shortly, a woman shows up claiming to be the missing wife (Virginia Keiley), and Barry, delighted with his success, phones Sir Basil and asks him to meet them. The phony Sir Basil and—as we suspect—the phony wife meet each other and both, for the moment, claim to recognize the other and leave Barry. When Barry calls his father with the good news, Charlie is appalled because he has just found evidence to prove that Sir Basil is not who he claims to be, and the woman, whoever she is, may be in danger. Charlie must act swiftly to solve the case before any further untoward activities to take place.

Congratulations to Richard Grey who penned this episode in the series. It is the most cleverly written mystery thus far in the series, and it explodes a bombshell of information at the conclusion that puts the whole episode in a new light. The fast-moving plot laced with intriguing characters and above-average production values makes for a fascinating thirty minutes that will delight Chan fans.

Episode 16: "Patron of the Arts"

Executive Producer: Leon Fromkess, Producer: Rudolph C. Flothow, Associate Producer: Herman Blaser, Director: Leslie Arliss, Teleplay: Lee Erwin.

CAST: J. Carrol Naish, James Hong, Lloyd Lamble, Adrienne Corri, Oscar Quitak, Bernard Rebel, Maurice Kaufmann, Reed De Rouen, Harold Arneil.

PLOT/COMMENT: Artist Paul Bretton (Maurice Kaufmann) offers his latest painting to art dealer François Duval (Lloyd Lamble) for five thousand francs, but Duval will only pay two thousand. The artist, angered by the offer but needing the money, accepts the two-thousand-franc offer and leaves. Another man, an art expert named André (Oscar Quitak), examines the painting and tells Duval that "someday the painting will be worth a million francs, maybe even more." Duval scoffs, "In a hundred years from now maybe." "No, Monsieur Duval, much sooner if something very sad were to happen, something like the sudden untimely death of Paul Bretton"—fade to opening credits.

Charlie and Barry are on a tour of a Brussels art museum when they happen to meet Paul and Monica Bretton (Adrienne Corri). When Charlie learns of the financial straits the couple is in, he offers to buy them a "sumptuous dinner" if they will continue the tour through the art museum with them and serve as knowledgeable guides; they agree readily. In the meantime, André is dunned for his large gambling debt by art lover and gambling house owner Renaud (Reed De Rouen). André proposes that Renaud buy up Paul's paintings and that they then arrange a fatal accident. "When the source of the supply is cut off," André states, "the value of the paintings will rise. You will make a fortune, and I am off the hook."

Later that evening back at Paul and Monica's apartment, they are having coffee with Charlie and Barry when Duval arrives and asks to see Paul's paintings. He soon buys all the paintings Paul has at hand and leaves. Charlie is suspicious of Renaud who does not appear to be a patron of the arts and yet has purchased so many of Paul's paintings. Later that night Paul is shot and slightly wounded when a burglar steals a painting of Monica that Paul has refused to sell. The next day Paul is almost pushed under an oncoming bus. Charlie then begins to investigate what appears to be a murder plot to do away with the artist.

While the episode is well executed in the acting, directing, and production values areas, the basic premise of the plot is hard to believe and/ or accept—that you could buy up a painter's work and then murder him to make a nifty profit upon his death. If it were that easy to gauge a painter's greatness during his lifetime and then to make a profit upon his murder, fine artists would have to be guarded day and night to avoid assassination attempts. This episode gets a "thumbs down."

Episode 17: "A Hamlet in Flames"

Executive Producer: Leon Fromkess, Producer Rudolph C. Flothow, Associate Producer: Herman Blaser, Director: Don Chaffey, Teleplay: Robert Leslie Bellem from a story by Herbert Purdom.

CAST: J. Carrol Naish, James Hong, Raymond Huntley, Walter Gotell, Carl Jaffe, Douglas Wilmer, Paul Hardmuth, Dervis Ward, Tony Thawnton.

PLOT/COMMENT: We are in Belgium in 1940 at a Nazi prison camp. Colonel Kurt Schmidt (Raymond Huntley), the commandant of the area, is talking with his prisoner, the Marquis Remy (Douglas Wilmer), who owns a first folio edition of Shakespeare's *Hamlet* valued at two hundred thousand dollars; the Colonel, who covets the *Hamlet*, has offered one hundred dollars for it. "Sign the bill of sale and I will cancel the order for your execution," the Colonel smugly promises. Reluctantly, the Marquis agrees and signs the bill of sale, which is back dated to 1937 so that it will not appear that the transaction had anything to do with the present situation. The Marquis is taken back to his cell as the Colonel scratches his signature onto a paper and then reaches for the phone. "Adjutant, the execution order for the Marquis Remy is now signed"—fade to opening credits.

The story now jumps to the present, 1957, and we are in Germany with Charlie and Barry as they enter the office of Baron Schmidt, owner of the first folio of Shakespeare's *Hamlet* that Barry wishes to photograph and then present the photos to his college library. "It would be a feather in my cap," the young man tells the Baron who, it turns out, is happy to let him take the photographs. He informs Barry and Charlie that the folio is going up for sale and Rudolph Zeigler (Carl Jaffe), who owns a rare bookstore, is serving as his agent in the sale and that Barry will need to take his photos at the store. That evening, however, the Baron himself breaks into the bookstore and attempts to steal the folio but is stopped by bookstore worker Conrad Weiss (Paul Hardtmuth) and the arrival of Charlie and Barry before he escapes into the night. Barry insists that the burglar was Schmidt and speculates that he might be after the insurance that is on the folio.

The next evening while Barry is taking his photos, he receives a bogus phone call that Charlie is ill and that he is to come at once. Later, when Barry, Charlie, and Police Inspector Steiner (Walter Gotell) return to the bookstore, they find the store on fire and the body of Baron Schmidt dead on the floor, shot through the heart. Charlie's investigation soon adds two wartime compatriots of the dead Marquis Remy to the suspect list who may be involved with the murder and the now-missing folio.

This is a well-produced episode in the series with excellent actors and a pace that keeps the story moving along at a brisk pace. In the climactic moments, however, the episode loses its way as Charlie reveals the murderer, but the motivation for the killing seems inadequate for the drastic crime that has taken place—and there is a sense of letdown.

Episode 18: "Dateline—Execution"

Executive Producer: Leon Fromkess, Producer: Rudolph C. Flothow, Associate Producer: Charles Bennett, Director: Leslie Arliss, Teleplay: Richard Grey.

CAST: J. Carrol Naish, Robert Raglan, Richard Caldicot, John Stratton, Mary Laura Wood, Oliver Burt, Arthur Howard, Hugh Williams.

PLOT/COMMENT: Father Dolin (Richard Caldicot) administers the last rites to prisoner Arthur Donald (John Stratton) and then meets with the warden outside the cell. He asks if there has been a reprieve granted. The answer is "no." "Then, Warden, you've got to stop this execution," Father Dolin insists. "Arthur Donald isn't guilty. He's innocent, I tell you. I know!"—fade to opening credits.

The warden reluctantly grants a stay on the execution for twenty-four hours—time for Father Dolin to bring in the one man he feels might find the real murderer in the few hours that Arthur Donald has yet to live, Charlie Chan. Charlie visits his friend Inspector Marlowe (guest star Hugh Williams) at Scotland Yard who explains the circumstances of the murder. It seems that Dr. Roy Beach had been found burned to death in his car. The autopsy showed that there were multiple head injuries but no carbon monoxide in the blood, meaning he was dead before the fire. Arthur Donald was the doctor's chauffer/handyman and was found nearby the burned car with a lot of unexplained cash on him, cash that the doctor had gotten from the bank that day. In addition, bloodstained clothes and towels were found in Arthur's room. It looks like an open and shut case to Scotland Yard, but the indefatigable Charlie thinks it might all be a frame up and starts to investigate. Dr. Beach's widow, Marilyn (Mary Laura Wood), claims to have had an affair with Arthur, but when Charlie talks to him, he denies it. A Mission Padre (Oliver Burt) tells Charlie that Arthur was a fine fellow and found it hard to believe that he could be a murderer, but he tells Charlie the police found the murder weapon hidden at the mission—more damaging evidence against Arthur. With little time to spare, the great detective finally unravels the baffling mystery.

This is another episode where Charlie is without the assistance (?) of his Number One Son whose absence is not explained. There is an unusual paucity of suspects in this episode which perhaps heightens the mystery aspects. There is the accused and the widow of the murdered man with no other likely suspects standing around. A fine cast, good direction, and a crisp script keep the story rolling along to the surprising climax.

Episode 19: "The Sweater"

Executive Producer: Leon Fromkess, Producer: Rudolph C. Flothow, Associate Producer and Director: Charles Bennett, Teleplay: Jack Sackeim.

CAST: J. Carrol Naish, Margot Grahame, Conrad Phillips, Robert Cawdron, Billy Milton, Sandra Francis, Nicholas Stuart.

PLOT/COMMENT: Troubled American couple Dick and Verna Martin (Billy Milton and Margot Grahame) check into their hotel suite in Amsterdam and continue their ongoing quarrel. Presently, Dick, trying to bring peace during their stay in Amsterdam says, "Look, Darling, snap out of it. Let's see if we can't make this thing work. Let's try again, a little bit harder. Maybe we can find some of those things we lost." Verna, softening, tells him, "That sounds like the Dick I used to know, way, way back," and turns to unpack. Opening his suitcase and withdrawing a small gun, Dick continues, "You see, I don't intend to lose you ever again." Her back to him, Verna replies, "Thank you, Darling."—fade to opening credits.

While shopping in an exclusive Amsterdam fashion house the next day, Verna and Dick Martin happen to see Charlie Chan, an acquaintance of Verna's from years before in Honolulu. (It is explained that Charlie is in Amsterdam on vacation and looking for a gown for one of his daughters.) Charlie and the Martins agree to meet again the next day after Charlie visits with his old friend Inspector Van Der Reyden (Robert Cawdron) of the Amsterdam police. Before they leave the fashion house, Verna buys a sweater from high-fashion designer Dirk (Conrad Phillips) that, through a mix up, was supposed to go to the Contessa Philzano (Sandra Francis) who later demands the return of the sweater that was designed for her. She is so insistent that she goes to the Martin hotel suite and demands the return of the sweater—a demand that Verna refuses to honor.

Later, Charlie is interrupted during his meeting with Inspector Van Der Reyden by a phone call from Dick, requesting that he come immediately because Verna has been killed and he is being held for murder by the Amsterdam Police. Charlie, working with the inspector, begins an investigation that reveals Verna was killed by a hard blow to the head, perhaps made by the gun that belongs to Dick; that the Contessa's sweater is missing; and that the murder may have something to do with a diamond smuggling operation.

This average episode in the series was directed by associate producer Charles Bennett with a clever script by Jerry Sackheim that has the distinction of being one of the few mysteries I've encountered where all the suspects turn out to be guilty of something. Charlie is again working without his Number One Son to complicate the investigation. Barry must be studying for final exams back at college.

Episode 20: "The Noble Art of Murder"

Executive Producer: Leon Fromkess, Producer: Rudolph C. Flothow, Associate Producer and Director: Charles Bennett, Teleplay: John K. Butler.

CAST: J. Carrol Naish, James Hong, Mary Kerridge, Ferdy Mayne, John Van Eyssen, André Maranne, Teresa Thorne, Malou Pantera.

PLOT/COMMENT: We are in Brussels and Barry is in a boxing ring engaged in a French form of boxing called savate, where both fists and feet are used in the competition. There is a group of tourists watching the exhibition, one of which, a young lady, takes a flash photo causing the fight to be stopped while the referee and owner of the gym, Georges Larue (Ferdy Mayne), cautions the lady not to take any more photos because they can temporarily blind the fighters. When the bout continues, Barry soon lands a double-foot blow which knocks out his opponent Henri (un-credited), ending the bout. Barry leaves to take his shower as the referee begins to examine the still-unconscious Henri. Suddenly, Georges cries out, "Wait, wait, this man is dead! We must call the police!" The young lady takes another photo and rushes out with her tourist group—fade to opening credits.

Charlie learns from Police Inspector Renal (John Van Eyssen) that Barry has been detained pending the cause of death of Henri. Later, when Barry has been released, he tells Charlie that he is mystified by the death and that he believes it might not have been just a boxing accident, that it may have been murder. He explains that when he came out of the shower, the body was not still in the boxing ring but was on the floor outside the ring. He speculates that the gym was very likely empty while Georges phoned the police and that anyone could have entered during that time.

Charlie and Barry seek out the lady with the tour group who took the photos in hopes that she/they will verify Barry's story about the location of the body and, also, that they may reveal other matters regarding the incident. Later, the death is ruled murder when it is found that Henri died of a skull fracture that most likely would not have been caused by Barry's double-foot blow. Nevertheless, Inspector Renal arrests Barry on suspicion of murder because Barry had jokingly said he was going to get even for the last three bouts when Henri had beaten him in the savate competition.

Charlie bails Barry out of jail and begins his investigation. The suspects soon include Mme. Dubois (Mary Kerridge), Georges' sister who loaned money to Henri which he lost gambling; Georges, who knew that Henri planned to start his own gym with money he got from Mme Dubois; Jock Flaubert (André Maranne), the tour guide operator; and maybe even Inspector Renal who may be in love with the victim's fiancée, Odette Dubois (Marlou Pantera), the niece of Mme. Dubois. Charlie soon finds the murder weapon, an Indian club missing from the gym wall, and shortly thereafter identifies the murderer.

This fast-moving and interesting episode is only compromised at the conclusion when Charlie presents his evidence as to who committed the murder. To this amateur detective it seems that Charlie's evidence—as written in the teleplay by John Butler—is no more than circumstantial and would be shot down later in a court of law. Since the accused does not challenge Charlie's claim and is taken off to jail, the episode closes with Charlie prevailing.

Episode 21: "Three Men on a Raft"

Executive Producer: Leon Fromkess, Producer: Rudolph C. Flothow, Associate Producer: Herman Blaser, Director: Leslie Arliss, Teleplay: Ted Thomas, Jan Leman.

CAST: J. Carrol Naish, Raymond Huntley, Maxine Audley, Stanley Van Beers, Ernest Clark, Nancy Roberts, Keith Crane.

PLOT/COMMENT: Charlie is in a London bookstore contemplating the purchase of a rare edition of Don Quixote when he sees a young boy (Clive Crane) of about ten draw a gun and prepare to shoot the famous author Tony Hathaway (Raymond Huntley) who is there signing copies of his book. Charlie stops the boy and takes him outside the store where he confesses to Charlie that he did it because of the awful lies Hathaway had written about his dead father in *Memory of Terror*: that his father, a captain in the army, had shirked his duty, "cracked up," and was a coward. (In the book his father is washed overboard from a raft he shares with the author and a Chinese steward.) As Charlie is about to take him home, the boy runs into the street and is hit by a car—fade to opening credits.

Charlie visits the boy, Ronnie Ramsden, and his mother (Maxine Audley) at Mercy Hospital where his injuries are serious, but he refuses to take his medicine and has little will to get better. Charlie talks with the boy and agrees to investigate the author to see if he lied about his father, but the boy must take his medicine and pay Charlie three pounds, his fee, on Waterloo Bridge when the investigation is complete. The boy agrees, knowing that he will have to be well to go to Waterloo Bridge to pay Charlie. The investigation turns up evidence that the author had indeed played fast and loose with the truth in his book, that the publisher knows this and doesn't want his publishing company embarrassed by the revelation—to the extent that he sends a couple of thugs to try to stop the meddlesome detective. Charlie also discovers that the Chinese steward who shared the raft with Ramsden and the author died six months before and had had no means of support other than money he received each month. But what puzzles Charlie most is that Ronnie's mother and her fiancé Sir Arthur Ruggles (Ernest Clark) try to stop Charlie's investigation to prove the boy's father, her first husband, was an honorable man.

The premise of the story is weak, and there is little criminal activity in the plot beyond the thugs that are sent to stop Charlie's investigation—and that comes across in the script as an over-the-top action by the publisher. Charlie is dealing mainly with plagiarism here, and there is little motivation for the great detective Chan to get involved in this situation with an upset little boy who believes his father has been maligned. Even when Charlie finds the evidence he is looking for, all he can accomplish at the end of the story is to get a signed statement by the author and his publisher that the book was a piece of fiction rather than a true story. With that signed paper, the boy is happy again—end of story.

Episode 22: "No Holiday for Murder"

Executive Producer: Leon Fromkess, Producer: Rudolph C. Flothow, Associate Producer and Director: Charles Bennett, Teleplay: Terence Maples from a story by Doris Gilbert.

CAST: J. Carrol Naish, James Hong, Alan Wheatley, Betty McDowall, George Margo, Althea Orr, Norah Gorsen, Peter Elliott.

PLOT/COMMENT: A tour group from Ohio is visiting Brussels and staying in the same hotel as the vacationing Charlie and Barry. The members of the group are anything but happy campers, mostly because of a blustery, obnoxious lady named Mrs. Remington (Althea Orr), who constantly browbeats her traveling companion and aid, Mary Ann Edwards (Betty McDowall). Not only is Mrs. Remington intolerant of Mary Ann's attempts to do her job properly, but she even gossips to others on the tour that Mary Ann has had a mental breakdown and spent six months in a mental home the previous year. The members of the tour have expressed their dislike and contempt for Mrs. Remington, and then Barry finds a letter addressed to an inmate in Sing Sing that contains a veiled threat to Mrs. Remington—fade to opening credits.

In the hotel lobby Charlie observes Mrs. Remington berating the head of the tour, Professor Ambrose (Alan Wheatley): "Another delay, Professor Ambrose, another example of your organizing ability. Since we left New York you haven't considered yourself responsible for anything—deplorable hotels, missed connections, poisonous food. Why I took your tour I shall never know." Immediately thereafter she panics and becomes more irritable when her handbag containing her money and jewels is missing, but it is found untouched a few moments later in the dining room. Charlie is taken aback when Max Willis (George Margo), a tough-talking prize fighter on the tour, tells Charlie, "One of these days I'll murder that dame."

Barry becomes friendly with attractive Sharon Prince (Norah Gorsen), a young and hip member of the group. When she invites Barry to go on their excursion to a Congo museum, Charlie agrees to go along, too. During the tour Charlie hears a scream and sees Mrs. Remington fall down a steep staircase. He rushes to her in time to hear her last words, "I was pushed!" Clutched in her hand is the drawstring from her jewel bag but the jewels, valued at more than ten thousand dollars, are gone. Soon, Inspector Verne (Peter Elliott) of the Brussels Police force arrives and, with Charlie's assistance, an investigation is begun to find her murderer.

The episode is weakened by the fact that several plot elements do not make much sense. Examples: the tour guide is supposedly a professor at an Ohio college, but then Charlie finds out that he isn't a professor and that there is no such college. It would seem that the company responsible for the tour would have done a better background check. Then, too, it seems unlikely that the prizefighter would confess to the murder to protect former mental patient Mary Ann just because he has taken a liking to her on the tour. And, finally, the fact that Mary Ann is a former mental patient only seems to exist so that the real murderer can try to push her mentally into another breakdown and suicide, which would further incriminate her and deflect attention away from him—yes, it's a "him."

Episode 23: "No Future for Frederick"

Executive Producer: Leon Fromkess, Producer: Rudolph C. Flothow, Associate Producer: Herman Blaser, Director: Don Chaffey, Teleplay: Terence Maples from a story by Brock Williams.

CAST: J. Carrol Naish, Hugh Williams, Derrick de Marney, Maggie McGrath, Genine Graham, Anita Sharp-Bolster, Derek Waring, David Markham, Peter Swanwick.

PLOT/COMMENT: We are in the London shop of palmist Madame Clara (Anita Sharp-Bolster) who is attempting to read the palm of boorish British actor John Frederick (Derrick de Marney). Distaining in his manner, he accuses her of being a fake and then demands, "Tell me about the future." She demurs until he presses her. Finally, she responds, "You have no future!" Furious, Frederick throws her fee on the table, "There's your money, not that you're worth a penny of it!" Rushing out into the street, he barely misses being hit by a passing car. He gasps, clutches his heart, and frantically searches for the medicine container in his pocket. Once opened, he swallows several pills to calm himself—fade to opening credits.

Charlie and Inspector Marlowe (guest star Hugh Williams making his second appearance as Marlowe) have tickets for a John Frederick performance at the theatre, but by the time they arrive, the actor has been found dead in his dressing room. At first thought to be the victim of a heart attack, Charlie soon determines the death to be a murder. Charlie and the inspector find themselves surrounded by suspects who all acknowledge that they hate Frederick enough to want to kill him: his female costar with whom he has had an affair but has recently dumped, his stage manager whom he has rebuked publicly for missing various cues at dress rehearsal, a fellow actor whom he accuses of having little or no talent, and his dresser whom he constantly criticizes for ineptness. In short, the man is not liked by anyone around him. Charlie soon discovers from a pharmacist that Frederick has been prescribed digitalis for his heart condition but also has been given a doctor's sample which has a dosage printed on it that would be poisonous if taken consistently over time.

This is an interesting episode in the series, really one of the better ones. It is a bit unusual to have the victim so hated by all those around him that they are all likely suspects. More often you get a couple of obvious suspects (usually red herrings) and several whose connection to the victim appears to be more nebulous. The plot follows the formulaic pattern of most mysteries but with a couple of twists that distinguishes it and makes it worthwhile viewing. Barry is not present for this episode and is never mentioned.

Episode 24: "Safe Deposit"

Executive Producer: Leon Fromkess, Producer: Rudolph C. Flothow, Associate Producer: Herman Blaser, Director: Leslie Arliss, Teleplay: Richard Grey.

CAST: J. Carrol Naish, James Hong, Hugh Williams, Wensley Pithey, James Raglan, Terence Kilburn, John Brooking, Jerold Wells, Godfrey Kenton.

PLOT/COMMENT: We are in London at Finlay's Band as a young man (later to be identified as Bill Shaw, uncredited) enters carrying a briefcase and stands near the door. Inside we see a bank messenger receiving bound bundles of payroll money that he is to deliver to the Allied Dairy Company in a similar briefcase. As the messenger starts to leave the bank, Shaw strikes him with a judo cut, grabs the briefcase, and as he exits tosses his own empty briefcase into the arms of the oncoming Barry Chan, who is immediately accosted by bank officials and guards. Shaw races down the street, tosses the briefcase with the money into an alley and rushes on only to be stopped by a police officer. A distinguished-looking older gentleman with hat and cane steps out of the alley with the briefcase, enters the bank, is greeted by bank officials as a familiar customer, and proceeds to the privacy of the safe deposit box room where he deposits the contents of the briefcase—fade to opening credits.

Charlie is discussing the recent rash of bank holdups with Inspector Marlowe (Hugh Williams, making another guest appearance on the series) when he discovers that son Barry has been involved accidentally with the latest holdup. The capture of Bill Shaw leads Charlie and the Inspector to a community club for under-privileged boys that Shaw frequented and whose chairman is a distinguished-looking older gentleman named Colonel Ross (uncredited) who we recognize as the depositor of the stolen money. Later, Ross turns up dead with a broken neck from a judo chop that Charlie says could only have been accomplished by someone with a black belt ranking. By the time we get two-thirds through the episode there is only one suspect who fits the description, and Charlie out judo chops him to resolve the case.

The cleverest aspect of the episode is the *modus operandi* of the criminals, and that alone makes the episode *almost* worth watching. Otherwise, the plot is pretty shallow and leads, as indicated above, to an obvious resolution. (At the start of a midway break in the episode, James Hong as Barry holds up a large card that says to stay turned for the upcoming commercial, and before the final credits J. Carrol Naish does a comic bit as Charlie, humbly requesting our presence in seven days for the next adventure.)

follow . . . .

The ADVENTURES of CHARLIE CHAN starring J. Carrol Naish

MONDAYS at 7 p.m. on WNAC 7 tv

Episode 25: "Voodoo Death"

Executive Producer: Leon Fromkess, Producer: Rudolph C. Flothow, Associate Producer: Herman Blaser, Director: Don Chaffey, Teleplay: Lee Erwin.

CAST: J. Carrol Naish, James Hong, Trevor Reid, Hugh Miller, John Harrison, Ann Sears, William Abney, David Peel, Richard Bebb.

PLOT/COMMENT: We are in England at the estate of wealthy Joseph Temple* who is about to be shaved by his African servant Bartoo. When Temple sees Bartoo fumbling with several voodoo trinkets, he rails against the dark-skinned man for believing in the ancient practice. Temple tells him to stop his voodoo hocus pocus "unless you want the beating of your life." With the shaving razor resting against Temple's throat, Bartoo gently cautions, "Do not beat me, master; do not even talk of beating me."—fade to opening credits.

Charlie and Barry, along with several other guests, are invited to Joseph Temple's home for dinner and bridge. Among those present are Temple's daughter Ann who is in love and plans to marry Michael Ross despite her father's displeasure and threat to cut her off from her inheritance, claiming that Michael is only a "fortune hunter." Also in attendance is a geologist named Payne who with Temple's nephew Harry Carr has discovered a uranium mine in Honduras, a project that was financed by Temple. During the evening Temple tells his nephew that he has purchased Payne's portion of the mine and gives it to Harry as a gift. Strangely, Harry does not seem too pleased at receiving this windfall. Later that night Temple receives a cablegram that the uranium mine has been salted, that it is a fake and worthless. The next morning Ann discovers her father dead in his bedroom, his head having been fractured with a heavy object.

Now Charlie, with the clumsy and frequently bungling assistance of an English inspector and son Barry, begins to investigate the murder. Utilizing a new twist on an old ploy, Charlie gathers all the suspects together in the murder room at midnight and, with Bartoo's assistance, practices a little voodoo to catch the murderer.

This is a routine episode in the series, but the voodoo hoodoo gives it a little spice. Frequent director Don Chaffey is able to conjure up a bit of atmosphere for the climactic scene: With Bartoo in an exotic costume and manipulating a menacing snake in the semi-darkness, the suspects and Barry shudder in dread anticipation until the guilty party is overcome by the "voodoo magic," as Bartoo has branded it, and confesses.

(* Character names are not provided on the cast list.)

Episode 26: "The Expatriate"

Executive Producer: Leon Fromkess, Producer Rudolph C. Flothow, Associate Producer: Herman Blaser, Director: Leslie Arliss, Teleplay: Peter Barry.

CAST: J. Carrol Naish, James Hong, Alan Gifford, Natalie Benesh, Delphi Lawrence, Anne Wakefield, Frederick Jaeger, Robert Henderson, Russell Napier, Murray Kash.

PLOT/COMMENT: We are in London with deported American racketeer Nate Peliter (Alan Gifford) who is seeking the lowdown on an English lawyer named Herbert Stevenson (Robert Henderson) from his cohort Benny (Murray Kash). Benny tells him that Stevenson's daughter Ellen (Anne Wakefield) wishes to marry Henry Mellar (Frederick Jaeger), the heir to an English Lord. Stevenson swears he won't let her marry Henry and threatens to tell Henry that Ellen is adopted and really the daughter of racketeer Peliter. Upon hearing this from Benny, Peliter pulls a pistol from a drawer and tells him, "I'm going back on my word. When I got out of prison, I swore I'd never use this gat again!" –fade to opening credits.

Charlie and Barry are checking in at the hotel where the Stevensons reside when a gunshot is heard from an elevator. They rush to the scene and discover Ellen Stevenson, gun in hand, standing over the body of her father, seriously wounded but not dead. Ellen claims she picked up the gun when she came upon the scene. In the midst of the crowd that gathers, we see Nate Peliter, who quickly turns and leaves. Back in the Stevenson suite Charlie and Inspector Parker (Russell Napier) from the London police begin an investigation. The mix of suspects soon includes Stevenson's young law partner Lisa Blanchard (Delphi Lawrence), a pushy, bitchy lady who tries to take control of the situation. Mrs. Stevenson claims she had had a headache and was asleep when the shooting occurred, but later points out to Charlie that she believes Blanchard is in love with her husband. Later it is discovered that the gun used was licensed to Blanchard in New York a year or so earlier. Charlie soon comes up with a plan to trap the murderer in the hospital room where Stevenson is in critical condition.

This episode had the potential of being one of the better episodes in the series, but by the twenty-minute mark in the plot, it is quite obvious who the guilty party is—most unusual for Chan movie or TV episodes— but little comfort for the viewer since the actor playing the murderer (yes, Stevenson died) acted guilty throughout and *was*!

Episode 27: "The Airport Murder Case"

Executive Producer: Leon Fromkess, Producer: Rudolph C. Flothow, Associate Producer: Herman Blaser, Director: Don Chaffey, Teleplay: Jerry Sackheim and Stuart Jerome from an original story by Brock Williams.

CAST: J. Carrol Naish, James Hong, Raymond Young, Arthur Gomez, Gene Anderson, Kay Callard, Alex Scott.

PLOT/COMMENT: We are in Rome as a train arrives from Paris with a young lady named Joan Marsh* aboard. She departs and moves among the crush of passengers out onto the street. A passing bus backfires—or was it a gun?—Joan Marsh clutches her heart and falls to the sidewalk as passersby stop to gawk—fade to opening credits.

Charlie and Barry are vacationing in Rome when Dino Rienzi (Raymond Young) knocks at their hotel door and requests Charlie's assistance in the investigation of Joan Marsh's murder. He tells Charlie he wants a private investigation because he has little confidence in the police. Despite Dino's comment about the police, Charlie calls his old friend Inspector Galvani (Arthur Gomez) and asks if Barry could work with him on the case—practicing his criminology skills from college—while Charlie does a private investigation.

Martha Recci, the owner of the nightclub where Joan sang, tells Charlie that Dino had recently dumped Joan for a rich American widow named Carol Vaine. When Charlie meets with the widow, she tells him that she and Dino plan to marry and that Dino had long-ago promised never to see Joan again. Carol shows disdain for Joan and calls her a "little tramp." Charlie returns to Dino's apartment to further question him, but Inspector Galvani and Barry arrive with a search warrant. The inspector finds what turns out to be the murder gun in Dino's apartment, and he is arrested. Charlie doubts Dino's guilt and continues his investigation which eventually leads him to a blackmail operation, messages hidden in lobster claws, and foreign spies searching for the location of a shoreline atomic reactor station—a much bigger case than was first envisioned!

This is a good episode in the series. The plot twists and turns are fascinating, and the climax with Charlie physically fending off a knife-wielding villain is more overt action than the series usually provides viewers. From a production standpoint, the outdoor location scenes are handled well, but interior scenes often reveal skimpy, underdressed sets that give evidence of the low budget.

(*Some character names are not provided on the cast list.)

Episode 28: "The Hand of Hera Dass"

Executive Producer: Leon Fromkess, Producer: Rudolph C. Flothow, Associate Producer: Henry Blaser, Director: Leslie Arliss, Teleplay: Lee Erwin.

CAST: J. Carrol Naish, James Hong, John Gabriel, David Ritch, Eunice Grayson, Robert Marsden, Alex Gallier, Martin Benson, Richard Golding, Michael Peake.

PLOT/COMMENT: We are in Nice, France, at the Hotel Negresco where Charlie and Barry are meeting with a Mr. Dubois.* Dubois wants to secure the services of Charlie to fly to Cairo, Egypt, and get the Hand of Hera Dass, a symbolic gold hand, from a man named Harown Ali and return with it to Nice within forty-eight hours. Charlie is reluctant to take on the assignment that a messenger boy could seemingly handle, but Dubois insists and tells Charlie that the Near East is a powder keg. "In the wrong hands the Hand of Hera Dass could be very dangerous indeed."

"But if I should fail?" Charlie asks. Dubois sighs, "Then it is war in the Near East"—fade to opening credits.

Charlie and Barry go to Cairo and check into the Hotel Continentale where Harown Ali soon arrives with the golden hand only to be stabbed to death as he exits Charlie's hotel room. Presently a beautiful, veiled young lady by the name of Jasmine arrives at Charlie's room professing love for the dead Harown and claiming that a one-eyed man by the name of Ahmed is responsible for the murder. Barry takes Jasmine back to her home and is then mugged by two thugs who find out where Charlie is staying and soon show up to steal the golden hand for the money that it will bring to them. By this time Charlie has been visited by the Grand Wazir of the Federated Tribes, an Oxford University graduate no less, who also seeks the golden hand. "Hera Dass," he says, "was the great Emir who brought peace to the warring tribes. Even now the symbol of his hand unifies my people." With the assistance of the local police, Charlie sets a trap to catch the killer of Harown Ali and then sees that the Hand of Hera Dass is returned to the proper hands.

This episode in the series is like no other, and perhaps that's just as well. While played seriously, the whole plot—with its stereotypical characters (with stereotypical names) running in and out of Charlie's hotel room, now through the front door, now through the French doors, looking and acting for all the world like an over-stressed company of *Kismet* actors searching for their camels—involves the search for the mysterious golden Hand of Hera Dass to prevent a tribal war in Egypt. I didn't believe a bit of it. Almost the entire episode took place in Charlie's hotel room in Cairo which reflected the limited budget allowed for settings and dressings—among other things.

(*Character names are not provided on the cast list.)

Episode 29: "The Chippendale Racket"

Executive Producer: Leon Fromkess, Producer: Rudolph C. Flothow; Associate Producer: Herman Blaser, Director: Don Chaffey, Teleplay: Gertrude Walker.

CAST: J. Carrol Naish, James Hong, George Howe, Ethel O'Shea, Harold Scott, Laurie Main, Robert Perceval, Rupert Davies, Stella Bonheur (uncredited).

PLOT/COMMENT: We are in London as American tourist Tom Steele (Robert Perceval) surprises his wife Martha (Stella Bonheur) at their London hotel with two antique silver candelabra he has just purchased from a silver shop to celebrate their silver anniversary. Tom mentions to Martha that he ran into Charlie and Barry, acquaintances from Honolulu, in the lobby and has asked them to come up to see the silver candelabra since Charlie, too, is a collector of silver. When Charlie examines them, he reluctantly tells Tom and Martha, "I deeply regret, although expert work-manship, they are not genuine period pieces." Ashen faced, Tom exclaims, "What, you mean they're fakes?"—fade to opening credits.

Charlie, Barry, and Tom return to the silver shop run by a man named Winkleman (George Howe), who calls in his silver expert Mr. Meadows (Laurie Main) who also proclaims that the candelabras are not genuine period pieces. Winkleman then acknowledges that occasionally his sil-versmith makes copies of pieces owned by Lady Abbott (Ethel O'Shea) and calls in his silversmith, Carstairs (Meadows White), to bring in the original candelabras—which he then discovers are missing, but he will check with Lady Abbott about their whereabouts.

Charlie soon learns that Carstairs is the estranged brother of Lady Abbott who suspects that his sister is in an illegal partnership with Win-kleman to export fake antique silver items. In addition, Barry, visiting Lady Abbott's house unannounced, overhears a conversation between her and Winkleman that supports the fact that they are working together to export fake antique silver. Suddenly, Barry is struck over the head by an unseen assailant and knocked out. By the time he regains consciousness, Lady Abbott has been murdered by someone using a fireplace iron, and Barry is being held at gunpoint by the butler Hitchens (Harold Scott). Charlie soon arrives at Lady Abbott's home with his old friend from Scot-land Yard, Inspector Duff (Rupert Davies), and gets busy on the case.

This is a nicely done episode in the series, well written and interest-ing. Visually, from a production standpoint, it gives the appearance of an infusion of cash in the budget. The sets for the upscale silver shop and Lady Abbott's home are more impressive than we have seen in recent episodes. Barry even drives up to the Abbot estate in a fancy convertible sports car. There is the usual high-quality acting from the British cast, all of which make this episode worthwhile viewing.

Episode 30: "The Invalid"

Executive Producer: Leon Fromkess, Producer: Rudolph C. Flothow, Associate Producer: Herman Blaser, Director: Don Chaffey, Teleplay: Jan Leman and Ted Thomas.

CAST: J. Carrol Naish, James Hong, Joan Rice, Philip Friend, Basil Dignam, Robert Arden, Susan Richmond, William Lucas, Victor Woolf, Rupert Davies (Uncredited).

PLOT/COMMENT: We are in London on the film set of a murder mystery starring Sybil Adams (Joan Rice) with Charlie Chan acting as technical advisor on the production. After Charlie does a stand-in bit for actor Cary Norton (William Lucas) as a murder victim in a stabbing, there is a heated discussion between the director Pinero (Robert Arden), the producer Howard Richards (Basil Dignam), and Charlie about the scene. During this discussion Sybil leaves the set to take a phone call. When the director is again ready to shoot the scene, Sybil is nowhere to be found; she has disappeared. "Disappeared," the intense director shouts. "She can't disappear in the middle of a picture!"—fade to opening credits.

As Charlie begins to informally investigate the young actress's disappearance, a gossip column suggests that she may be trying to escape the amorous attentions of the director and producer, lovesick rivals for her attention. But the truth is soon uncovered when Charlie finds out that she has rushed to her home after receiving a phone call from her housekeeper (Susan Richmond) that her crippled husband, former actor Don McGruder (Phillip Friend), has accidentally fallen out of his wheelchair. This information leads to the fact that Sybil's marriage has been a secret from everyone because, as angry Producer Richards soon states, "Just one leak and my million dollars is down the drain" if the public finds out that this beautiful young actress is married to a cripple, her public image and all that.

During filming the next day, with Sybil's husband visiting the set, there is a scene where Sybil is called upon to shoot a prop pistol. In the staging of the scene, Pinero tells Sybil to aim the pistol towards him off camera. She does so, with an unexpected *real* bullet striking the director in the shoulder. Now the set turns into a crime scene, and Inspector Duff of Scotland Yard (Rupert Davies) soon arrives. How the real bullet got into the prop gun and why someone should want to kill the director or anyone else in the story, puzzles our Chinese detective as he and the inspector carry on their investigation.

The overheated craziness of the plot works against this episode, and I suspect it would even in 1958. Would the public quickly lose interest in a movie star who is married to a crippled man in a wheelchair? Would a movie star even try to keep such a situation secret? Would the situation cause the producer to lose a million dollars at the box office? Would the producer, director, and leading man all fall in love with the beautiful leading lady? Well, sure—and that happens too before all is said and done. When the final moments arrive and we discover who put the real bullet in the gun and why, and then in the denouement the crippled actor/husband miraculously (and with a great soap-opera-ish flurry) regains his ability to walk, many viewers may be left with an overriding feeling of disbelief and, perhaps, annoyance.

Episode 31: "The Man in the Wall"

Executive Producer: Leon Fromkess, Producer: Rudolph C. Flothow, Associate Producer: Henry Blaser, Director: Leslie Arliss, Teleplay: Rik Vollaerts from a story by Rik Vollaerts and Jerry Sackheim.

CAST: J. Carrol Naish, James Hong, Norman Shelley, Terence Alexander, Melissa Stribling, Alison Leggatt, Graham Stuart, Rupert Davies.

PLOT/COMMENT: We are in London as the old Anthony Torrance mansion, blitzed during World War II, is finally being excavated for the construction of the new, upscale Packer Towers Apartments. Suddenly, as a wall collapses, we see a suit of armor fall among the rubble. Two Englishmen on the site rush over, clear some of the debris away, and open the grated head piece to reveal a bony human skull—fade to opening credits.

Charlie and Barry have been summoned by Irving Packer (Norman Shelley), builder of the new Packer Towers Apartments, because he fears that the discovery of the corpse in the suit of armor is already causing bad publicity for his new apartments—"People are talking about the ghost of Packer Towers." Packer wants Charlie to get to the bottom of the situation so that a public explanation can be forthcoming. Before Charlie can contact Inspector Duff (Rupert Davies) of Scotland Yard to see what he has discovered regarding the skeleton in armor, Duff calls him to say that the death was caused by a bullet that had pierced the armor, and it now appears that they are dealing with a seventeen-year-old murder case.

The back story on the situation reveals that on the night of a Nazi air raid, a fancy dress masquerade party was being held at the Torrance Mansion and that Anthony Torrance was dressed in armor for the occasion. Among those present who survived the air raid are Torrance's business partner Christopher Morgan (Graham Stuart), Mrs. Torrance (Alison Leggatt), and two children, Gerald Torrance (Terence Alexander) and Virginia (Melissa Stribling), now grown and married to each other. When examining the list of those present that died in the attack, Charlie discovers that there was a Scotland Yard inspector at the party working on a case. Inspector Duff reveals that the case concerned the possibility that Torrance and Morgan were black marketing British currency to America.

Soon all of the living suspects in the death of Torrance request and then demand that Charlie drop the investigation—to the point where they seem to be threatening Charlie's own wellbeing. He comments to Barry the strangeness of the situation; usually it is only the guilty party who wishes a case to be dropped, but here everyone wants it dropped. Further investigation by Charlie and Duff reveals that the bullet hole in the armor was made by a machinegun, such as those mounted on Nazi dive bombers during the war. Inspector Duff now believes that there never was a murder; Charlie is not so sure—maybe it was the Scotland Yard inspector who was murdered!

This is a first-rate mystery in the series, well developed and executed by the writer, nicely performed by an excellent cast, and carefully nuanced by a creative director. Here is a fine example of a mystery where each twist and turn in the plot tweaks the viewer's curiosity in a new direction and makes the final outcome more and more a puzzle until the smart detective resolves it. This is one of the finest episodes in the series.

Episode 32: "Something Old, Something New"

Executive Producer: Leon Fromkess, Producer: Rudolph C. Flothow, Associate Producer: Henry Blaser, Director: Leslie Arliss, Teleplay: Lawrence Louis Goldman and Brock Williams.

CAST: J. Carrol Naish, James Hong, Brenda Hogan, Derek Aylward, Rupert Davies, Mary Merrall, Patrick Troughton, John Salew, Diana Fawcett.

PLOT/COMMENT: We are at the Regina Apartments in London; it is night as a shadowy figure dressed in black, flashlight in hand, scurries up a fire escape, raises an unlocked window, and enters a darkened bedroom. A quick search of the room produces cash from a woman's purse. As the lone figure opens the door a crack to the adjoining room, an angry woman's voice demandingly states to another in the room, "I'm going to stop it, I tell you. So get out of my way." The burglar shrinks back into the darker shadows to listen more. "What are you doing with that? Don't," the lady screams and falls to the floor, her lifeless hand extending to the light of the cracked door. Beating a hasty retreat, the burglar exits the window, rushes down the fire escape, and into the arms of an awaiting police officer—fade to opening credits.

Charlie and Barry are just arriving at the Regina Apartments for their appointment with Mrs. Helen Crane (Diana Fawcett) when they hear the cries of elderly Alice Gardner (Mary Merrall), Mrs. Crane housekeeper, who has just discovered the body of Mrs. Crane; she has been stabbed. By the time Charlie has examined the body, Inspector Duff (Rupert Davies) of Scotland Yard arrives with the stolen money that the police officer has found on "Second-Story Pete" Wilson (Patrick Troughton), the burglar who was in the next room when Mrs. Crane was murdered. Duff, of course, immediately assumes that the murder was part of the robbery, but Charlie demurs.

It soon develops that Mrs. Crane had hired Charlie to investigate the father of her stepdaughter Julie Crane's (Brenda Hogan) fiancé, Dr. Dennis Pearson (Derek Aylward). Mrs. Crane, Charlie learns, was against the engagement and eventual marriage because half of the family business income Mr. Crane inherited will go to the stepdaughter when she marries. Charlie's investigation of Dennis's father revealed that the father had gone insane and killed his wife, Dennis's mother, years before. Mrs. Crane felt that the disclosure of the murder in Dennis's family would destroy his doctor practice and probably the engagement. The dead Mrs. Crane is held in such little regard that Charlie is told by Mr. Crane, "All of us are much better off now that my wife is dead." Charlie thus has an abundance of suspects from whom he must ferret out the murderer.

This is another fine episode nicely directed by series regular Leslie Arliss. Again, it can be said that the production values (sets, dressing, lighting, camerawork) for these later episodes are a considerable improvement over some of the mid-series entries. The script is well acted by an experienced cast of English performers, including an outstanding performance by future Dr. Who, Patrick Troughton, as the cockney burglar "Second-Story Pete" Wilson.

Episode 33: "The Man with a Hundred Faces"

Executive Producer: Leon Fromkess, Producer: Rudolph C. Flothow, Associate Producer: Henry Blaser, Director: Charles Bennett, Teleplay: Rik Vollaerts.

CAST: J. Carrol Naish, James Hong, Alan Wheatley, Eric Pohlmann, Peter La Trobe, Arthur Brander, Harry Tardios, Michael Mellinger.

PLOT/COMMENT: We are in Venice, Italy, as a jewelry shop owner oversees the transfer by armed guards of seventy million lira's worth of jewels to an armored truck for delivery to the purchaser. As the transfer is completed and the guards leave, a swarthy figure enters from a side room and moves to a closet where we see an unconscious man bearing the likeness of the jewelry store owner. The swarthy man chuckles, "When you wake up, my friend, just try to convince the insurance investigators that you had nothing to do with this affair." He turns to his accomplice, whose appearance matches the comatose man, "Let's go"—fade to opening credits.

Charlie, Barry, and Inspector Rietti (Michael Mellinger) of the Venice Police enjoy a nightclub performance by Pietro Monti (Alan Wheatley), "The Man of a Hundred Faces," after which the performer passes a note requesting Charlie's help. Shortly thereafter, while Charlie and Barry are enjoying a gondola ride in Venice, the gondolier turns out to be Pietro who tells Charlie of his problem. It seems that Pietro's brother Vitorio has gotten into legal problems for writing bad checks which Pietro has been able to keep from the police. A man named Vincente Donati (Eric Pohlmann), an import/export dealer who on the sly runs a slick robbery operation, has threatened to expose Vitorio unless Pietro, using his ability to impersonate people, assists in the committing of robberies. Pietro tells Charlie that he will help to expose Donati's crimes if the police will give him a reduced sentence for his involvement.

Charlie agrees to work with Pietro and meets with Inspector Rietti to inform him of the situation. Soon Charlie is informed by Pietro of a robbery that is to take place of a valuable painting entitled "Virgin and Child." Charlie, Barry, and the police stand by to make the arrests when suddenly there is an unexpected complication that tests the observational skills of even the great Charlie Chan—and turns up an unexpected culprit to the robbery.

The highlight of this episode is the outdoor filming that actually takes place in Venice, Italy, and adds enormously to the enjoyment of the episode. The plot is clever and quite well executed with a conclusion that only gets telegraphed to the viewer slightly ahead of Charlie's explanation. Again, in this episode, the production values are first rate. The only troublesome aspect of the episode is the continued writing for Barry's character that paints him as a yipping, overly-eager puppy dog next to the wise, thoughtful father/detective to the degree that the viewer is annoyed by the son's insistent yammering to his pop. This was, of course, used in the Chan movies to provide comic relief, but it was generally handled with some finesse so that, usually, the son was not too offensive. The writers for the television series, to a great extent, have lacked this finesse and have made Barry almost demented and certainly childish. My sympathies go to the young James Hong who worked gamely with what the writers provided him.

Episode 34: "The Point of No Return"

Executive Producer: Leon Fromkess, Producer: Rudolph C. Flothow, Associate Producer: Herman Blaser, Director: Don Chaffey, Teleplay: Jack Dawe, Homer McCoy, and Edward E. Seabrook.

CAST: J. Carrol Naish, Jeanette Sterke, John Witty, John McLaren, Cyril Chamberlain, Arthur Gomez, David Lawton.

PLOT/COMMENT: We are in Venice, Italy, as Alice Benson (Jeanette Sterke) and Paul Durrant (John Witty) are locked in a passionate kiss. As their lips part, Paul says, "We must always be together, my darling." "I feel the same way, too," she responds. "We'll speak to John, get him to set you free," he assures her. Alice breaks from John's embrace as he asks, "What's the matter; don't you want to be free?" Her face turns cold and stark, "I'd do anything to be free of John Benson!" –fade to opening credits.

Charlie meets his friend Inspector Bernini (Arthur Gomez) of the Venice Police in a posh gambling casino and asks the inspector if he knows a gambler that Charlie has been observing prior to the inspector's arrival. Bernini tells Charlie that the man is John Benson (John McLaren) who arrived in Venice some months before with his wife and rented a villa. Charlie is sure that he had seen Benson before in Honolulu or California.

Later in a meeting with Benson, Charlie tells him that he looks very much like a swindler named Arthur Whelan who is wanted in California and elsewhere. Benson denies the charge and leaves angrily—but carelessly forgets a wine glass with his fingerprints that Charlie confiscates for analysis. When the analysis proves Benson to be Whelan, Charlie and Inspector Bernini go to his house to arrest him. They find Benson's wife Alice and Paul Durrant there but are told that Benson has gone spear fishing and is long overdue. Shortly, a servant arrives with the aqualung Benson was using that he found on the beach, but no Benson. When the aqualung is examined, it is determined that the air supply has been poisoned by cyanide—later discovered to have been purchased by Alice Benson. No body is found, but it appears to be a case of murder, with Alice Benson and her lover Paul Durrant the prime suspects, since it is known that Mrs. Benson was trying to get a divorce from her husband so that she could marry Paul. The case looks a bit too pat for Charlie, and his continued investigation proves his suspicions are well founded.

Barry's absence from this episode is explained early on when Charlie gets a telegram from him from Paris where he is supposedly studying French culture ("I hope he has some of it rub off on him," says his sighing pop) and requests more money. Again, the location filming in Venice adds considerably to the production values and viewing enjoyment of the episode. The plot is not quite up to the previous one set in Venice, but it is serviceable and has an intriguing climax.

Episode 35: "A Bowl by Cellini"

Executive Producer: Leon Fromkess, Producer: Rudolph C. Flothow, Associate Producer: Henry Blaser, Director: Leslie Arliss, Teleplay: Lee Erwin.

CAST: J. Carrol Naish, Arthur Gomez, Peter Bennett, Richard Goolden, Stanley Van Beers, Martin Benson, Richard Dunn, Guy Deghy, Catherina Ferraz, Lala Lloyd.

PLOT/COMMENT: We are in Rome where an elderly Englishman named Archibald Meeker (Richard Goolden) is taking photographs of the ancient sites in the city. Presently he encounters a street hawker named Guido (Peter Bennett) who tries to sell him postcards and other trinkets that he has on his stand. When Meeker shows no interest, Guido takes a small "good luck" charm from his pocket and states, "This offers infallible protection on a day such as this." Chuckling at the pitchman's absurd claim, Meeker asks, "My good man, how is this day different from any other?" "It's Friday the thirteenth," Guido responds. Suddenly panic stricken, Meeker exclaims, "Friday the thirteenth! This is murder!"—fade to opening credits.

The little Englishman explains to Guido that today is his twenty-fifth wedding anniversary and he has forgotten, but he knows that his wife Martha (Lala Lloyd) will not have. She will expect an appropriate gift—and now the stores have closed for the day. Guido says that he can help and soon provides Mr. Meeker with a somewhat tarnished silver bowl that he offers for the "low price" of twenty thousand lire. Because he is in a bind, Meeker reluctantly agrees and returns to his hotel suite where Martha awaits. Martha, overbearing and somewhat shrewish, shows disdain for the tarnished bowl and insists that Archibald return it.

Guido, of course, is nowhere to be found, so Meeker goes to a jewelry store to try to sell it—a jewelry store where Charlie Chan just happens to be purchasing a watch. The jeweler immediately recognizes the silver bowl as an original Cellini, the master worker in metals from the sixteenth century. The jeweler makes an offer of eight hundred thousand lira, but Meeker feels he needs to take it back to Guido because the street hawker obviously didn't know its worth when he sold it to the gullible Meeker.

Charlie gets involved because he suspects that there may be a crime ring selling fake Cellini bowls by showing the genuine bowl to the customer and then doing the old switcheroo to a fake bowl when the customer isn't looking. In this case it appears that Guido, none too swift of mind, accidentally sold Mr. Meeker the original. With the assistance of Inspector Galvani (Arthur Gomez) of the Rome Police, Charlie goes looking for the ring leader and finds murder along the way.

This is an enjoyable and frequently humorous episode in the series. The humor comes mostly from fuddy-duddy Mr. Meeker—whose name is very appropriate, since he is extremely meek in disposition and saddled with a wife who is a termagant. There is a lighthearted atmosphere to the episode up until the late-in-coming murder and subsequent hasty conclusion. Director Leslie Arliss frequently gets his actors outside so that he can take advantage of the many famous sites in Rome, which adds to the overall production quality of the episode. Son Barry is nowhere to be seen in this episode. He must be still studying French culture in Paris, as he was in the last episode.

Episode 36: "Without Fear"

Executive Producer: Leon Fromkess, Producer: Rudolph C. Flothow, Associate Producer: Herman Blaser, Director: Don Chaffey, Teleplay: Leon Fromkess and Sam Neuman.

CAST: J. Carrol Naish, Dermot Walsh, Jane Griffiths, Viola Keats, Rupert Davies, Coral Fairweather, Edward Dentith.

PLOT/COMMENT: We are in the office of Dr. Alfred Black* on Harley Street in London. It is June 5, 1950. He is telling his attractive, twenty-something patient Margaret Holmes, "All I can say is that it's a great pity, but the consolations will be there too. I'll see you again July fifth, a month today." Margaret leaves the doctor's office, crosses to the street, and calls out for a taxi—then suddenly screams as an onrushing truck almost strikes her. Dr. Black, inside, hears her urgent scream and hurries to the window—fade to opening credits.

It is now June 5, 1957, as Charlie stops at his travel agency to inquire about his plane ticket which was to be delivered to his hotel the day before. Richard Stanton (Dermot Walsh), the travel agent, explains that his assistant and fiancée, Ann Meadows, was to deliver the ticket and make a bank deposit the day before but has disappeared. He has been frantically looking for her.

Presently Ann arrives with a crippled lady, who identifies herself as Ann's sister-in-law Cecilia and tells Richard and Charlie that Ann has just recovered from amnesia and now realizes that seven years ago she was Margaret Holmes, pregnant, and married to a lout of a husband named Anthony Holmes who was unfaithful to her. His background included a car accident back in 1948 which resulted in his sister Cecilia being paralyzed and forced to live in a wheelchair. We learn that Margaret/Ann seven years ago, right after leaving the doctor's office, lost the baby while in a similar car accident with Anthony in which he was killed and Margaret acquired her amnesia.

The police investigation of the accident revealed, however, that Anthony had been poisoned with a slow-acting medication before the accident actually occurred, that he had been given an overdose of a painkiller that was his sister Cecilia's medicine. The container with the remaining pills was found in Margaret's handbag. The police found that they could not bring criminal action against her because she was an amnesia victim and remembered nothing of the accident. She has spent four of the last seven years in a sanitarium but disappeared three years ago and has been living under the name Ann Meadows, a name she had given a doll when she was a child, according to Cecilia. Now, in 1957 with her memory back, the police may wish to charge her with the murder of her husband Anthony.

Charlie does some investigating with Inspector Duff (Rupert Davies) of Scotland Yard and is able to show that Margaret really lost her memory on the day of her June 5, 1950, appointment with Dr. Black when she was almost hit by the truck and, therefore, would have had no memory of her husband's philandering ways at the time of the accident and thus no motive to kill him. If Charlie is correct, there is another murderer out there that has escaped punishment for seven years.

The reader can see from the above summary that we are dealing with a *very* complicated and, basically, unbelievable plotline—not to mention some extreme coincidences I have not even touched upon. The result is an episode where much of the twenty-six minutes of plot time are spent with characters sitting or standing around talking about what happened seven years ago while others listen along with us, the viewers; there is little movement or action. Weighted down with so many details, there is a temptation about midway to throw up one's hands in frustration. Yes, the plot is clever and, overall, intriguing, but one cannot escape the feeling that the author, Lawrence Huntington, from a story by Sam Neuman, got carried away with his own ingenuity. (As an aside, the IMDb lists executive producer Leon Fromkess as the writer of "Without Fear," but the show's credits indicate Lawrence Huntington wrote the episode. Lawrence Huntington was a writer, producer, and director in England during this time period, but his résumé does not list this episode. In 1957 he was busy as a director for the British TV series entitled *The Adventures of Sir Lancelot*, directing six episodes of the series that year. Mysteries continue to abound!) By the way, Charlie was picking up only one plane ticket at the start of this episode. There is no mention of the whereabouts of son Barry.

(*Character names are not provided for the entire cast.)

Episode 37: "Kidnap"

Executive Producer: Leon Fromkess, Producer: Rudolph C. Flothow, Associate Producer: Herman Blaser, Director: Leslie Arliss, Teleplay: Doreen Montgomery.

CAST: J. Carrol Naish, Bryan Coleman, Ingeborg Wells, Marne Maitland, Ann Hanslip, John Stuart, Arthur Gomez.

PLOT/COMMENT: We are in Rome where Janet Curtis ((Ingeborg Wells) and her father Professor John Curtis (John Stuart) are on vacation and registering at a hotel. The hotel attendant then escorts them to the elevator where he first takes Janet to her floor. As she exits, a distinguished-looking man with a blond goatee gets on the elevator and moves to behind Professor Curtis. As the elevator door closes, the man with the blond goatee takes out a cloth, and firmly places it over the mouth and nose of the startled Professor Curtis who struggles in vain to break free. The hotel attendant calmly turns to observe—fade to opening credits.

Later, when Janet goes to the room assigned to her father, she discovers a distinguished-looking man with a blond goatee residing there who claims that he has had the room for several days. Victor Gasperi,* the hotel attendant, tells Janet that she registered alone—that there was no man with her. When the police will take no action, Janet goes to Charlie Chan at the Hotel Florino and asks for his assistance. It seems that her father is a scientist working on a highly secret ultrasonic project, and Charlie suspects that agents from a foreign government might have kidnapped him to discover secrets regarding the project.

Charlie goes to the hotel attendant's home to question him but at first only finds his wife Roxanne who is fearful that her husband is up to no good—as has happened in the past. Victor arrives and physically threatens Charlie with a wine bottle but is dispatched by the wily detective with a single judo chop. Roxanne agrees to meet Charlie for further questioning at the Roman Forum later at five o'clock when her husband is working. When Charlie arrives at the Forum, he is accosted by a thug (later identified as Guido Catcho) whom he also dispatches with a single judo chop. He then discovers the body of Roxanne among some rubble; she has been stabbed to death. Charlie now calls upon the assistance of Inspector Galvani (Arthur Gomez) of the Rome Police to help solve Roxanne's murder and to locate the missing Professor Curtis.

This episode is moderately interesting but at times is bogged down by trite, overused devices—for example, getting information from the faint impressions on a notepad that is dealt with hurriedly and improbably—and weak, illogical plotting, as when the loving husband is apparently not going to his wife's funeral because of the need for Charlie's questioning and seems little concerned. On the plus side, the overall production is greatly enhanced by location filming at various historical sites in Rome, Italy. There is no mention of lost son Barry.

(* Character names are not provided for the entire cast.)

Episode 38: "Rhyme or Treason"

Executive Producer: Leon Fromkess, Producer: Rudolph C. Flothow, Associate Producer: Herman Blaser, Director: Don Chaffey, Teleplay: Rik Vollaerts.

CAST: J. Carrol Naish, Ralph Michael, Hugh Miller, Lisa Daniely, John Dearth, Oliver Burt, Mary Laura Wood, Richard Waring, Robert Raglan, Laidman Browne, Rupert Davies.

PLOT/COMMENT: It is 1942 and we are in London in a jail cell at Pentonville Prison where the condemned man, James Coslow,* is conferring with a priest. Suddenly, a guard opens the wooden cell door and admits the governor who tells Coslow, "In view of your service to the nation, the King has seen fit to set aside the sentence of death passed on you for treason." "And instead?" the prisoner asks. "You will remain in prison for the rest of your natural life." "All my life! And I'm innocent; I'm innocent!"—fade to opening credits.

It is now the present, 1957, and Coslow's now twenty-one-year-old daughter Linda, with her winnings from a television quiz show, has enough money to hire Charlie to conduct an investigation into the justification for the execution of her father. "Will you go back into the past to prove that my father James Coslow was not guilty of treason against his country?" she asks. The venerable Chinese detective, of course, cannot refuse her sincere plea for assistance.

Charlie soon finds out from Inspector Duff (Rupert Davies) of Scotland Yard that Coslow was a member of a security unit during the war that was especially chosen for their reliability. He then questions Sir Aubrey Talbot, the commanding officer of the security unit, who tells Charlie that the unit worked out of Benham House which hasn't been used again since the war. Soon Charlie has the five members of the unit—not counting Coslow—at Benham House for questioning. Miss Mernock, the secretary, it turns out was in love with Coslow, but he did not return her affection. Maxwell Duggan, impatient and self-important, suspected Coslow first and was the person who found the book and code that eventually convicted him. Cecil Barrows, an alcoholic who wishes the questioning hurried so that he can go get a drink, states that he liked Coslow and felt that he knew his job better than some of the others. As he talks to Charlie, he adjusts a large, heavy painting on the wall which suddenly breaks loose and almost strikes Charlie.

Soon Charlie has determined that the guilty party was a proficient typist (not a hunt-and-peck one) and most likely was the British quisling who was to take over England for the Nazis after the invasion of the country. With the aid of a fake document typed on a German typewriter, Charlie sets a trap for the guilty party.

This is a nicely handled mystery—no murders this time—that has a solid plot and a limited number of suspects whose backgrounds are clearly revealed providing the viewer with an excellent chance of discovering the bad guy right along with Charlie in the time-honored device of bringing all the suspects together in one room and having it out with them. Director Don Chaffey keeps the mainly talky plot moving at a fast clip through nice staging and utilization of plot gimmicks to give a sense of real action—paintings falling and lamps being overturned, etc. There is a brief, superfluous bit at the beginning of the story where the daughter Linda appears on a TV quiz show in London entitled *What's Your Answer* and wins 375 pounds—a not-so-subtle acknowledgment of the popularity of American quiz shows in 1957-58 such as *The $64,000 Question*. Again, there is no mention of son Barry in the episode.

(*Character names are not provided on the cast list.)

Episode 39: "Three for One"

Executive Producer: Leon Fromkess, Producer: Rudolph C. Flothow, Associate Producer: Herman Blaser, Director: Leslie Arliss, Teleplay: Stan Silverman.

CAST: J. Carrol Naish, Derek Bond, Ronald Leigh-Hunt, Jerry Verno, Delphi Lawrence, Ernest Clark, Robert Cawdron, Billy Milton.

PLOT/COMMENT: We are in London at the Ames Treasure House when a gentleman with a black patch over one eye comes in and asks to see samples of the rare antique china that the shop has recently acquired. When the clerk brings out a particularly beautiful china piece, the gentleman removes a small hammer from his coat and smashes it. The manager, Peter Ross (Derek Bond), enters as the clerk cries out, "Another of your vandal friends, Mr. Ross. Look what he has done!" Ross gazes at his friend with the hammer in disbelief, "But, Cosgrove, why?" The bewildered Stephen Cosgrove (Ronald Leigh-Hunt) stammers, "I don't know, Peter. I honestly don't know"—fade to opening credits.

Charlie Chan meets with Peter Ross to discuss the several strange occurrences at the Ames Treasure House. Cosgrove is the third friend to come into the shop and destroy an object. Herbert Hodges, a taxidermist, slashed a painting, and Doris Tillman, the manager of the Hastings Grill, poured acid over a valuable tapestry. Because the friends seem to have no motive for committing the acts, Charlie asks if he has any enemies. Ross can only name Marilyn Marsh, who was in love with him and became emotionally upset when Ross married another person. Marilyn is now in a mental institution. When Charlie interviews each of the parties who destroyed merchandise at the shop, he discovers that none of them has any remembrance of the event. In the interim there is another attack at the shop. This time it is by Ross's friend Colin Prentice (Billy Milton), who destroys an antique chair and in the process also breaks his eyeglasses.

Charlie soon discovers that Cosgrove, Hodges, and Prentice are all patients of an eye specialist named Dr. Hilary Saunders (Ernest Clark), who just happens to have been engaged to Ross's wife Betty before their romance and marriage broke up the engagement. Only Doris Tillman seems to have no connection to Dr. Saunders, except that the Hastings Grill is located below Dr. Saunders' office. During Charlie's questioning of Doris about this, he is introduced to Walter Hastings (Robert Cawdron), the owner of the grill and a former performer in vaudeville.

Charlie's suspicion of hypnosis as the method used to cause the suspects to act without remembrance is confirmed when Ross, in a hypnotic state, attempts to shoot Charlie but is thwarted by the agile detective. Soon Charlie gathers all the suspects together at the Hastings Grill for dinner and the denouement of the case.

This final episode in the series is an above-average one with some interesting and unexpected twists and turns for the viewer—nothing unusual in that, of course. In this case the viewer is led down a path that seems to implicate one of the suspects rather conclusively (red-herring alert!) only to later discover that there is an even more devious path to the real culprit. And that's what mystery stories are all about, aren't they? The only unresolved mystery is the whereabouts of son Barry who disappeared in Paris six episodes ago.

The Amazing Chan and the Chan Clan with Keye Luke

This animated series from Hanna-Barbera Productions ran on the CBS Television Network as a Saturday morning, thirty-minute kids' show from September through December of 1972, with a total of sixteen episodes produced.

Each episode found Charlie, his ten children, and family dog Chu Chu in a different location—Greece, London, India, New Orleans Mardi Gras, wherever—where they encountered a criminal act, usually the theft of some valuable article native to the area visited in that episode. The kids, usually in groups of three, "helped" their detective father by looking for suspects and clues while Charlie conducted his own investiga-

tion. In all episodes the kids received the most face time on screen with Charlie usually on camera only at the beginning and end. The kids always got into trouble during their part of the investigation and ended up being chased repeatedly by ethnic-type villains all the while innocuous music

The Chan Clan Band.

was played frantically in the background. In most cases the scriptwriting made the villains cardboard cutouts of stereotypical scoundrels with not a nickel's difference among them except for changes in costume. It was established in the first episode that several of the kids performed in a band known as "The Chan Clan," and they sang a song or two in most episodes in a style that would be appealing (apparently) to youngsters of the early 1970s and might be called "bubblegum rock."

Many considered the casting of Keye Luke as the voice of Charlie Chan a breakthrough, since this was the first time that a Chinese actor portrayed the venerable detective. (There were two Japanese actors who played Chan in the silent films of the late 1920s, a Korean-American actor in the first sound film, and Caucasian actors after that.) Luke had, of course, a lot of familiarity with the role having played Number One Son Lee in the Warner Oland film series.

The clan kids in this animated series are each of a type: Henry Chan is the oldest (in his late teens) and the leader of the kids. He plays drums in the band. Stanley Chan is the second oldest of the kids and is somewhat a comic sidekick to Henry. He plays the guitar in the band. Suzie Chan is the oldest of the girls, likeable and very pretty, and she is the tambourine player in the band.

Then there are the mid-teen members of the clan: Alan Chan is the inventor of the clan having invented the Chan Van which can change shapes depending on the circumstances. He wears sunglasses and is the clarinet in the band. Anne Chan is also in her mid-teens, wears a baseball cap, and is the tomboy of the girls, always with a smart remark for the others. Tom Chan is the smarty pants of the clan, an intellectual who wears horned-rimmed glasses and plays the trombone in the band.

The leader of the youngest contingent of the clan is Flip Chan, not yet a teen and the most eager to help his old man solve a case. His younger brother Scooter calls him "Chief." Nancy Chan is a pony-tailed preteen who is the klutz of the clan, always running into one kind of accident or another. Sweet little Mimi Chan is the youngest of the girls, very girlish with a penchant for bossing around little Scooter. The youngest of the clan is Scooter, a cute little boy whom Flip considers "second-in-command." And then, of course, the eleventh member of the clan is the family dog Chu Chu, probably a Shih Tzu, which can make unusual sounds for a dog—for instance, howling like the siren from a police car while in the Chan Van.

The series was trouble-prone from the start. Perhaps wanting to deflect any racial criticism by casting Asian children in the kids' roles, the producers created a problem that soon manifested itself. While it was commendable to cast Asians in the ten roles, it was soon discovered that the children cast in the roles had thick accents that were hard to understand. Thus, the ignominious task of recasting was undertaken for all of these roles. Young Jodie Foster, ten or eleven at the time, was one of the people cast in the redo. Then there was the criticism of the music, that it was too much like other Hanna-Barbara cartoons—mainly *Scooby-Doo* (which also had that group chasing crooks much as the Chan clan did) and *The Archie Show*. In fact, the Archies' lead singer Ron Dante provided vocals for The Chan Clan. Charlie, as presented in the series, was rather bland and depicted in a costume that made him look more like a traditional (Caucasian) detective: he wore a blue suit, tie, and a snap-brimmed fedora hat that looked like a Sam Spade leftover.

And then there was the general feeling that the whole project was somewhat misguided—that it contained nothing resembling the Derr Biggers stories or the motion pictures. Gary H. Grossman in his excellent book *Saturday Morning TV* commented: "Most noticeably airing in an altered state was Oriental movie-sleuth Charlie Chan in the 1972 Hanna-Barbera-produced CBS series *The Amazing Chan and the Chan Clan*. The ill-conceived format revolved around gumshoe Chan and his ten musical children who solved a case or two, then played contemporary tunes with an Oriental flavor." Viewers commenting on the International Movie Data Base (IMDb) were more straightforward in their feelings: "Why the animators had . . . to make Charlie into an incompetent figurehead when he was portrayed on the big screen as so much more is very hard to understand"—rpaca. "Unlike the excellent films, this cartoon version has Charlie Chan and his family solving crimes committed by moron villains."—latronic. It is perhaps emblematic that Charlie Chan's first name is never mentioned in the series except in the title of one episode. He is always referred to as "Mr. Chan" or "The Amazing Chan."

The Amazing Chan and the Chan Clan
The Episodes

Episode One: "The Crown Jewel Caper" September 9, 1972.

Producers and Directors: Joseph Barbera and William Hanna, Series Writers: Eddie Carroll, Jamie Farr, Willie Gilbert, Max Hodge, Mark Kammerman, Dennis Marks, Sidney Morse, Ray Parker, Henry Sharp, Harry Winkler.

SERIES CAST: **Regulars throughout series**: Keye Luke (Charlie Chan), Robert Ito (Henry Chan), Don Messick (Chu Chu the Dog), Brian Tochi (Alan Chan). **Original Clan voices:** Debbie Jue (Nancy Chan), Jay Jay Jue (Flip Chan), Leslie Juwai (Mimi Chan), Leslie Kumamota (Anne Chan), Virginia Ann Lee (Suzie Chan), Michael Takamoto (Tom Chan), Robin Toma (Scooter Chan), Stephen Wong (Stanley Chan). **Redubbed Clan voices:** Gene Andrusco (Flip Chan), Jodie Foster (Anne Chan), Johnny Gun (Tom Chan), Beverly Kushida (Nancy Chan), Cherylene Lee (Suzie Chan/Mimi Chan), Michael Morgan (Scooter Chan), Len Weinrib (Stanley Chan), Cynthia Adler, Lisa Gerritsen, Hazel Shermet, Janet Waldo, Len Wood (various characters).

PLOT/COMMENT: The Burmese Crown Jewels have been brought from England by Lord Buckley for a museum display. Chan is in charge of security for the exhibition and, sure enough, suddenly the jewels disappear and a ransom demand is made. Three of Chan's suspects have voices that sound a lot like Boris Karloff, Peter Lorre, and Humphrey Bogart.

The plot from this episode was utilized for the first *The Amazing Chan and the Chan Clan* comic book published by Gold Key in 1972. Chan Clan song: "Undercover Man."

Episode Two: "To Catch a Pitcher" September 16, 1972.

PLOT/COMMENT: While Charlie and his five boys are at the World Series, famed pitcher Boo Blew is kidnapped by a couple of hoods. Shortly, Charlie gets a call from the team manager asking him to investigate the kidnapping. He and the clan get to work on the case.

The song in this episode sounds a lot like the "Shaft" movie theme. In this instance the lyrics describe Henry Chan as a "Super Sleuth." This plot was adapted for the second Gold Key comic book published in early 1973.

Episode Three: "Will the Real Charlie Chan Please Stand Up?" September 30, 1972.

PLOT/COMMENT: While Chan and the clan are on vacation in Hawaii, Pop is accused of stealing Mrs. Kingsley's black pearls from the hotel where they are staying. Could it be that the famed Chinese detective has become a thief—or is there a Chan imposter up to no good?

While the plot doesn't hold up very well (Chan has been sunning himself on the beach for all to see while the robbery is taking place), it is nevertheless an entertaining chapter in the series. There is no song by the Chan Clan in this episode.

Episode Four: "The Phantom Sea Thief" September 30, 1972.

PLOT/COMMENT: Charlie and his kids meet wealthy Mrs. Van Norton while on a cruise. She tells Charlie she is nervous about a million-dollar painting that she has on board ship. Later, while the Chan Clan is performing on the ship, the painting mysteriously disappears, and Charlie finds himself on another case.

This is a funnier than usual episode. Stanley Chan (Len Weinrib) gets some laughs when he impersonates a blond, curly-headed maid while trying to pilfer a glass for its fingerprints. The song is "I Got My Eye on You (Yes, I do)."

Episode Five: "Eye of the Idol" October 7, 1972.

PLOT/COMMENT: Charlie and the clan go to the shipyards to watch the arrival of a Buddha idol which contains the most valuable piece of jade in the world in its eye. Suddenly, a thief uses a smoke bomb as a distraction while he steals the jade eye. Chan and the Clan must retrieve the eye and bring the robber to justice.

There is no song by the Chan Clan in this episode. The storyline was later utilized for the fourth issue of the Gold Key comic book series.

Episode 6: "Fat Lady Caper" October 14, 1972.

PLOT/COMMENT: While Chan and the clan are visiting the side-show at the Zambini Circus, Dimples the Fat Lady disappears. Mr. Zambini suspects that a rival circus, the Ding-A-Ling Brothers' Circus, is trying to close him down by kidnapping Dimples. Charlie and the Clan come to Zambini's assistance to find Dimples.

This episode is a more fast-moving adventure containing a higher level of excitement. The song "Let's Give a Hand to the Family Chan" is heard during a chase sequence rather than as a performance of the Chan Clan Band.

Episode Seven: "Captain Kidd's Doubloons" October 21, 1972.

PLOT/COMMENT: While on vacation in Trinidad, Chan and the clan visit Buccaneer Days where the Captain Kid Doubloons, gold coins over three hundred years old, are on display. Jeremiah, the last surviving member of the Kidd family, shows up and demands the Doubloons that belonged to his kin. Soon the Doubloons are stolen, and Chan and the clan must find their whereabouts.

A funny moment occurs in this episode when Stanley (Len Weinrib) does an impersonation of John Wayne and Jimmy Durante while interrogating a suspect, to which the suspect responds, "If you'll stop, I'll turn myself in." There is no song by the Chan Clan in this episode.

Episode Eight: "Bronze Idol" October 28, 1972.

PLOT/COMMENT: Charlie and the clan are sailing on a boat that makes a stop at an island trading post. The tribal chief on the island tells Charlie that Ona Bona, a bronze idol known as "The Great One," is taking everything that they have and telling the natives that they must find more pearls. Chan and the Clan discover that a conman is at work to bilk the natives out of the pearls.

This is a routine episode in the series, no better and no worse than the others. Apparently the plot ran a bit short because the song, "(You Make Me So) Happy to Be with You," is performed twice by the Chan Clan Band. Once would have been plenty.

As usual, the Chan Clan comes to the rescue to save dear old pop.

Episode Nine: "Double Trouble" November 4, 1972.

PLOT/COMMENT: Chan and the clan are watching an auto race when racer Prince Hareem, an auto racer driving car number thirteen (and friend of Henry Chan), is kidnapped and replaced with an imposter for the big race. Prince Hareem's racing rival is suspected of the skullduggery as Charlie begins his investigation.

During the song "Who Done it?" in this episode, Henry, the drummer in the Chan Clan Band, shows remarkable skill when his left hand mysteriously disappears behind his back, but his drumming continues unabated (an animation goof?).

Episode Ten: "The Great Illusion Caper" November 11, 1972.

PLOT/COMMENT: Charlie and the clan go to see a magician, Alusio, and his magic troupe. Charlie, at the behest of the police, is looking for Hamid Bey, one of the performers who is wanted for stealing a ruby worth a million dollars. During Alusio's performance his dog Fifi disappears—only this time it's for real and not one of Alusio's allusions—and there's still the ruby to be found.

Twin magic troupe performers Alli and Baba get the prize for cutest names if not for the best performance. "Number One Son" is the song performed by the Chan Clan Band.

Episode Eleven: "The Mummy's Tomb" November 18, 1972.

PLOT/COMMENT: Charlie, the clan, and Lord Redgrave are in ancient Egypt visiting an archaeological dig of the three-thousand-year-old

Temple of Ramosses. While they are inside the temple, the lights go out and Ramosses seems to speak to them, warning of an ancient curse and telling them to leave immediately. Lord Redgrave asks Charlie to investigate the strange occurrence.

As is usually the case in these episodes, many chases occur involving the kids—this time the kids and a spooky mummy—while Charlie dithers about trying to solve the mystery. The Chan Clan Band performs "I Got the Goods on You."

Episode Twelve: "The Mardi Gras Caper" November 25, 1972.

PLOT/COMMENT: Charlie and the clan are in New Orleans for the Mardi Gras celebration. During their stay a ring that once belonged to Marie Antoinette is stolen, and Charlie is asked to interrogate the usual subjects. While that's going on, the kids decide to follow some of the suspects.

It's the same-old same-old: continuous innocuous music, the kids following suspects, the kids being chased by suspects, Charlie finding the real culprit in time for the fadeout. In the Mardi Gras Parade the Chan Clan performs "I Got My Eye on You (Yes, I Do)."

Episode Thirteen: "The Gypsy Caper" December 2, 1972.

PLOT/COMMENT: While Charlie and the clan are visiting a small village in an unnamed country (could be Switzerland, Bavaria), the community's most highly-prized possession, The Golden Icon, is stolen and a band of Gypsies is suspected of the crime. The village mayor asks Charlie to help find the missing icon.

There's a little lesson in prejudice in the episode with the assumption by the village that the disdained gypsies must be the culprits in the heist of the Golden Icon. Actually, the gypsies seem a rather merry band with their dancing bear. The "Number One Son" song is reprieved in this episode.

Episode Fourteen: "The Greek Caper" December 9, 1972.

PLOT/COMMENT: Charlie and the clan are vacationing in Greece in this episode. While visiting the Parthenon, the kids see the Winged Venus of Athens disappear while they are looking at it through a telescope. When they return the next morning with Charlie, they discover that the Winged Venus of Athens is back in place. Closer examination reveals it to be a plaster replica of the real Venus. Charlie begins an investigation.

There are the typical number of inane chase scenes involving the Chan kids and bad guys. It's the usual missing object plotline for this episode with the intrepid detective ultimately finding the object and bringing the thief to justice in time for another song by the Chan Clan Band. This time they render repeats of two songs: "Who Done It?" and "Undercover Man."

Episode 15: "White Elephant" December 16, 1972.

PLOT/COMMENT: Charlie and the clan are in India to visit Habeeb, Charlie's old friend. While there, Charlie asks to see the White Elephant Ceremony. Before the ceremony can begin, someone releases rats, causing the white elephant and other elephants to stampede. Later, when the white elephant cannot be found, it is suspected that the pachyderm has been stolen. If the Sultan doesn't ride the white elephant during the ceremony, he loses his power. Charlie is asked to help with the investigation.

This is another cookie-cutter episode in the animated series. About the only thing that is a bit different this time is that all of the kids appear on screen together for the inevitable chase scene. Usually the ten kids are broken down into smaller groupings for simpler animation in the chase sequences. "I Got the Goods on You" is the Chan Clan song.

Episode 16: "Scotland Yard" December 30, 1972.

PLOT/COMMENT: While Chan and the clan are in England on vacation, the Stone of Scone, the coronation stone where all the kings of England have been crowned, is stolen from Westminster Abbey. Chan and the clan are soon on the path of the thieves.

One clever bit in this final episode is the transformation of the Chan Van into a double-decker bus by Henry and Stanley. Soon they are stopped by a bobby who demands that they pick up passengers at the bus stop. "(You Make Me So) Happy to Be with You" and "Mystery Woman" are the two tunes used to wrap up the series.

The Return of Charlie Chan with Ross Martin

The Return of Charlie Chan
(Universal TV, 1973) 96m.

Executive Producer: John J. Cole, Producer: Jack Laird, Director: Daryl Duke, Screenplay: Gene R. Kearney, based on a story by Kearney and Simon Last.

CAST: Ross Martin, Richard Haydn, Louise Sorel, Joseph Hindy, Kathleen Widdoes, Don Gordon, Peter Donat, Leslie Nielsen, Rocky Gunn, Virginia Ann Lee, Ernest Harada, Soon-Taik Oh, Patricia Gage, Ted Greenhalgh, Graeme Campbell, Neil Dainard, Otto Lowy, Pearl Hong, Adele Yoshioka.

Ross Martin as Charlie Chan.

The Return of Charlie Chan *was subtitled* Happiness Is a Warm Clue, *which should be warning enough for the discriminating viewer.* – Hal Erickson, *All Movie Guide*

PLOT/COMMENT: The film has never been released on video and is very rarely shown on TV, so I have not had the opportunity to view it; I can, however, provide some basic information on the film from those who have seen it—and apparently we haven't missed much. Charlie Chan (Ross Martin) is now sixty and retired but nevertheless is summoned back to detective work when an Onassis-like shipping magnate is murdered on his luxury yacht. Charlie, with the assistance of Rocky Gunn as Number One Son Peter (yes, that's right, Peter!) and several other siblings that include Doreen Chan (Virginia Lee), Stephen Chan (Soon Taik-Oh), Oliver Chan (Ernest Harada), and Mai-Ling Chan (Adele Yoshioka), takes on the case. Suspects and red-herring characters within the plot are played by several well-known names, including Richard Haydn (from *The Sound of Music* fame), Louise Sorel (who later became a popular TV soap-opera actress on such day-timers as *Santa Barbara*, *Port Charles*, and, most recently, *Days of Our Lives*), Don Gordon (a TV regular as thug or cop, depending on the whims of casting directors), and Leslie Nielsen (of the *Naked Gun* films, *Spy Hard*, and other roles of all types).

The Return of Charlie Chan was a 1973 made-for-television pilot with ambitions of becoming a series again, as with *The New Adventures of Charlie Chan* back in 1957. That syndicated series had never been popular, but hope springs eternal, and in the early 1970s detective series experienced a revival with such flourishing examples as *Columbo, Barnaby Jones, The Rockford Files*, and *Mannix*—and the list goes on, but you get the idea.

So why not a return of Charlie Chan? Very simple. The times were changing, and pressure groups were almost immediately in a snit when they

Rocky Gunn as Number One
Son Peter.

heard that yet *another* white actor was going to play Chan, as, of course, had been the habit since the Charlie Chan franchise took off in movie land back in the early 1930s. Chinese groups, in particular, felt that the character was demeaning to them. Such ire was aroused that plans for a series were quickly dropped, and the film was put on the shelf until 1979 when it first got an airing on ABC television. (*The Return of Charlie Chan* had been released theatrically in Europe back in 1973 in an attempt to recoup some of its investment.)

If you were going to cast a Caucasian in the role of Charlie, Ross Martin seemed a likely candidate. He was a good actor who had recently come off the popular *Wild Wild West* TV series playing a character named Artemus Gordon, a master of disguises, working as an undercover government agent for President Grant. It's likely that the producers of *Return* felt that for most viewers this would be seen as Ross Martin playing Artemus Gordon in a Chinese disguise as Charlie Chan. For the young Asian actor, Rocky Gunn (birth name Roderick Wong Gunn), who played Number One Son Peter Chan in the film, it was to be his first and last film. He died in 1983 of undisclosed causes just three months shy of his forty-third birthday. Ross Martin, who had a history of heart problems, preceded him in death in 1981 of a heart attack during his sixty-first year.

Peter Lorre as Mr. Moto.

The Case Files
of Mr. Moto

John P. Marquand
and the Novels

SEVERAL PEOPLE WERE INSTRUMENTAL in the creation, development, and success of the Mr. Moto character in literature and films: John P. Marquand, the author/creator, who saw the Moto novels as a quick and easy money-making diversion from his *important* writing; Sol M. Wurtzel, B-picture film producer at Twentieth Century-Fox, who saw the character as just another company assignment; young film director/screenwriter Norman Foster, who wanted to direct A-budget pictures but by reluctantly agreeing to direct six of the eight B-budget episodes in the Moto series established himself as a respected director/screenwriter in Hollywood; and, of course, actor Peter Lorre, who had only slight interest in the role of the little Oriental and feared being typecast but nonetheless created a character that is still fondly remembered decades later. None of the participants was particularly interested in the Mr. Moto property, but as is so frequently the case in the creative process, a serendipitous situation occurred that made for an international success.

Mr. Moto, the fictional Japanese secret agent, first came to life in the pages of the *Saturday Evening Post* in 1935 in a story from the pen of future Pulitzer Prize winner, John Phillips Marquand (1893-1960). The serialized story, first titled *No Hero*, would later be published in book form as *Your Turn, Mr. Moto*. But by this time, 1935, Marquand was an old hand at writing stories for the *Post,* having written his first one, "The Right that Failed," in 1921. By 1922 he was writing serialized novels that ran in the *Post* (sometimes in the *Ladies' Home Journal, Collier's,* and other popular magazines of the day) and then were published in book form afterwards.

Soon Marquand was a familiar name among *Post* readers, and he began to make big money for the twenties and thirties (reportedly five

John P. Marquand wrote six Mr. Moto novels between 1935 and 1947, but he is probably best known for his Pulitzer Prize-winning novel, *The Late George Apley* (1937).

hundred to three thousand dollars for each story and thirty to forty thousand dollars for novels) cranking out these stories and novels, most of which concerned America's upper class and the efforts of those on the lower echelons to claw their way up to that elevated station. Marquand told their stories with, as one commentator put it, "a mix of respect and social satire." By 1938 this type of writing would win Marquand the Pulitzer Prize for a satirical novel of Boston's social elite, *The Late George Apley*.

The impetus for creating Mr. Moto came when Earl Derr Biggers, the creator of the hugely popular Charlie Chan novels, died in 1933. Marquand's editor, George Lorimer, suggested to him that a new Oriental sleuth would be very marketable with the passing of Biggers, and, who knows, they might even get a film series out of it the way Biggers did. To seal the deal with Marquand, Lorimer gave the author a cash advance and per diem to go to the Orient to soak up some Asian ambiance and to come back with a suitable sleuth/secret agent or whatever. You know, just do it!

While he was in Japan, Marquand was constantly shadowed by a polite little Japanese detective. According to Marquand's account, "Suddenly, it dawned on me that he was just the protagonist I was looking for—and while my shadow did his duty very conscientiously, 'Mr. Moto,' the shrewd, the polite, the efficient sleuth was born." This was the way Marquand described it to writer David Zinman for his book *Saturday Afternoon at the Bijou*.

As mentioned, Marquand created Moto for the novel *No Hero*, and it was serialized in the *Saturday Evening Post* in six installments starting on March 30 and running until May 4, 1935. Following the serialization, the novel was published in book form by Little, Brown and Company as would be the rest of the Moto stories. With the success of *No Hero*, Marquand set about writing sequels, publishing *Thank You, Mr. Moto* in 1936, *Think Fast, Mr. Moto* in 1937, *Mr. Moto Is So Sorry* (1938), and *Last Laugh, Mr. Moto* in 1942 (first serialized in *Collier's* under the title *Mercator Island*). With the arrival of World War II, novels featuring a Japanese secret agent were no longer appealing to the *Post* or any of the other leading magazines, so Marquand closed the book on his popular Oriental character. It would not be until 1957 that he would again feature his polite little Japanese in a *Saturday Evening Post* series first entitled *Rendezvous in Tokyo* but then published in book form as *Stopover: Tokyo*, with later editions taking the titles *The Last of Mr. Moto* and, finally, *Right You Are, Mr. Moto*.

Interestingly, Mr. Moto, like Charlie Chan, was never the main character in the novels. The stories were usually told by a Westerner who gets involved with some sort of intrigue in one of the Pacific Rim countries and encounters Moto along the way, not realizing that he is a Japanese agent but soon realizing his capabilities and resourcefulness. In the first five novels Mr. Moto is an agent of the Japanese empire. For the sixth novel, set in Japan long after World War II during the 1950s, Moto is a senior intelligence official in the pro-western Japanese government. As a good example of the fact that Moto was never the key character in the novels, when the final novel was filmed as *Stopover Tokyo* by Twentieth Century-Fox in 1957, the Moto character was cut *entirely*. The Mr. Moto films, supposedly based on the novels, bore little resemblance subject-wise to their source material, and for the screenplays, of course, the character of Moto was placed front and center.

According to numerous sources, Marquand was little concerned about changes to the character. He didn't much care what Hollywood did to his stories after they were completed. His main interest was always the money that could be generated by the licensing of the novels and the character. As he blithely put it, "I wrote about him [Moto] to get shoes for my baby."

John P. Marquand continued writing right up to the end, still mostly concentrating on the vagaries of the Boston social elite with little thought given to his Oriental creation who, as usual, resided on the back shelf of the author's mind. On July 16, 1960, Marquand had dinner with his son John, Jr. and went to bed. Sometime during the night he died in his sleep. He was only sixty-six years old.

The Mr. Moto Novels

No Hero (1935) (Serialized as *Your Turn, Mr. Moto*) Publisher: Little, Brown and Company.

PLOT/COMMENT: Casey Lee, a World War I American flying ace now reduced to stunt work with planes, is in Tokyo on assignment for a tobacco company to fly a plane across the Pacific as a publicity stunt. When the deal collapses on Casey, he relapses in his accustomed manner with alcohol and outspoken bitterness about life's vagaries. Soon Casey falls for a White Russian refugee, gorgeous but treacherous, and somehow becomes involved with the Japanese Emperor's future plans for his country. Enter Mr. Moto, an agent of the Imperial Japanese government, who befriends the out-of-luck fly boy and soon has him and his White Russian lovely involved in an espionage caper that may or may not make Casey Lee a hero back home.

It has been noted that the novel would have made an excellent Alfred Hitchcock film, with its plot of an innocent man succumbing to a sultry *femme fatale* and then being thrust into the hands of forces dealing with matters beyond his control—think *North by Northwest* or *Saboteur*. The title, *No Hero*, becomes somewhat ambiguous because as the plot unfolds, it could apply to both Moto and Casey Lee.

Thank You, Mr. Moto (1936)

Published by Little, Brown and Company.

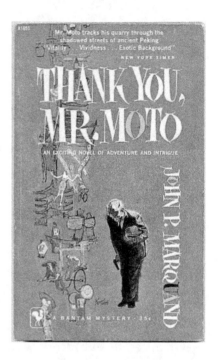

PLOT/COMMENT: American Tom Nelson has been living in Peking for some years, speaks Japanese fluently, and feels that he has a grasp of the Oriental mind. Tom encounters an American museum buyer named Eleanor Joyce who has arrived in Peking seeking eight ancient silk scrolls. Soon, despite Tom's cautionary remarks, she meets with a former British military man named Major Jamison Best who is known to sell Chinese art treasures and artifacts. Eleanor is able to get one of the scrolls from Major Best, but the next day Best is discovered murdered by someone using a Chinese crossbow. Tom and Eleanor take the scroll to Prince Tung, a friend of Tom's, who is shocked to learn that Eleanor is after all eight scrolls, seven of which are in his private vault. Mr. Moto turns out to be the investigating officer in the matter of Major Best's murder and warns Nelson not to get involved with the situation. Later, Tom discovers that Moto has made the murder look like a suicide, and then Nelson himself barely survives a similar crossbow attack. Before the case is resolved, Tom Nelson, Eleanor Joyce, and Mr. Moto come to the knowledge that they are involved not only in a murder mystery but in a political espionage plot against the ruling party in Japan.

Shortly after returning from a trip to China, Marquand wrote the novel in the first person from the point of view of Tom Nelson. Using the framework of murder and international intrigue, Marquand takes the opportunity to delve into additional matters of concern to the author. His protagonist Tom Nelson, an American expatriate living in Peking, becomes our guide and the voice of Marquand in his delineation of culture clashes between the East and the West and the even bigger portrait of Sino-Japanese relations, matters that the escapist Mr. Moto films rarely ventured into.

Think Fast, Mr. Moto (1937) Publisher: Little, Brown and Company.

PLOT/COMMENT: Wilson Hitchings—the young heir to the American Banking firm of Hitchings Brothers, Bankers and Commission Merchants: Honolulu, Shanghai, Canton—is sent by his uncle to Honolulu to deal with the "Hitchings Plantation," a gambling casino started by a black sheep in the family who, when he died, passed on the operation of the establishment to his beautiful daughter named Eve. Wilson's uncle feels that the gambling operation is giving the Hitchings family and business a black eye from a public relations standpoint. Wilson's instructions are to close it down ASAP. Mr. Moto, a Japanese government agent, also has his reasons for wanting the plantation shut down. It seems that gambling money is being channeled through the plantation to Chinese and Russian agents who then transfer it to anti-Japanese forces in Manchuria. Mr. Moto is able to help Wilson accomplish his goal and, at the same time, serve the interests of the Japanese empire.

Although this was Marquand's third Mr. Moto novel, it was the first one to be filmed, and the book and the movie bear only the slightest resemblance. In the film Mr. Moto picks up the trail of diamond smugglers in San Francisco's Chinatown who lead him to Honolulu and then Shanghai on board the *Marco Polo*, a luxury passenger ship. On board and undercover, Moto encounters Bob Hitchings, the young son of the ship line owner. Soon it becomes apparent that his family's ship line has inadvertently gotten involved with an international crime ring. Well, they kept the Hitching family name in the film—if little else.

Mr. Moto Is So Sorry (1938) Publisher: Little, Brown and Company.

PLOT/COMMENT: American Calvin Gates, running away from robbery accusations back home, is hoping to connect with the Gilbreth Expedition, a scientific archeological team working in Mongolia. While on the train to Mongolia, Gates meets up with Sylvia Dillaway, a sketch artist who is also on her way to the expedition and who is accompanied by her Russian guide Boris. When the mysterious Mr. Moto shows up on the train, Boris

appears noticeably nervous at the sight of Moto and gives Sylvia a silver cigarette case that has a curious design on its cover. During a train stopover Boris is murdered in Calvin's hotel room, and suddenly the cigarette case becomes an item of desire for several mysterious individuals on the train, including Captain Sam Hamby, an Australian Army officer who is in the employ of Prince Wu, the ruler of the province of Ghuru Nor where the expedition is located; General Shirov, Boris's brother and a Russian spy; and Major Ahara, a Japanese Army officer. It is soon revealed that the cigarette case has a coded message regarding Japanese Army movements in Mongolia that the Russians and others would like to put their hands on.

Here, Marquand offers up another case of international intrigue, including an Alfred Hitchcock-type "MacGuffin," the cigarette case, that adds to the mystery and huggermugger of the goings-on. In the plot formula that Marquand has by now established for the Moto novels, an American man, the protagonist in the story, usually stumbles by happenstance into an international situation that involves powerful figures and forces from competing countries that put him in grave peril. It is through the intervention of Mr. Moto that the situation is resolved and the protagonist's life is saved.

Last Laugh, Mr. Moto (1942) Publisher: Little, Brown and Company.

PLOT/COMMENT: Our protagonist in this novel is an ex-Navy pilot from America, Bob Boles, who is drifting and drinking his way through the Caribbean on his sailboat. Presently he is hired by a suspicious-acting, wealthy American couple to take them and their Swedish butler

on a voyage to a remote location known as Mercator Island. Why do they want to go to this dreary little island? Why does the Charterer's wife seem to fall for the yank yachtsman? Could the Swedish butler really be an undercover Nazi? And why is all of this of such great interest to a Japanese government agent named Mr. I. A. Moto?

On the surface some of this sounds like a variation on Hemingway's *To Have and Have Not*, and a young Bogart might have been good casting for the Bob Boles role. But, alas, this was not to be. The screenwriters of the Moto film series took their little Japanese character on other adventures that never involved a Bob Boles or his for-hire sailboat.

Stopover: Tokyo (1957) (also known as *Right You Are, Mr. Moto* and *The Last of Mr. Moto*) Publisher: Little, Brown and Company.

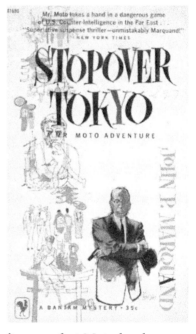

PLOT/COMMENT: It is now the mid-1950s and America is embroiled in a "Cold War" with its nemesis communist Russia. Two American agents, Jack Rhyce and Ruth Bogart, are sent to Japan on a secret mission to thwart a communist effort to create an international anti-American incident. The nefarious plot involves the assassination of a popular Japanese political figure that would be damaging to the American authority in the country and cause a Japanese backlash. Mr. Moto works with the couple in their efforts to infiltrate the enemy organization and foil their plans.

Fittingly, in this final Marquand Mr. Moto novel, Moto is depicted older than in the earlier novels that were written more than a decade earlier. This doesn't mean that Moto has become "soft" or much "mellowed" in his middle years. He is as lethal in dealing with the bad guys as he ever was, but there is more of a tendency for him to delegate some of the lethalness to his professional cohorts.

The Mr. Moto Films

Sol M. Wurtzel, Film Producer

When the screen rights to Mr. Moto were purchased by Twentieth Century-Fox in 1937, the plans were to make an A-budget movie out of the material. When none of the A-unit producers on the lot showed any interest in the project, it was assigned to B-unit producer Sol M. Wurtzel (1890-1958), a veteran on the Fox lot whose career went all the way back to 1915 when he joined the studio as private secretary to mogul William Fox.

Wurtzel was the personification of the "company man" and spent his entire career on the Fox lot. In 1917 Fox sent "Solly," as he was nicknamed, to California to oversee the studio's West Coast productions. In 1933 he was promoted to producer on the lot and had a hand in furthering the careers of such Fox contractees as Will Rogers, John Ford, and even little Shirley Temple, among others. In 1935 Wurtzel took over the B-unit at the studio and successfully turned out the low-budget, meat-and-potatoes features

Twentieth Century-Fox's B-unit producer Sol M. Wurtzel produced seven of the eight Peter Lorre Mr. Moto films and is considered instrumental in the success of the series even though it was "just a job" to him at the time.

that sometimes kept the studio afloat when expensive A-pictures bombed at the box office. Wurtzel was tight-fisted with the funds to produce his Bs and believed, according to Hal Erickson in *All Movie Guide*, "that his B-films would post a profit no matter how much time or money was spent on them, so why endeavor to make his films any better?" This belief by Wurtzel didn't always make him popular with his actors or directors, but the front office loved him *and* the box-office returns that came rolling in from his pictures. Writer Erickson quotes comic Harry Ritz's summation of the artistic quality of Sol Wurtzel's films: "Things have gone from bad to Wurtzel." Never fazed by such disparaging remarks, Sol M. Wurtzel continued to ply his trade of turning out B-picture potboilers until his retirement from Fox in 1949. He lived in happy retirement until his death in Los Angeles, California, in 1958.

Fledgling director and screenwriter Norman Foster only reluctantly accepted the Mr. Moto assignment from producer Sol Wurtzel, but the B-budget series helped to cement his career as a solid director and screenwriter.

Norman Foster, Director and Writer

Actor and future director Norman Foster (1903-1976) had had a middling career on the stage during the 1920s and came to Hollywood and the Fox Studio around 1930 where he continued to have a middling career, this time acting in films. He had married Claudette Colbert back in 1928 and by 1935 the marriage had soured and was headed to the divorce court. He would marry Sally Blaine, Loretta Young's older sister, in 1937 and remain with her until his death.

Foster felt he might refresh his career by turning to directing and was finally given a B-picture entitled *I Cover Chinatown* (1936) for which he both directed and played the lead role—a tour guide in Chinatown who with his girlfriend gets involved with jewel thieves and murder.

The picture wasn't much, but it was a start in directing. Following that picture Foster wrote and directed another low-budget murder mystery entitled *Fair Warning* (1937) that had J. Edward Bromberg, Betty Furness, and John Payne in the cast. These two forays into directing were okay to get his feet wet learning the director's trade, but Foster had higher ambitions and wanted A-budget pictures on his résumé.

So when producer Sol M. Wurtzel approached Foster about directing the first Mr. Moto picture, the fledgling director was underwhelmed by the assignment. In addition, he felt that the actor being touted for the Moto role, Peter Lorre, a Hungarian, was a bad case of miscasting. "Why not find an Asian actor to play the role?" he queried. But the studio was intractable. Then when Foster went to talk to Lorre about the role, he found that the actor was in a sanitarium coming off a morphine addiction, the result of appendicitis and the removal of his gall bladder. The diminutive performer appeared so weak to Foster that the director feared he would never be able to handle the physical demands of the role (and, in fact, stuntman Harold Parry *did* ultimately perform most of the physical feats required by the judo-trained Mr. Moto).

With no better assignments in the offing, Foster reluctantly agreed to direct the first Moto film and to co-write the screenplay with Howard Ellis Smith—which gave Foster a chance to enhance his director's salary a bit with the writing assignment, since as an actor he had been paid two thousand a week and he was now making about a fourth of that directing. Smith and Foster keep only minimal elements from Marquand's novel for their screen adaptation, tightening the plot, changing the focus to Moto, and making it "move" with action and suspense. Foster proved to be a skilled writer and director in the mystery/detective/secret-agent genre, bringing the film in on time and on budget. As a plus, the reviewers and the public greeted the film positively, making *Think Fast, Mr. Moto* a critical and box-office success. So what do you do when you have a hit film? You make sequels. Mr. Moto was now a series!

Norman Foster took pleasure in the success of his first Mr. Moto film and agreed to carry on with a second film, *Thank You, Mr. Moto*, again co-writing the screenplay (this time with Willis Cooper) and directing. Foster would stay with the series through 1938 and 1939, directing and co-writing six of the eight Mr. Moto films that were produced prior to America's worsening relations with Japan leading to World War II and Peter Lorre's desire to move on to other roles before he became totally typecast as the little Japanese; thus the series ended. The Norman Foster entries in the Mr. Moto canon are generally judged to be the best in the series, with *Thank You, Mr. Moto* usually placed at number one.

The two episodes not directed by Norman Foster are *Mr. Moto's Gamble* and *Mr. Moto in Danger Island*. *Mr. Moto's Gamble* is a reworked Charlie Chan script that was put in the Mr. Moto schedule when Warner Oland became ill and couldn't continue with the film that was already well-underway. Sol Wurtzel produced the film which was helmed by another studio director, James Tinling. *Mr. Moto in Danger Island* was produced by John Stone (who had produced other Bs on the Fox lot including many of the Chan features) and directed by Herbert I. Leeds, also no stranger to B pictures but a director who had a rather spotty track record. *Mr. Moto in Danger Island* is generally considered the weakest of the Moto films and *Charlie Chan in the City of Darkness*, also directed by Leeds, bears the same dubious distinction among the Chan Twentieth Century-Fox features.

With the ending of the Moto series, Norman Foster took on the task of directing three Charlie Chan features with Sidney Toler: *Charlie Chan in Reno, Charlie Chan at Treasure Island*, and *Charlie Chan in Panama*, judged by many to be three of the best Chan films made by Twentieth Century-Fox. His future directing years included the Orson Welles feature *Journey into Fear* in 1943, *Rachel and the Stranger* in 1948, and *Kiss the Blood off My Hands,* also in 1948. In the 1950s Foster began directing in television and spent a lot of his time at the Disney Studio cranking out episodes for *The Wonderful World of Disney*, including the Davy Crockett, Zorro, and *The Nine Lives of Alfego Baca* films along with several television features such as *Hans Brinker or the Silver Skates*. He continued directing on television (occasionally taking on an acting role, too) up to 1976. Among his credits are episodes of *Batman, The Green Hornet, The Monroes, The New Loretta Young Show, Cannon*, and *It Takes A Thief,* just to name a few. Norman Foster died of cancer in 1976.

Peter Lorre as Mr. Moto

Peter Lorre (1904-1962), like Norman Foster, was not sure that accepting the role of Mr. Moto was a good career move when it was first offered to him. After all, he had been born in Rózsahegy, Hungary, with the name Lásló Löwenstein, which didn't seem to make him an obvious choice for an Oriental sleuth—although he was looking for a role that might break him out of the "mad men" and other sinister roles with which he seemed to be typed.

It all went back to his early years as a theatre actor in Vienna, Austria, and later in Berlin during the 1920s when he had adopted the stage name of "Lorre." His big opportunity came in 1931 in his breakthrough perfor-

Peter Lorre portrayed Mr. Moto in eight films for Twentieth Century-Fox.

mance as child murderer Hans Beckert in Fritz Lang's film *M*. Lorre's performance as the serial killer who preys upon little girls was so frightening that it was said many viewers could not separate the actor from the real-life Beckert and that there were occasional calls to the police when Lorre was seen in public. Other German film roles followed, most in a sinister vein, as the young actor achieved some fame. By 1934 Alfred Hitchcock, directing still in England at Gaumont British studio, sought Lorre for the villain's role in his first production of *The Man Who Knew Too Much* (1934). Lorre, who did not yet speak English, had to learn much of his role phonetically.

With the rising Nazi power in Germany during the early 1930s, Lorre decided that perhaps America might be a better place for him to continue his acting career and, without too much delay, received a contract from Columbia Pictures—his reputation as a fine actor had obviously preceded him to Hollywood. Soon he was loaned to MGM for the macabre role of Dr. Gogol in *Mad Love* (1935), but soon frustration ensued when the studio seemed unable to come up with suitable roles for their enigmatic young actor.

In early 1937 Lorre moved to Twentieth Century-Fox and received assurances from Darryl F. Zanuck, the head of the studio, that he would be given roles of a "lighter" nature than he had had at Columbia and in Europe. In his first assignment for Fox, *Crack-Up* (1937), Lorre played the role of Randolph Maximilian Taggart, a master spy, who during much of his screen time is disguised as Colonel Gimpy, a crippled halfwit who goes around blowing a bugle and reciting "The Walrus and the Carpenter." Lorre's performance—ranging from sinister to outrageously comic—provided the actor with a rare opportunity to demonstrate his tremendous range. Then came *Nancy Steele Is Missing!* (1937) in which he played another despicable villain role, this time involving attempted murder and extortion—the old typecasting frustration started to reemerge for Lorre.

It was at this point in time that the studio acquired the rights to *Mr. Moto* from John P. Marquand and set Sol M. Wurtzel as the producer. Wurtzel then assigned Norman Foster as director and selected contract player Peter Lorre for the leading role of Mr. Moto. Foster's earlier hesitation regarding Lorre in the Moto role was soon calmed when he noted that the actor's short stature matched the character and with appropriate makeup, false buck teeth, his hair slicked down, and wearing wire-rimmed glasses, Lorre very much took on the persona of Mr. Moto as described by Marquand in the novels.

The two years that Peter Lorre spent in the guise of Mr. Moto were turbulent years for the actor. He was still suffering from his addiction to morphine related to his appendix and gallbladder health issues that continued to plague him. Often he was so weak that he found it difficult to even climb stairs. All of his physical acting in the films was covered by stuntman Harvey Perry, or, occasionally, John Kascier. To save the actor's strength, Delmar Costello, a would-be actor of Mexican descent who was Lorre's exact height and body type, was employed as his stand-in for all eight films. And there were bouts with mental depression. Author Howard M. Berlin in *The Complete Mr. Moto Film Phile* comments on the tormented Lorre listening to Adolph Hitler's speeches on the radio in his dressing room and then crying out when called for a scene, "The whole world is falling apart, and you want me to make a picture!" And then there was Lorre's growing concern that he was being typecast in the role of the polite little Japanese detective.

With the completion of *Mr. Moto Takes a Vacation* in 1939, the decision was made not to continue the series. As stated previously, America's precarious relations with Japan as the war eased ever closer and the desire of both Norman Foster and Lorre to move on in their careers were undoubtedly the main reasons for this decision. Lorre would move on to greater acting acclaim in the 1940s, his glory years as an actor, with roles in such outstanding films as *The Maltese Falcon* (1941), *Casablanca* (1942), and *Arsenic and Old Lace* (1944). By the 1950s and '60s his career evolved into to a series of lesser roles that were typically madmen, sinister villains, and creepy scoundrels that were deemed "Peter Lorre roles."

In his last years he was cast with Vincent Price and Boris Karloff in two Edgar Allen Poe-based films for American International Pictures entitled *Tales of Terror* (1962) and *The Comedy of Terrors* (1964). The three master actors, all trapped in their stereotypical roles, hammed it up for the camera outrageously. American International touted the three as "Your Favorite Creeps Are Together Again." But Philip K. Scheuer in the *Los Angeles Times* saw it differently. His headline was "Aging Actors Chew Scenery." Within his review he went on to say, "I felt ashamed to watch once reputable actors hamming it up all over the place, making a mockery of whatever is left of their poor images."

Peter Lorre ended his career frequently mocking his own image in roles that were sometimes outrageous send-ups from an earlier and better time in his career. He knew what he was doing, and he accepted it as par for the course when you are a "face maker"—as he liked to refer to himself rather than as an actor. It was his way of saying that he didn't take it seriously anymore—that he just made faces for the stipend he was given. But even with his great disappointment regarding what he considered his "limited" career—and certainly many actors would have given their eyeteeth for such a career—Lorre was known to reveal a dark sense of humor, particularly about the vainness and vagaries of actors like himself. The story goes, according to Vincent Price, that when he and Peter Lorre went to view Bela Lugosi's body during Bela's funeral, Lorre, upon seeing Lugosi dressed in his famous Dracula cape, quipped, "Do you think we should drive a stake through his heart just in case?" The story, listed in

Lorre's International Movie Data Base as trivia, is no doubt apocryphal, but suggests Lorre's brand of humor and is certainly what he *might* have said, even if he didn't *actually* say it.

Peter Lorre died suddenly of a stroke in the spring of 1964. He was only fifty-nine years old.

The Mr. Moto films of Peter Lorre

Think Fast, Mr. Moto (Twentieth Century-Fox, 1937) 66m.

Producer: Sol M. Wurtzel, Director: Norman Foster, Screenplay: Howard Ellis Smith and Norman Foster (Wyllis Cooper and Charles Kenyon, uncredited) from a novel by John P. Marquand.

CAST: Peter Lorre, Virginia Field, Thomas Beck, Sig Rumann, Murray Kinnell, John Rogers, Lotus Long, George Cooper, J. Carrol Naish, Frederick Vogeding, Philip Ahn , Richard Alexander, George Hassell.

To have a Japanese man out-thinking all the sneaky Caucasian minds around him is really quite startling for 1937, considering the casual xenophobia of the time. – Jemmytee

PLOT/COMMENT: In this first entry in the Mr. Moto series, international diamond smuggling is the concern, particularly as it involves the Hitchings Ship Line as the means to transport the diamonds to the United States. In what amounts to a prologue to the film, we discover Moto in disguise as a seeming panhandler on the busy streets of San Francisco during the Chinese New Year celebration. His attempt to sell a diamond in a curio shop results in the discovery of a dead body in a wicker basket and a violent physical confrontation marked by jiu-jitsu and fisticuffs involving Moto, the shop owner, and a police officer before the wily Japanese

makes his escape, removes his disguise, and books passage for an overseas voyage.

And now a different Mr. Moto emerges as he travels on the Hitchings' *Marco Polo* luxury liner from San Francisco to Honolulu to Shanghai in the guise of a seemingly meek and mild, milk-drinking, cultured Kentaro Moto. His fellow passengers include the ship owner's son Bob Hitchings (Thomas Beck), a callow, shallow playboy-type who is more interested in wine and women than business responsibilities, and a beautiful woman who immediately attracts Bob's eye when she boards in Honolulu, Gloria Danton (Virginia Field), a more mysterious lady than she lets on to Bob and Moto. Later we learn that she is a "white Russian" expatriate working with Nicolas Marloff (Sig Rumann), a kingpin in the smuggling operation and owner of the International Club in Shanghai where Gloria is a singer going by the name of Tanya Barov. During the voyage Mr. Moto recognizes a ship steward (John Rogers) as the murderer of the wicker-basket dead man in the curio shop back in San Francisco. When Moto discovers the steward trying to steal an important letter from Bob's stateroom, a vicious fight ensues where Moto again demonstrates his skill at jiu-jitsu and ends the encounter by callously throwing the steward overboard to his death.

In Shanghai Bob delivers the letter he has been carrying for his father to the company's branch manager Joseph Wilkie (Murray Kinnell), which turns out to be a blank sheet of paper—presumably Moto has retained the real letter after discovering the steward trying to steal it. A transatlantic call from Bob's father to Wilkie explains that the purpose of the letter was to have Wilkie carefully examine all ships in the line for smuggled diamonds because government agents are investigating and there would be a possible two-hundred-thousand-dollar fine if smuggled jewels were found on any of their ships. In Shanghai Mr. Moto's search for the ringleader of the international smuggling operation leads him and all of the possible suspects directly to the International Club where he shortly (with some police assistance) handcuffs his prey.

Mr. Moto clearly enjoys mixing it up physically with his adversaries more than the docile Charlie Chan and Mr. Wong. As one viewer commented, "Moto is the Dirty Harry of the Oriental detective set." The biggest asset in the Mr. Moto series is the casting of Peter Lorre in the role. He so embraces the role physically and vocally that it is hard to imagine that J. Edward Bromberg, reportedly considered for the role, or anyone else could capture the essence of the character better than Lorre. There is elegance in his dress and manner along with intelligence and a wry humor; these qualities, coupled with a sense of danger, make the character fascinating to watch.

The masterminds behind the film series, producer Sol M. Wurtzel and director/co-writer Norman Foster, despite working with a relatively low budget, provide a fast-moving story, excellent production values, a large cast, and dozens of extras to flesh out the street scenes during the Chinese New Year, the passengers on the *Marco Polo*, and the crowded and atmospheric International Club. Watching the film you rarely have the feeling that you are on the back lot of Twentieth Century-Fox.

The acting by the large cast is first rate throughout. Much of the cast is comprised of Fox contract players and/or well-known character actors such as Thomas Beck, Sig Rumann, Virginia Field, and J. Carrol Naish (who twenty years later would assume the role of Charlie Chan for the television series *The New Adventures of Charlie Chan*).

Interestingly, this first film in the series does not make clear where Mr. Moto gets his authority to operate as a crime fighter. When Bob Hitchings asks Mr. Moto at the end of the film if he is a detective, Moto hands Bob a business card that states he is the managing director for the Dai Nippon Trading Company of San Francisco, and he then tells Bob he is only an amateur detective. This is in contrast to his behavior throughout the film where he seems to be a government agent working closely with American and Shanghai Police in the rounding up of the smuggling ring. If he is doing all of this strictly as a private citizen, we have to wonder about his murder of the steward on the *Marco Polo*—don't we!

Thank You, Mr. Moto (Twentieth Century-Fox, 1937) 67m.

Producer: Sol M. Wurtzel, Director: Norman Foster, Screenplay: Willis Cooper and Norman Foster from a story by John P. Marquand.

CAST: Peter Lorre, Thomas Beck, Pauline Frederick, Jayne Regan, Sidney Blackmer, Sig Rumann, John Carradine, William Von Brincken, Nedda Harrigan, Philip Ahn, John Bleifer, Richard Loo, Dale Van Sickle, Victor Sen Yung.

Nervous or squeamish souls may be disturbed by the continual thud of falling bodies... – NY Times

PLOT/COMMENT: In this episode Mr. Moto, in the employ of parties unknown, is after seven ancient scrolls which, when brought together, provide a map leading to the location of the long-hidden tomb of Genghis

Khan where it is believed that a huge treasure resides. When the story begins, Moto is traveling in disguise as a Mongolian with a caravan of pack camels in the Gobi Desert, heading for Peiping, China. While camped at night in a tent, Moto reveals that he has one of the scrolls in his possession. As he is about to turn in, he becomes embroiled in a fight to the death with a camel driver named Ning (Charles Stevens) who tries to steal the scroll. Moto is forced to stab him to death and bury him in a hastily dug grave in the tent.

Soon Moto arrives in Peiping, China, where he removes his disguise and becomes the cultured, erudite Mr. Moto residing in a posh hotel. He has waiting for him an invitation to a garden party that evening by the wealthy but shady Colonel Tchernov (Sig Rumann). Knowing the Colonel and his partner Eric Koerger (Sidney Blackmer), Moto suspects that there must be an ulterior purpose for the party. That evening the Colonel introduces guests as they arrive, including Tom Nelson (Thomas Beck), of an American delegation in Peiping, to the guest of honor, Eleanor Joyce (Jayne Regan), the daughter of a well-known importer (with the pair soon to be our romantic love interest in the plot). We discover when Mr. Moto arrives that he knows Tom who introduces him to Eleanor. Moto seems fascinated that Eleanor is in Peiping writing a book on Chinese art and hoping to pick up a few antiques.

The reason for the party soon becomes apparent when Colonel Tchernov greets guests Madame Chung (Pauline Frederick) and her son Prince Chung (Philip Ahn) and asks to speak with the Prince in the library. There the Colonel attempts to purchase the scrolls that are owned by the Prince and his mother. The Prince refuses to sell the scrolls and explains that he and his mother see it as their sacred trust to protect the scrolls from falling into the hands of unscrupulous treasure hunters. When he sees that the Prince will not sell the scrolls, the Colonel becomes angry and threatens Prince Chung's life with a pistol. Shortly, the Prince leaves the library and exits the party hurriedly with his mother. A few moments later the Colonel is discovered slumped over his desk, dead from a stab wound—not administered by the Prince, we learn, but by Mr. Moto who leaves the body as an apparent suicide.

Eric Koerger and Colonel Tchernov's unfaithful wife now attempt to secure the scrolls by going to the home of the Prince and his mother. When their torture of Prince Chung to get the location of the hidden scrolls is not fruitful, they threaten him with the death of his mother unless he reveals the hiding place. Though she pleads with her son not to do so, he relents and tells them where the scrolls are hidden. Then, tragically, his mother is shot by Koerger when she makes one last effort to stop him.

Prince Chung, in anguish over what has transpired, commits suicide with a dagger. Before he dies Moto and Tom arrive, and Moto makes a promise to the dying Prince.

Mr. Moto and Tom Nelson pursue Koerger and Madame Tchernov and have a final encounter with them on a Chinese junk where—shades of *Think Fast, Mr. Moto*—the Japanese detective throws one thug overboard to his death and, ultimately, concludes a vicious fight with Koerger by shooting him dead. Then keeping the promise he made to the dying Prince Chung, Mr. Moto takes the scrolls and burns them so that they will cause no temptation or harm to others.

This is a fast-paced episode in the Mr. Moto series, directed and co-written by Norman Foster. The film has the look of an A-budget picture with its early sandstorm scene with camels and Mongols in the Gobi Desert, then realistic scenes of crowded Peiping streets (really the Fox back lot) filled with hurrying Chinese rickshaws, quaint antique shops, and wealthy foreigners in their white suits living in a posh, modern hotel. Later, the film turns to atmospheric *noir* with deep fog, dark shadows, and a creaky Chinese junk waiting at anchor for the denouement. It's a tip-top job of filmmaking and Norman Foster deserves the credit for the care taken to make it all seem real.

Again, we are puzzled throughout the story as to where Mr. Moto gets his authority to pursue and kill the evildoers. In this film alone he racks up four killings—all of them quite brutal and without hesitation or remorse. At one point he displays his business card which states that he is "Kentaro Moto, Confidential Investigator for the International Association of Importers"—hardly a license to kill. Early in the film Eleanor asks Tom about Mr. Moto. Tom explains that he is "an adventurer, explorer, soldier of fortune, and one of the Orient's mysteries"—hardly appropriate for his business card, but probably fairly accurate, as far as it goes. Late in the film Mr. Moto tells a gate guard that he is with the "International Police," whatever that means specifically, but the guard quickly accedes to Moto's demands. Whatever his authority, he gets the job done!

As an aside: within a few months of the release of *Thank You, Mr. Moto,* Victor Sen Yung would acquire the role of Number Two Son Jimmy Chan in *Charlie Chan in Honolulu.* In *Thank You* he can be seen in two non-speaking bit parts: as a Peiping street person and later as the elevator operator in the hotel where Mr. Moto is staying.

Mr. Moto's Gamble (Twentieth Century-Fox, 1938) 71m.

Producer: Sol M. Wurtzel, Director: James Tinling, Screenplay: Charles Belden, Jerry Cady from a story by John P. Marquand.

CAST: Peter Lorre; Keye Luke; Dick Baldwin; Lynn Bari; Douglas Fowley; Jayne Regan; Harold Huber; Maxie Rosenbloom; John Hamilton; George E. Stone; Ward Bond; Lon Chaney, Jr.; Paul Fix; Pierre Watkins; Irving Bacon; George Chandler; Olin Howland.

What you get is the usual made-in-four-weeks murder mystery in glorious black and white with the usual Fox suspects as actors.
– jonfrum2000

PLOT/COMMENT: Mr. Moto, Charlie Chan's Number One Son Lee (Keye Luke), and Police Lieutenant Riggs (Harold Huber) are off to a boxing match that has Bill Steele (Dick Baldwin) pitted against Frankie Stanton (Russ Clark), a bout that has the high-rolling gamblers laying down some heavy bets. Nick Crowder (Douglas Fowley), who manages the heavyweight champ Biff Moran (Ward Bond), has a "hunch" that Bill Steele will knock out his opponent by the fifth round and makes a thirty-thousand-dollar bet with high-powered gambler Clipper McCoy (Bernard Nedell). Phillip Benton (John Hamilton), president of the corporation that runs the boxing operation, bets ten thousand dollars on Stanton, although he claims to Lt. Riggs that the ten-dollar bet between them is about as much as he likes to gamble. In this mix we also have a love interest: Newspaper reporter Penny Kendall (Lynn Bari) and Linda Benton, (Jayne Regan), Phillip Benton's daughter, both have a serious crush on fighter Bill Steele, and he seems to have a when-I'm-not-near-the-girl-I-love,-I-love-the-girl-I'm-near problem.

So the grudge match begins with both fighters about equally matched. When Stanton's small cut over his eye begins to bleed, his manager Jerry Connors (George E. Stone) puts some collodion on it to stop the bleeding. The next round, without a clear punch being thrown, Stanton goes down for the count—the long count; he's dead! An autopsy is performed, and it is determined that a poison called amarone, found on Steele's boxing glove, killed the boxer. Steele is arrested, later indicted, and then suspended as a boxer.

Through some behind-the-scenes maneuvering by Mr. Moto, Lt. Riggs, and the district attorney, Steele's suspension is lifted for a match with the heavyweight champion Biff Moran. Moto makes it known to all the likely suspects for the murder of fighter Stanton that he will arrest the culprit at ringside that night.

This third episode in the Moto series is a victim of unfortunate circumstances. As has been well chronicled elsewhere, this was supposed to be a Warner Oland/Charlie Chan film entitled *Charlie Chan at the Ringside*. Several days of shooting took place and then the much-troubled Warner Oland said he was leaving the set for a glass of water and never returned. When it became certain that Oland would not be returning to the studio for some time, it was decided to save as much film footage as possible by modifying the script somewhat—mostly by writing Moto where it had previously said Chan—and converting it into a Mr. Moto film. The actors assigned to the Chan film were called back (except for a couple who had started new jobs during the hiatus), and Keye Luke continued as Lee Chan, becoming a criminology student of Mr. Moto who is seen teaching such a class in several new scenes added to the script.

The flaw in this tactic to save a few bucks was that Mr. Moto was a very different character from Charlie Chan. In his first two episodes Mr. Moto had distinguished himself as a man of action who practiced jiu-jitsu on his enemies and was a master of disguises. Moto is seen as a far more complex character and somewhat amoral in that a confrontation with an enemy was usually a fight to the death. Remember, in the first two episodes he had occasion on board ship to throw men overboard to their deaths when there were lesser alternatives. Unfortunately, the reworked Chan script called for a passive, more stolid Mr. Moto who is not a man of action, thereby denying the character the very qualities that distinguished him from Mr. Chan. In fact, the very essence of the Moto character was cut away in this episode.

In the first two Mr. Moto films Moto didn't have to suffer the foolishness of comic sidekick characters such as the Chan sons or the over-the-top performances of Harold Huber, who was a frequent irritant in the Chan cases. In *Mr. Moto's Gamble* he not only has Luke and Huber but there is the oafish Wellington character played with mindless goofiness by former boxer Max "Slapsie Maxie" Rosenbloom, a totally annoying and unrealistic character who is pitted with Keye Luke in many supposedly comic scenes. You can see a bemused smirk on Peter Lorre's face in several of the scenes where his Mr. Moto suffers these fools.

Despite all of this nay-saying, the film does have its pleasures. The boxing scenes are handled nicely and, generally speaking, the proceedings move along at a decent clip. The plot has some interesting twists that hold the viewer until the very end when there is an unexpected last-minute murder. In addition, it's always great to see some of the wonderful character actors of the era at work, people such as John Hamilton, George E. Stone, Ward Bond, Cliff Clark, Pierre Watkins, Irving Bacon, and Olan Howland in a tiny bit part.

Mr. Moto Takes a Chance (Twentieth Century-Fox, 1938) 63m.

Producer: Sol M. Wurtzel, Director: Norman Foster, Screenplay: Lew Breslow and John Patrick from a story by Willis Cooper and Norman Foster.

CAST: Peter Lorre, Rochelle Hudson, Robert Kent, J. Edward Bromberg, Chick Chandler, George Regas, Frederick Vogeding, Gloria Roy, Victor Sen Yung.

Take away Peter Lorre as Moto and we'd have a tired jungle drama of nefarious natives, banana plants, and the occasional crocodile. The only real mystery is how Mr. Moto keeps his white suit so clean in the jungle. – Terrell-4

PLOT/COMMENT: In this episode the indomitable Mr. Moto finds himself in Cambodia posing as an archaeologist but really investigating a possible uprising by native tribes against the colonial government and searching for a hidden munitions base that will supply weapons for the

anticipated uprising. Into this jungle setting flies Victoria Mason (Rochelle Hudson), an Amelia Earhart-type pilot who is supposedly making an around-the-world flight, who mysteriously sabotages her plane and parachutes to within a few yards of Moto's dig. At the same time two American wildlife documentary filmmakers, Marty Weston (Robert Kent) and Chick Davis (Chick Chandler), are in the area gathering stock footage that they plan to sell back in the States—if they survive their own bungling incompetence as they traverse the jungle. They are what passes for comic relief, especially Chick, who runs into trees, falls into a tiger pit, and even attempts feeble magic tricks to entice chuckles. Marty, not quite so comically obnoxious, functions additionally as the romantic interest for Victoria, called "Vicki" by those who know her well. The bad guys are Rajah Ali (J. Edward Bromberg), the high muckety-muck of the Village of Tong Moi, and his High Priest, Bokor (George Regas), both of whom seek to be the number one power broker when the uprising begins, each having no love for the other—and each overacting egregiously.

Moto functions in disguise about half the time as an elderly "god" of the nearby ancient temple—and looks for all the world as if he must have been the model for George Lucas's later creation of Yoda. The resemblance is striking, especially in long shots. By the end of the film we discover Victoria's purpose for parachuting into the jungle: she has been sent by the British Intelligence Service to stop the uprising. (Apparently, the BIS has quite a budget, since it can afford to crash her plane just to parachute her into the locale.) Anyway, Moto, Vicki, Marty, and Chick prevail at the ending shootout involving handguns, Tommy guns, machine guns, and a massive explosion at the hidden munitions dump. The natives are no longer restless!

Reportedly, this was the second Moto episode filmed, but the studio withheld it because it was thought not up to the quality of *Think Fast, Mr. Moto*—and they were right! *Thank You, Mr. Moto* was filmed and released second. Then, with the loss of Warner Oland in the Charlie Chan series, *Mr. Moto's Gamble* was rushed into production and released prior to *Takes a Chance*.

A few minutes into *Mr. Moto Takes a Chance* and the viewer soon becomes aware that the story is not progressing, that we have no idea why Mr. Moto and Victoria are out in the Cambodian jungles, and we don't find out until near the very end. Then as we meet the rest of the cast and see their involvement with Moto and Victoria, what little interest that has been generated soon wanes and the proceedings become tedious. These are not believable characters with whom we want to spend much time.

One viewer of *Mr. Moto Takes a Chance* mentioned the "dopey moments" in the film; another, the "sappy dialog"; and perhaps most damning of all, "the script took a nosedive and crashed like Rochelle Hudson's plane did at the beginning." It is interesting that the same basic team that brought to life the earlier outstanding Mr. Moto films could screw up the works so badly.

Mysterious Mr. Moto (Twentieth Century-Fox, 1938) 63m. (AKA *Mysterious Mr. Moto of Devil's Island*)

Producer: Sol M. Wurtzel, Director: Norman Foster, Screenplay: Philip MacDonald and Norman Foster.

CAST: Peter Lorre, Mary Maguire, Henry Wilcoxon, Erik Rhodes, Harold Huber, Leon Ames, Forrester Harvey, Fredrik Vogeding, Lester Matthews, John Rogers, Karen Sorrell, Mitchell Lewis.

He's a one-man Hawkshaw who performs miracles, these not excluding the way he escapes from traps laid for him, from flocks of hoodlums, from gunfire, and from wet feet, or a head cold. Nothing can touch him… – Char. Variety

PLOT/COMMENT: The film begins with Moto, in disguise as Ito Masuke, and Paul Brissac (Leon Ames) escaping from Devil's Island through the dense jungle and murky waterways to a Portuguese tramp steamer in Cayenne, on to Lisbon, and then to London where Brissac takes on the distinguished guise of a man named Romero. Moto finagles himself into the position of houseboy for Brissac/Romero in order to keep an eye on him, since Moto knows that he is one of the founders of an organization in Europe known as the League of Assassins. The back story for all of this is that Moto, an agent of the International Police, was sent to Devil's Island undercover as a murderer in order to ingratiate himself to Brissac, escape with him, and then stay with him in the hope that he would lead Moto to the ringleader of the organization. (It may seem like an unlikely, dangerous, and slightly overblown approach to getting in good with the bad guy, but be that as it may.)

In his disguise as Ito Masuka, Moto becomes Romero's houseboy in London and becomes acquainted with other members of the League, namely George Higgins (Forrester Harvey), a cockney Londoner who has the bad habit of talking too much and soon gets eliminated by his own

pals; Ernst Litmar (Harold Huber), a higher up in the League, but by no means the brains behind the operation; and Gottfried Brujo (Fredrik Vogeding), a little classier than his associates but still not the head honcho.

Mr. Moto soon discovers that the likely next subject for the assassins is Anton Darvak (Henry Wilcoxon), the "steel king of Prague" and a pacifist who refuses to provide the formula for a new steel his company has developed that is sought by European armament people—read Nazis—who are now threatening his life through the League of Assassins. Darvak's secretary Ann Richman (Mary Maguire) fears for Darvak's life and tries to persuade him to take precautions, but he blithely refuses (to the point of idiocy, a weakness in the plotting). David Scott-Frensham (Erik Rhodes), a stereotypical silly-ass Englishman who is handling some business affairs for Darvak, pops in every once in a while during the plot development.

An elaborate plot to lure Darvak to an art gallery exhibit so that he can be cleverly assassinated—by the "accidental" dropping of a heavy ceiling chandelier—is foiled by the indomitable Moto (in yet another disguise). He maneuvers the League kingpin beneath the chandelier at the precise moment of its descent—thus procuring his immediate demise.

Mysterious Mr. Moto is a welcome return to the high-quality, action-full plotting and direction of the first two episodes in the series. The refreshingly straightforward plot is easy to follow, and the characters are intriguing—some even Dickensian when the action moves to the seedy streets and smoke-filled dives of the Lime House district of London where Moto meets his Eurasian underground compatriot Lotus Lio (Karen Sorrell). The sets and street scenes are so authentic-looking that it seems impossible that we are really on the back lot of Twentieth Century-Fox. This is the first episode that clearly establishes that Mr. Moto is an Agent of the International Police, thus giving him legal cover when he chooses to dispatch an opponent.

Mr. Moto's Last Warning (Twentieth Century-Fox, 1938) 71m.

Producer: Sol M. Wurtzel, Director: Norman Foster, Screenplay: Philip MacDonald and Norman Foster.

CAST: Peter Lorre, Ricardo Cortez, Virginia Field, John Carradine, George Sanders, Joan Carrol, Robert Coote, Margaret Irving, Leyland Hodgson, John Davidson.

> *Mr. Moto's glasses really cling to his face. He gets tossed off the pier in a bag, escapes and swims to the surface, and his glasses remain undisturbed on his face. He then gets into a struggle on the dock with the bad guy and takes a couple of blows to the face. Cut to a close up of Mr. Moto and the glasses rest solidly on his nose. I guess they must be some type of specially designed spy spectacles.*
> – cutterccbaxter

PLOT/COMMENT: In this episode a gang of international spies, working for an unnamed foreign power (I wonder who that could be in 1938?), is seeking to cause a rupture between the English and French, longtime allies, by blowing up the French fleet when it arrives at the English-controlled Suez Canal at Port Said. There is never any mystery as to who the malevolent spies are; the only question is whether Mr. Moto and his operatives will be able to stop them.

The gang is headed by Fabian the Great (Ricardo Cortez), a music hall ventriloquist when he isn't planning international intrigue. His closest compatriot is Eric Norvel (George Sanders), a monocle-wearing, waxed-mustache-adorned, continental type—may we guess German? (Sanders' accent hovers between French and German throughout the film.) Danforth (John Carradine) is a sort of undercover spy for Fabian, but later it turns out that he is really Richard Burke, a British undercover agent working with Moto. Unfortunately, Burke's cover is blown and he ends up at the bottom of the sea in a diving bell with no oxygen, one of the more grisly murders I've seen in adventure films of this era. The last of Fabian's major cohorts is the swarthy Hakim (John Davidson), an underling who eagerly does the bid-

ding of Fabian, whether it means closing a door or planting a ticking bomb in Moto's quarters. The only significant female in the plot is Connie Porter (Virginia Field), a British expatriate who runs a sleazy dive called Connie's Place where much of the planning for the sabotage takes place. Connie is Fabian's inamorata, a basically good girl who has gotten mixed up with the wrong crowd. One commentator on the film accurately described her as "a kind of dime-store version of Joan Blondell—blond, plump, good-hearted, and luscious."

The sabotage plot is supposed to work as follows: The crew of the *Vulcan*, a salvage ship, is supposedly working a salvage mission on a sunken cargo ship a couple of miles off shore at the mouth of the Suez Canal. In reality divers are planting explosives so that the whole area is mined with depth charges which can be controlled by the saboteurs from shore. If all goes according to their plan, the French fleet will be destroyed as it starts through the canal. But, of course, the bad guys had not planned on the resourceful Mr. Moto to foil their plot.

Again director Norman Foster has brought together the elements of a fine adventure story and told that story in an effective and action-full manner. The atmospheric feel of the film is palpable: the narrow, darkened streets of Port Said; the onstage and backstage hurly-burly of the Sultana Theatre of Variety where Fabian the Great performs with his cockney dummy Alfred; Connie's Place in the crowded underbelly of Port Said where nefarious deeds are hatched and, hopefully, not brought to fruition; and on board the *Vulcan* where murder is calmly and quietly executed in the narrow confines of an airless diving bell.

Peter Lorre and the outstanding supporting cast mentioned above keep it all seemingly real, even when plot strands seem to fray beyond the realm of probability—in the real world would Moto have detected the ticking bomb *just* at the last moment and disposed of it before it went off? We hope so. It should be mentioned that the supporting cast includes a fine comic turn by Robert Coote, playing the "silly-ass Englishman" who bobs in and out of the swirl of activity but in the end actually assists Moto in the roundup of the saboteurs.

Mr. Moto in Danger Island (Twentieth Century-Fox, 1939) 64m.

Producer: John Stone, Director: Herbert I. Leeds, Screenplay: Peter Milne based on story ideas by George Bricker and John Reinhardt from the novel *Murder in Trinidad* by John W. Vandercook.

CAST: Peter Lorre, Jean Hersholt, Amanda Duff, Warren Hymer, Richard Lane, Leon Ames, Douglass Dumbrille, Charles D. Brown, Paul Harvey, Robert Lowery, Eddie Marr, Harry Woods, Willie Best, Ward Bond.

This corner has long since allowed that Peter Lorre is superhuman in every conceivable respect when he slicks down his hair, stains his face, puts on those steel-rimmed "specks" and goes around playing Mr. Moto, the yellow peril among sleuths. – NY Times

PLOT/COMMENT: Diamond smuggling is the caper this time for Mr. Moto. Cheap South American diamonds are being smuggled through Puerto Rico and are flooding the world market. It is already an international problem, and if it continues, diamond values will collapse. A special investigator sent from Washington has been murdered, and now Mr. Moto has been put on the case. While sailing to the island, Moto acquires a shipboard pal and bodyguard, Twister McGurk (Warren Hymer), a slightly dim-witted wrestler who is fascinated by Moto's skill at Judo. Together they take on the diamond smuggling racket.

After a failed attempt on his life, Moto determines that there is an informant (or maybe the ring leader) among Governor John Bentley's (Paul Harvey) inner council, since only they knew Moto was on his way to the island. The council includes numerous suspects. Major Thomas Castle (Charles D. Brown) has been leading the ineffective investigation of the smuggling for the governor. He is greatly troubled that the governor appears to want him off the case now. Commissioner Gordon (Richard Lane) is something of an opportunist and would, apparently, like Castle's job. Commissioner Madero (Leon Ames) claims he did not know

of Moto's assignment to the case, but later we see him burn the information that told him so. In addition, he is known as an excellent knife thrower, and that was the method used to kill Moto's predecessor. Mr. Sutter (Jean Hersholt) is the owner of a shipping line, and it is known that much of the smuggling is taking place on his ships. Then there is the governor's nephew, Lt. George Bentley (Robert Lowery), who would seem to have no motivation for involvement with the bad guys, and, besides, he is in love with the Governor's beautiful daughter Joan (Amanda Duff), and we know the love interests are never guilty in these films.

Moto and his buddy Twister soon determine that the smuggling ring's hideout is in the Great Salinas Swamp, thought to be haunted by the ghosts of pirates who used to hide out there. Just when things are looking up for Moto and the case, the governor himself is murdered by a thrown knife. Moto uses a clever ruse to go undercover with the smugglers and then in a rousing speedboat chase all but the ringleader are captured. With another show of cunning, Moto wraps up the case by luring the brains of the operation to try to murder a dead man.

Both producer Sol M. Wurtzel and regular director and co-scriptwriter Norman Foster are missing from this episode, and very possibly that accounts for the diminished returns. Director Herbert I. Leeds was part of the B unit at Fox and has the unfortunate credit of later directing *Charlie Chan in the City of Darkness*, generally thought to be the nadir of the Fox Chan pictures. Leeds would go on to direct such other B features for Fox as a Lloyd Nolan Michael Shayne mystery, and several Cesar Romero Cisco Kid films. John Stone, the producer, has some outstanding credits in the Warner Oland Chan series, producing such episodes as *Charlie Chan in Paris,... at the Race Track,* and... *at the Opera.*

One of the major weaknesses in the film is that we are never provided enough verisimilitude to really believe that the story was taking place on the island of Puerto Rico. In previous Moto films when he was supposedly in the Gobi Desert heading for Peiping, China, or in Port Said in Egypt protecting the Suez Canal, or escaping from Devil's Island and traveling to London, the production values were such that there was almost total believability—we were *there*. Not so here; we could be almost anywhere. As one viewer commented, "I cannot remember seeing anyone who even resembled a Puerto Rican." The exception to this was the scenes in the Salinas Swamp that were handled nicely with appropriate jungle atmosphere and creatures.

But I don't wish to paint too bad a picture of this episode. It's still a good adventure/mystery with an extremely talented cast of topnotch character actors. Even Warren Hymer's Twister character is humorous at times, and, for one film, could be tolerated without too much annoyance. Peter Lorre is, of course, delightful in the leading role and is so appealing as Mr. Moto that one is happy to sit through a less-than-stellar Moto mystery just to savor his performance.

Mr. Moto Takes a Vacation (Twentieth Century-Fox, 1939) 65m.

Producer: Sol M. Wurtzel, Director: Norman Foster, Screenplay: Philip MacDonald and Norman Foster.

CAST: Peter Lorre; Joseph Schildkraut; Lionel Atwill; Virginia Field; John King; Iva Stewart; George P. Huntley, Jr.; Victor Varconi; John Bleifer; Honorable Wu; Morgan Wallace; Anthony Warde; Harry Strang; John Davidson; Willie Best; Stanley Blystone; George Chandler.

> *Dark, sinister characters lurking in the rainy night; gunshots fired from open windows that narrowly miss the hero's head; sophisticated and supposed foolproof alarm systems just begging for someone to test them; and master criminals believed to be dead—these are the kind of elements found in a lot of the really good 1930s mysteries that I love.* – bensonmum2

PLOT/COMMENT: Although produced before *Mr. Moto on Danger Island*, for some never-explained reason the release of the film was held up until several months after *Danger Island* played theatres. All of the original top people—producer, director, and screenwriters—are on hand for this episode that is slightly different in format. Usually there is one group of bad guys who are attempting to take over the world or are after a valuable something-or-other and must be stopped, of course, by Mr. Moto. In *Takes a Vacation* Mr. Moto has to contend with three totally separate entities trying to steal the priceless ancient crown of the Queen of Sheba, recently unearthed by archeologist Howard Stevens (John King) in the Arabian Desert and brought to the Fremont Museum in San Francisco. Mr. Moto closely watches the return of the crown in anticipation that it will be tempting to robbers, especially the cunning and long-sought-after thief Mr. Mataxa, who Moto describes as "a psychopathic—a kleptomaniac on a grand scale. The more unattainable the object, the more determined he grows to possess it."

And, indeed, Mataxa *is* after the crown, but he is not alone in this endeavor. Three gangsters, led by Joe Rubla (Anthony Warde) working out of Chinatown in San Francisco, try to steal the crown by hijacking an armored truck supposed to be transporting the crown from the ship to the museum. Their mission fails but, never discouraged, they try other means to secure the crown until they are eventually caught by Moto and the police. The clumsiest operatives trying to get their hands on the crown are Paul Borodoff (Victor Varconi), who claims to be a special investigator from an insurance company, and Eleanore Kirke (Virginia Field), who uses her sexual assets to gain closeness to the handsome archaeologist Stevens (who really only has eyes for the museum curator's secretary Susan French (Iva Stewart). They never really come close to stealing the crown, but they do muddy up the plot a bit. But back to Metaxa. Moto's suspects include the museum curator Professor Hildebrand (Lionel Atwill), fairly new in the position since he took the job after the recent death of the previous curator. Hendrik Manderson (Joseph Schildkraut) is a museum benefactor, donating the funds needed to finance the expedition that led

to the discovery of the crown. Manderson appears elderly and walks with considerable discomfort with a cane. And then there is Archibald Featherstone, a "silly-ass Englishman," who Moto refers to as "ubiquitous" because he is constantly showing up unexpectedly throughout the film and complicating things for Mr. Moto. Finally, through some clever detective work dealing with wet footprints and the use of a clever ruse to throw suspicion elsewhere and draw out the elusive Metaxa, Moto brings the case to a successful conclusion.

If there had only been the Metaxa plot to steal the crown, the film would have had a duration of about fifteen minutes, but, nevertheless, the other plots are fairly interesting and divert the viewer's attention in a somewhat red-herring manner from Metaxa. Director Norman Foster keeps the action moving throughout and lends the film a nice atmospheric touch with many of the Chinatown scenes taking place at night with a drizzly rain lending a *noir* feel to the setting. Then, too, the climactic scene is set late at night in the otherwise deserted and shadowy museum with artifacts tumbling thither and yon during Moto's forceful and violent fight with Metaxa. As one viewer commented, "Moto is like a whirling dervish of activity as he goes after his prey." It's an exciting conclusion to the series.

The only really unpleasant aspect to the film is the so-called comic relief, this time provide by George P. Huntley, Jr. in the form of yet another silly-ass Englishman. English actor Robert Coote played a similar role in *Mr. Moto's Last Warning* and was also annoying, but not nearly so much as the buffoonish Huntley. One viewer described Huntley's character as having "all the intelligence and acumen of a brain-damaged turnip." I don't think he has overstated this description. Nevertheless, while this final episode with the wonderful Peter Lorre as Mr. Moto may not be the best in the series, it is still an interesting and diverting hour and five minutes of mystery adventure.

The Return of Mr. Moto with Henry Silva

The Return of Mr. Moto (Lippert Films, 1965) 71m.

Producers: Robert L. Lippert and Jack Parsons, Director: Ernest Morris, Screenplay: Fred Eggers.

CAST: Henry Silva, Terence Longdon, Suzanne Lloyd, Marne Maitland, Martin Wyldeck, Brian Coburn, Stanley Morgan, Peter Zander, Harold Kasket, Anthony Booth, Gordon Tanner, Henry Gilbert, Richard Evans, Ian Fleming, Denis Holmes, Tracy Connell, Alister Williamson, Sonya Benjamin.

The Return of Mr. Moto *is one sad, drab, lifeless affair.* – bensonmum2

PLOT/COMMENT: This twenty-six-year afterthought to Peter Lorre's Mr. Moto series takes its cue from the hugely popular James Bond spy films that had exploded onto the film scene in the early 1960s. With a very jazzy-bouncy-under-credits music theme similar to 007's, we meet the new Mr. Moto, Henry Silva, a Hispanic with maybe, I say *maybe*, a tiny tinge of Asian about his appearance. Okay, so Lorre was Germanic and not Asian. At least makeup, costume, and dialogue steps were taken to give his appearance and actions the allusion of an Asian. None of these were utilized for Mr. Silva.

The plot concerns oil leases in the Persian Gulf. America's Beta Oil Company lease is up for renewal by the Shah of Wadi Shammar (Harold Kasket), and a group hoping to get the oil leases has been sabotaging the

wells leased by Beta, thus causing the Shah and his people to lose money on the leases. Moto is brought in to find out who is responsible for this and to assist in removing the obstacles that would cause Beta Oil to lose its leases. Early in the plot we learn that the head of this conspiracy is the Shah's own secretary Wasir Hussein (Marne Maitland), supplemented by his gang of toughs. With that information out of the way, the viewer then is free to just watch—no thinking required—as Mr. Moto eventually thwarts their efforts and gets Beta Oil back into the good graces of the Shah. While there are some secondary revelations that come out near the end of the plot, once we know who the good guys and the bad guys are—as we do early in the plot—it is all downhill from there.

Viewer vexation emerges as the story unwinds: there are just too many characters to keep straight. One needs a scorecard and pencil to keep track of them. Moto has his assistant Charles Ginelli (Peter Zander). Then there is Chief Inspector Marlow (Richard Evans) of Scotland Yard. Another Scotland Yard Inspector, Jim Halliday (Stanley Morgan), is mugged by a man named Chapel (Denis Holmes) who pretends to be Halliday to kidnap Moto. In addition, there are David Lennox (Henry Gilbert), the Chairman of the Board of Beta Oil, and Jonathan Westering (Terence Longdon) of British Intelligence who has something or other to do with the case. And these are only the good guys! There are about as many bad guys (with funny names) to keep straight. The distaff side

Mr. Moto (Henry Silva at center) confers with the Shah of Wadi Shammar (Harold Kasket) about oil leases in the Persian Gulf as leading lady Suzanne Lloyd and others try to show interest in the tedious conversation.

is a cinch: Maxine Powell (Suzanne Lloyd), secretary to the oil company chairman, and a nightclub belly dancer (Sonyia Benjamin)—who is well-qualified for her role.

As stated earlier, Henry Silva does very little to make Mr. Moto the soft-spoken, polite, intelligent, cunning, man-of-mystery-and-disguises that John P. Marquand created many years before. There is none of the Lorre stellar acting skill and charm that permeated the earlier Moto films. Even the use of a disguise is clumsily handled. Late in the film's plot Silva adopts the disguise of a Mr. Takura to inject himself into the oil cartel meeting as the representative of Japan. He dons black horn-rimmed glasses, a mustache and goatee, and affects a Japanese accent. Any five-year-old would recognize him as Moto, but other cast members are blithely fooled into believing that he is Takura—as the viewer very likely sighs and rolls his eyes in total disbelief, as I did.

The Return of Mr. Moto is a sad ending to the film files of the Mr. Moto character. As one viewer commented, "[It's] the only film I've walked out from."

The Radio Case Files
of Mr. Moto

THE **MR. I. A. MOTO** (frequently referred to as simply *Mr. Moto*) radio series was created by writer/director Harry W. Junkin for NBC as a 1951 summer series. It premiered on May 20, 1951, and ran each week as thirty-minute episodes, ending its run on October 20, 1951. The program was on a sustaining basis for its entire run of twenty-three episodes. It should be noted that the "I. A." initials for Mr. Moto in the radio series were a throwback to the novels where John P. Marquand identified Mr. Moto in that way without ever explaining what the I. A. stood for. In the movie series with Peter Lorre, the character was given the first name of Kentaro, but it was only used infrequently. It has been mentioned that the I. A. may have stood for International Agent, but I could find no verification to support that. The series was written and directed for the most part by radio veteran Harry W. Junkin, and starred James Monks in the title role.

Harry W. Junkin, Director and Writer

Harry W. Junkin already had a good reputation at NBC when the *Moto* series came along. In the mid-1940s he had directed some of the episodes of the popular *Adventures of Frank Merriwell* program. Then came his creation of the highly-acclaimed 1948 radio drama series entitled *The Radio City Playhouse*, where he adapted the works of some of America's outstanding writers—people such as Ray Bradbury, Cornell Woolrich, and Stephen Vincent Benét—

Writer/director Harry W. Junkin had an impressive background in radio prior to creating the *Mr. I. A. Moto* radio series in 1951.

for the radio series. When Junkin later created the *Mr. I. A. Moto* series, he brought along from *Radio City*, among others, the announcer Fred Collins and actor John Larkin, who had been a mainstay on *Radio City* and then played Moto's boss in several episodes.

Junkin moved into television in the 1950s working on such dramatic series as *Studio One*, *Philco Television Playhouse*, and *Kraft Television Theatre*. He moved to England in the 1960s and wrote for such television series there as *The Saint* with Roger Moore, *Gideon's Way* with John Gregson, and *The Persuaders* with Tony Curtis and Roger Moore. Junkin retired in the 1970s.

James Monks as Mr. Moto

James Monks (1913-1994), who portrayed Mr. Moto in the radio series, had a brother John who became a stage manager, actor, producer, and playwright of note who was instrumental in bringing about James's debut on Broadway in his 1936-1938 production of *Brother Rat*. James went on to play Owen Morgan in director John Ford's film of *How Green Was My Valley* in 1941; the following year he was Splinter in the 1942 film *Joan of Paris*, which starred Michele Morgan and Paul Henreid. On Broadway in 1943 he played Cassio in Paul Robeson's acclaimed *Othello*, with Jose Ferrer as Iago. His longest-running Broadway role was in *Aun-*

James Monks is seen here with Paul Douglas in 1946 in a very early television appearance. As one might surmise from the use of this picture, photos of James Monks are scarce.

tie Mame (1956-1958) starring Rosalind Russell. On radio James was the main character, Jim Brandon, in the mid-forties twenty-six-episode radio series entitled *The Avenger*, sometimes mentioned as a weak rip-off of *The Shadow* (and written by the creator of *The Shadow*, Walter Gibson AKA Maxwell Grant).

James Monks appeared with Rosalind Russell in the hit Broadway show *Auntie Mame* in the late 1950s.

Monks started early in television—appearing in an episode of the ABC television series called *Hour Glass* (1946-1947), and he had the lead in one episode ("You Have Been Warned") in the briefly-aired 1950 mystery/suspense TV anthology series, *Stage 13*, telecast live from New York—but he only worked occasionally in television over the years. The stage and radio were his favorite places to work. In 1950 just prior to the *Mr. Moto* series, James worked in several episodes of NBC radio's highly-respected science-fiction series, *Dimension X*. Following the *Mr. I. A. Moto* radio series in 1951, Monks played Ted White on *The Guiding Light* soap series for a while in the fifties.

In the mid-sixties, when ABC tried to resurrect radio drama with the *Theatre Five* series, a five-a-week, thirty-minute series named for its 5:00 p.m. time slot, Monks joined many other radio veterans (Mary Jane Higby, George Petrie, Jackson Beck, William Redfield, Vicki Vola, and others) for repeated appearances on the series. Although he never became a household name, James Monks made his mark, particularly in radio. He died of cancer on October 2, 1994, in the place of his birth, New York City.

Mr. I. A. Moto on Radio

It seems astounding today that so soon after World War II there would be a *Mr. I. A. Moto* radio series about a Japanese-American secret agent whose task was to root out communist agents who were plotting the downfall of our American way of life. Only a few years previously Japanese-Americans were considered a potential danger by the United States, and many had been detained in federal camps until the war was concluded. Regardless, six years later in 1951, *Mr. Moto, Mr. I. A. Moto* was on the side of the Americans and doing his job diligently. The standard format for the *Mr. I. A. Moto* radio series—with frequent variations, of course—was as follows:

Mr. Moto: "This is Mr. Moto, Mr. I. A. Moto."

Orchestral Music Intro.

Announcer: "NBC presents the world's greatest international secret agent, Mr. I. A. Moto, the popular Japanese character created by Pulitzer Prize-winner John. P. Marquand. With the straightforwardness of his American heritage and with the subtlety of his Oriental ancestors, Mr. Moto is fighting the war against communism ruthlessly and bravely. His only weapons are his brains, his courage, and his fabulous knowledge of the world from Nome to Cape Horn, from Cape Town to Murmansk. Tonight's story: (Title of episode) starring Mr. Moto, Mr. I. A. Moto." (Sample alternate opening by announcer: "Once again NBC brings you Pulitzer Prize-winner John P. Marquand's fabulous and mysterious Mr. Moto, international agent extraordinary—the inscrutable, crafty, and courageous little Oriental whose exploits have endeared him to millions of Americans—in another adventure in the world of mystery and international intrigue.")

Orchestral Music Bridge.

Mr. Moto: (His first-person narrative leads the listeners into and through the episode.)

Announcer: (At end of episode) "You have just heard the world's greatest international secret agent, Mr. Moto, Mr. I. A. Moto in (title of episode)." (Then credits for program) "And here with a preview of next week's episode is Mr. I. A. Moto."

Mr. Moto: (He starts with a Japanese aphorism which links to a brief description of the next episode. On most episodes Mr. Moto concludes with an epilogue unrelated to the episode, generally restfully pastoral in nature. Several of the actual epilogues are included in the following commentary on the individual episodes.)

Orchestral Music ends the episode.

There are a number of books and websites that can provide the reader with an episode guide to the *Mr. I. A. Moto* radio series. Most of the episode guides agree on the number of extant Mr. Moto episodes, but frequently disagree on how many episodes were produced in the summer and fall of 1951. It appears to this writer that the episode guide provided by the website The Digital Deli Too (Preserving the Golden Age of Radio for a Digital Future) is the most carefully researched and documented, and I have thus used it as my primary source for the *Mr. I. A. Moto* episodes.

Episode 1: "A Force Called X07" (5-20-1951)

Producer: Carol Irwin, Writer/director: Harry W. Junkin.

CAST: James Monks, Peter Cappell, John Larkin, Gavin Gordon, Scott Tennyson.

Announcer: Fred Collins.

PLOT/COMMENT: As Professor Howard Carlton, head of the Manhattan Atomic Research Foundation, tells Mr. Moto, "Project X07 makes the atomic bomb as obsolete as a sailing ship." The atomic-powered weapon, small and portable, is a death ray that evaporates the water from your body so that "you shrivel, you dry up; you become a shriveled, hard, little calcium doll about three feet long." When the professor is assassinated, Moto begins an investigation to stop the weapon from falling into communist hands.

The well-written and fast-paced episode gets the series off on a high level of excitement even if the denouement is a bit of a letdown: the sinister death ray X07, it turns out, can be deactivated by simply shutting off the electrical power to the building where it is being implemented—too, too easy for Mr. Moto, Mr. I. A. Moto.

Episode 2: "A Flight from Istanbul" (5-27-1951)

This is a lost episode.

Episode 3: "Smoke Screen" (6-3-1951)

Producer: Carol Irwin, Writer/director: Harry W. Junkin.

CAST: James Monks, Ross Martin, Bob Haig, Bernard Grant, Edwin Bruce.

Announcer: Fred Collins.

PLOT/COMMENT: The overall subject of this episode is racial prejudice and the crime of peddling drugs to minors. Specifically, the story deals with a communist plot to hook thirteen- and fourteen-year-old kids on drugs. In the end we find out that the kid Moto saves from addiction is the son of the villain, Arrington, who has no trouble peddling drugs to kids, but is very sensitive regarding racial prejudice. Arrington reveals that he is a Eurasian, meaning of mixed blood, and he has experienced prejudice all his life. When one of his henchmen refers to Moto as a "Chink," Arrington strikes him and says, "You know how I react to that kind of word. It's bigoted and disgusting. He's not Chinese; he's actually an American of Japanese descent."

Arrington goes on to reveal, "Yes, I'm surprised you didn't guess. I really look very white, don't I? Gifted, educated, but I committed an unpardonable sin: my mother was a Singaporean peasant."

This is another well-written and executed episode that is remarkably graphic in its depiction of drug use by the teenagers. The head villain, Arrington, is played by Ross Martin who would become famous years later for his role of Artemus Gordon on TV's *The Wild Wild West* in the late 1960s. Martin was featured in several of the *Mr. I. A. Moto* radio episodes.

Mr. Moto's epilogue: "May sleep fall upon your eyes as softly as poppy petals on a placid pool. May your soul be blessed with repose, your dreams with enchantment."

Episode 4: "Blackmail" (6-10-1951)

Producer: Carol Irwin, Writer/director: Harry W. Junkin.

CAST: James Monks, Bill Lipton, Grace Cuddy, Ralph Bell.

PLOT/COMMENT: Moto is called upon by an elderly lady friend in New York, Ilene Deklet, to find out why her youngest son Paul has stolen a valuable necklace from her library wall safe. Moto soon discovers that Paul stole the necklace as a blackmail payoff to a former nightclub owner named Raidek. It seems that Raidek has a threatening letter that Paul sent to his girlfriend Mary Louton when he discovered that she had been cheating on him with Raidek and other men. Subsequently, Mary was found murdered in her apartment. In his efforts to help Paul Mr. Moto uncovers the real murderer of Mary.

In this episode Mr. Moto functions as a detective rather than as a government agent. The story is plotted as a mystery with several possible suspects for Moto to interrogate until he comes to his surprise conclusion—as with most mysteries, the least likely person turns out to be the murderer. The episode has the usual twists and turns associated with a mystery, but the outcome seems a bit unlikely.

Episode 5: "The Dead Land" (6-17-1951)

This is a lost episode.

Episode 6: "The Braziloff Paper" (AKA "The Karilov Paper") (6-24-1951)

Producer: Carol Irwin, Writer/director: Harry W. Junkin.

CAST: James Monks, John Larkin, Ross Martin.

PLOT/COMMENT: Mr. Moto becomes a grave robber at the Yokohama cemetery where a Commander Driscoll is buried. It seems the brave commander went to his grave carrying the Kuriloff Papers in the heel of his right shoe—papers sought by the Communist Chinese and Russian governments. The papers could affect the entire balance of power in the Pacific. If the enemy gets the information that is on the papers, it would be possible for an enemy battleship or submarine to cross the Pacific, bombard our West Coast, and return without refueling.

This is another fast-paced and atmospheric episode in the series, quickly moving from one foreign location to another as the action unfolds. Ross Martin is again a major player in this episode. The episode is sometimes identified as being entitled "The Karilov Paper" for the West Coast broadcast and "The Braziloff Paper" for the East Coast. It appears more likely that "The Karilov Paper" was a recorded rehearsal (which still exists) and for some reason the title was changed prior to the actual broadcast to "The Braziloff Paper." The two programs are exactly the same except for the name change. (See David Goldin, RadioGOLDINdex for more.)

Mr. Moto's epilogue: "And now may I wish you a goodnight blessed with sleep, charmed with contentment."

Episode 7: "The Victim" AKA "The Gleason Case" (7-1-1951)

No credits available.

PLOT/COMMENT: Mr. Moto is asked to rescue an American industrialist who has been kidnapped and taken to the Soviet zone of Germany by the communists. While there he is to be brainwashed into espousing the glories of communism as compared to the "oppression" of workers in America. In addition, he is to claim that evil American imperialists are preparing for an atomic attack on Europe. Moto has his work cut out for him.

This excellent episode in design and development very closely resembles plots that were common on such other dramatic radio series of the day as *Dangerous Assignment* with Brian Donlevy, which had started just the year before on NBC, and the long-running *The Man Called X* with Herbert Marshall, which started on CBS in 1944 but was also running on NBC in 1950.

Episode 8: "Project 77" (7-08-1951)

Producer: Carol Irwin, Writer/director: Harry W. Junkin.

CAST: James Monks, Bill Smith, Connie Lemke, Bill Lipton, Scott Tennyson, Ian Martin.

Announcer: Fred Collins.

PLOT/COMMENT: Enemy agents in Japan have captured Commander Freer who has knowledge of the secret Project 77 that is in development. Project 77 is an underwater missile that can travel in excess of 200 miles per hour. Moto is told by the officer who is giving him background on the project, "It isn't a torpedo; it's an underwater bullet. Small, jet propelled with an atomic warhead, it will end submarine warfare. No submersible in the world can elude a guided missile traveling at that speed." Moto discovers that the enemy agent is the Reverend James Teasdale, a phony protestant minister serving Japanese natives, but who, undercover, ruthlessly tortures Commander Freer (with a sunlamp that burns his flesh) to get the secrets of Project 77. Moto, with the help of the minister's Japanese wife, thwarts the efforts to get the secret plans.

The gruesome torture depicted in the episode is surprisingly vivid for radio episodes of this era. It is also surprising to have the villain be a protestant minister, albeit a phony one, who is really instructing the natives in the ways of communism.

Episode 9: "Sabotage" (7-15-1951)

Producer: Carol Irwin, Writer/director: Harry W. Junkin.

CAST: James Monks, Hadley Rainey, Ross Martin, Rita Lind, Bernard Grant, Lyle Sudrow.

Announcer: Fred Collins.

PLOT/COMMENT: Mr. Moto tells us at the beginning, "Sabotage is to be expected wherever there are top secrets or experiments." In forty-eight hours one of the greatest inventions of modern warfare, identified as the Zirconium Project, is to be tested in the Manhattan Research Foundation. Two midget nitrogen bombs, not much bigger than hand grenades but with two hundred times the power, have been stolen, and Moto suspects they will be used to sabotage the testing of the Zirconium Project. We soon learn that enemy agents plan to place the midget nitrogen bombs in the subway system below the Research Foundation building where the test is to take place. With his usual cleverness and tenacity Mr. Moto saves the project from destruction.

There seems to be a nod to the House UnAmerican Activities Committee that was conducting investigations in the early 1950s to root out communists or those suspected of being communists. In the plot the head of the Manhattan Research Foundation, referring to Mr. Moto's earlier suspicion of a British agent working with them, says to Moto, "I hate witch hunts." To which Moto replies, "Yes, I hate them, too, Dr. Andrews. I hate to see an innocent person unjustly accused. On the other hand, the price of freedom is eternal vigilance."

Mr. Moto's epilogue: "May you sleep in grace and wisdom and arise to greet the dawn renewed and strengthened, confident in the words of the poet that the spirit of the worm beneath the sod, in love and worship, blends itself with God."

Episode 10: "Escape" (7-22-1951)

Producer: Carol Irwin, Director: Harry W. Junkin, Writer: Jim Haines.

CAST: James Monks, Joyce Gordon, Adelaide Klein, Joe Helgeson, Ralph Camargo, Merrill E. Jolles, Brad Barker.

PLOT/COMMENT: Vinchenzo DePietro, the leader of the Italian Christian Democrat Party and all his life a vehement anti-communist, is assassinated while making a speech on the streets of Rome. A well-known American syndicated sportswriter is kidnapped during the turmoil of the assassination and later charged by the Italian pro-communist press of the crime. If the pro-communists who are holding the American can force a confession, Mr. Moto believes that it will allow "the same old propaganda" that attempts to prove that "capitalist America sends gangsters abroad to murder and kill." Thus, fearing an international incident designed to embarrass America, Mr. Moto is sent to Rome to investigate and get to the truth of the situation.

The story seems incomplete when the climactic music signals the end of the episode without the bad guys being captured and brought to justice. From a little way past the midpoint of the episode, Mr. Moto and the accused American are trapped in the catacombs of Rome by the bad guys. From that point to the end, the plot is only concerned with how they escape from the catacombs (with the assistance of an also-trapped cat) rather than bringing the villains to justice. As they escape, Moto indicates that now he can concern himself with bringing the bad guys to justice. The listener cannot help but feel that the main point of the story is left unresolved—unless the story was continued in the next episode which, unfortunately, is among the missing episodes.

Mr. Moto's epilogue: "May the tender arms of sleep enfold you as gently as the moonlight creeps from flower to sleeping flower. And may the new dawn, blessed with God's good light, renew and prove your faith that right and right alone is might."

Episode 11: "The Wheel of Life" (7-29-1951)

This is a lost episode.

Episode 12: "Waltzing Matilda" (8-5-1951)

This is a lost episode.

Episode 13: "The Beauty and the Avenger" (8-12-1051)

This is a lost episode.

Episode 14: "The Shen Tsung Fan" (8-19-1951)

This is a lost episode.

Episode 15: "The Three Numbers" (8-26-1951)

This is a lost episode.

Episode 16: "The Unhappy Firebug" (9-2-1951)

This is a lost episode.

Episode 17: "The Blue Cigarettes" (9-9-1951)

This is a lost episode.

Episode 18: "The Kants of Kailua Neohe" (6-16-1951)

This is a lost episode. (See The Digital Deli Too for more on this title.)

Episode 19: "The Schraum Method" (9-23-1951)

Producer: Doris Quinlan for Carol Irwin, Director: Arthur Hanna, Written by Robert Tallman.

CAST: James Monks, Alice Frost, John Larkin, Eileen Eckart, Walter Greaza.

Announcer: Fred Collins.

PLOT/COMMENT: While in Honolulu, Mr. Moto receives a call from his chief in Washington, Captain Barrisford, asking him to catch the next clipper to Hong Kong where he is to check on a man named Max Mason. Mason, the senior partner in a firm called The Inter-Ocean Company which imports tea and spices, is concerned that his Hong Kong representative, Donald Rossmoor, may be secretly running a major smuggling operation through Inter-Ocean. Mason has gone to Hong Kong to confront Rossmoor with his belief. Mrs. Mason, under psychiatric care by a Dr. Schraum, has an overriding fear that her husband will kill Rossmoor when he finds him. It is into this messy situation that Mr. Moto is hurled. Before the situation is resolved, Moto encounters two murders, too much evidence, and a "man who never was."

The resolutely complicated plot with its many twists and turns—by the midpoint you need a scorecard with all the character names and relationships—*does* have a clever denouement—if you have kept the characters and their interactions straight in your head.

Mr. Moto's epilogue: "May sleep fall upon your lidded eyes as lightly as the falling of an autumn leaf, and may your dreams be as a fragrance of sandalwood in the clear air of an October morning."

Episode 20: "The Crooked Log" (9-30-1951)

No credits available.

PLOT/COMMENT: Mrs. Lila Clausen contacts Mr. Moto about a painting she has seen in the window of a New York art gallery that she feels reveals clues to the fact that her husband, who was thought to have died in an explosion on the *SS Emily Landis*, may still be alive. The title of the painting is "The Crooked Log." Mrs. Clausen also informs Moto that Clifford Landis, the owner of the line under which the *SS Emily Landis* was listed, received a million dollars in insurance money upon the supposed death of Landis and that the surviving first officer of the ship has been promoted to vice president of the company. Garner, the first officer, testified at the inquest that Mrs. Clausen's husband, the captain, was drunk and that his negligence caused the explosion. She suspects that the whole thing was a plot for the insurance money. During Mr. Moto's investigation two murders occur and there is the discovery of a very different type of log.

Mr. Moto again seems to function in this episode as more of a private detective than a government secret agent. As the series winds to a close (only two episodes remain), there seems to be a growing lack of focus as to the main character's "mission" and the types of situations he is asked to resolve. As stated earlier, at the end of each program Mr. Moto gives a preview of the next episode. The preview he describes for the next week is entitled "The Stolen Convertible." No such episode exists in the radio case files of Mr. Moto, so we have another "lost" or never-produced episode in the series. It would appear from the rushed ending of this episode ("The Crooked Log") that the credits were eliminated and Moto's benediction was rushed to meet the time constraints.

Mr. Moto's epilogue: "May the serenity of an October evening bring sleep to your weighted eyes and bear you away upon a fragrance of night-blooming jasmine in the tranquility of a summer garden, reflected in the still pool of untroubled dreams."

Episode 21: "The Case of the Stolen Convertible" (9-30-1951)

This is a lost episode.

Episode 22: "The Strange Elopement of Professor Sloan" (10-13-1951)

Producer: Doris Quinlan for Carol Irwin, Director: Arthur Hanna, Writer: Robert Tallman.

CAST: James Monks, Julie Stevens, Florida Freebus, Mason Adams, Bill Smith, Frank Silvera, Gene Gillespie.

Announcer: Ray Barrett.

PLOT/COMMENT: Moto is informed that a prominent atomic scientist, Professor Thaddeus Sloan, has disappeared from the H Bomb Project in Ellenton, South Carolina, and that his young female assistant, Helen Martin, has vanished with him—possibly in a romantic tryst. When Moto visits the site of the project to investigate, he discovers that the Professor's wife is an invalid in the care of a Nurse Goff and that a local jeweler, Hal Lloyd, is engaged to Helen and has provided cheap industrial grade diamonds to the professor to accommodate his private hobby. Through his investigation Moto uncovers evidence to prove that the cheap, yellow, industrial grade diamonds are being converted to valuable blue diamonds via atomic radiation and made available to international smugglers. In addition, the culprits are planning to transport Professor Sloan to an iron curtain country.

The well-developed plot provided Mr. Moto with another exciting adventure. Included in the cast was Mason Adams whose distinctive voice had been heard for many years on radio's *Pepper Young's Family*, in which he played Pepper Young from 1945 through the series end in 1959. Later in television Adams appeared in many roles, most notably as the managing editor of the *Los Angeles Tribune* on *Lou Grant* starring Edward Asner. Also for many, many years on radio and television, Mason Adams' voice told us "with a name like Smucker's, it has to be good!"

Episode 23: "The Case of the Dry Martini" (10-20-1951)

No credits available.

PLOT/COMMENT: This final episode in the Mr. Moto radio series is a strange one, indeed. Played coyly and with comic tongue-in-cheek by all of the characters except Mr. Moto, the plot unfurls in San Francisco where Moto has been sent to investigate an anonymous letter claiming that the Monsoon Trading Company is smuggling drugs into the country. Jerome Pearson, the head of the company, greets Moto and claims to have no knowledge of such goings-on while he fixes himself two pitchers of dry martinis. The next day Pearson is shot to death in Moto's presence by a drive-by shooter. We soon learn that Pearson's scatterbrained, flighty wife is having an affair with their chauffeur Ernie and that the car involved in the shooting is owned by Mrs. Pearson. When Moto goes to inspect the car in the garage, he discovers Ernie's dead body between the seats, shot. Furthermore, Moto discovers that the company vice president and treasurer, Mr. Harper, has been juggling the books and that the business is bankrupt *and* that the company lawyer, Mary Donohue, prior to Pearson's murder, fleeced him out of company stock and is now the majority stockholder of the worthless company. And, finally, there is a thousand-dollar check signed by Pearson to a strung-out junkie, "Pusher" Martin, who confesses to both murders.

Moto discovers that Pearson was dying from a brain tumor and wanted to get even with the unfaithful, unscrupulous people around him and hired the hapless Martin to kill him. Pearson's supposed "drunkenness" was really caused by the tumor and the dry martinis were only colored water. Oh, yes. The thousand-dollar check to "Pusher" Martin bounced.

It's a cleverly written final episode in a short-lived series that deserved better. But it was 1951 and radio, by and large, was now gasping for air as television began to mesmerize the public.

The Graphic Novel
Case File

Welcome Back, Mr. Moto by Rafael Nieves and Tim Hamilton

Publisher: Moonstone Books in 2008.

PLOT/COMMENT: (Plot as summarized by Moonstone) Ken Ta Kashi, an angry young man of Japanese descent, is released from an Idaho detainment camp at the end of World War II. Estranged from his mother and sister, enraged at the mysterious death of his beloved father, Ken is easily trapped in a web of deceit, double-cross, and death by sinister forces in the U. S. Government.

Originally published in 2004 as a three-part comic book series, the graphic novel version (containing all three parts) was then published in 2008 as a softcover book by Moonstone Books. As in the Marquand novels, the Mr. Moto character only enters the scene occasionally, moving in and out of Ken Ta Kashi's story. But that's the only similarity to the Marquand stories. This writer found *Welcome Back, Mr. Moto* dark, grim, hard to follow, and lacking any of the mood, atmosphere, or charm of the original Marquand novels, the films, or the radio series.

Boris Karloff as Mr. Wong.

The Case Files
of Mr. Wong

Hugh Wiley and the Short Stories

THE CREATION OF THE MR. WONG character by Hugh Wiley was very likely a copycat exercise building on the already existing popularity of the Earl Derr Biggers' Charlie Chan stories and films that had first appeared in the late 1920s. Many assume that next on the scene were the John P. Marquand Mr. Moto stories and films. In fact, the Hugh Wiley Mr. Wong creation came in 1934, a year *before* the Mr. Moto stories, and was very likely an attempt to appeal to the Charlie Chan murder mystery readers after the death of Earl Derr Biggers in 1933. The Wong films, however, *did* lag behind the Moto films by over a year and had less stellar production values than either the early Chan or Moto films. Nevertheless, Mr. Wong, in the eyes of many, seems to be an Oriental sleuth afterthought, and the character, of course, never reached the popularity of the other two sleuths.

Mr. Wong author Hugh Wiley (1884-1968) apparently couldn't make up his mind for a long time whether he wanted to be an engineer or a writer. As it turned out, engineering came early and late in his career. While a young man he became an engineer, and during World War I he served in France as the captain of B Company, 18th Engineering. In his later years he returned to engineering and began to write on the subject. But following his service in World War I and running through the 1940s, Wiley concentrated mainly on his writing career, starting with an adventure story, "Four Leaved Wildcat," which was published in the *Saturday Evening Post* in March of 1919. Other stories for the *Post* followed, mostly in a similar vein. In 1920 he published his first book, *The Wildcat*, which was inspired by his war experiences and concerned the escapades of an African-American fighting in Europe during the war—a depiction that would be very politically incorrect in today's world. Several of Wiley's other early works also dealt with blacks and the war in a manner that Bruce Eder in his *All Movie Guide* commentary referred to as "depicting black life in a comic and exaggerated manner, somewhat akin to minstrel show entertainment though perhaps a bit more subtle."

In 1934 Wiley created the character for which he is best-remembered today, the Chinese sleuth, Mr. James Lee Wong. Mr. Wong first appeared in *Collier's* magazine in March of 1934 in a short story entitled "Medium Well Done." There would be eleven more short stories in the *Mr. Wong* series, all of them published in *Collier's* over a four-year period ending in June 1938. The first Mr. Wong film, *Mr. Wong, Detective*, would not be released until November of 1938 after all twelve of the short stories had been published. Wiley wrote no *Mr. Wong* novels; however, the twelve short stories were collected into book form and were published by Popular Library in 1951 under the title *Murder by the Dozen*. [Author's note: Hugh Wiley apparently had an aversion to cameras, since even a diligent search revealed no photographic depiction of the author.]

The James Lee Wong character in the short stories is quite different from the five Boris Karloff films produced by Monogram Pictures from 1938 through 1940, with a sixth starring Keye Luke as a younger version of the Chinese detective. The Wong of the short stories is a man of action, more comparable to Mr. Moto than to Charlie Chan. He is an agent of the Department of Justice and sometimes utilizes fisticuffs to dispatch the villains or, more frequently, resolves a case by dispatching the bad guys with his ever-ready pistol. In the stories Wong also has a team of government agents working with him and can call upon them when his resolution of the case requires some assistance.

Mr. Wong is described by Wiley as tall and slim and of an indeterminate middle age, well-educated at Yale (in the films it is Oxford, probably due to Karloff's British accent) and prone to use scientific deduction whenever possible in solving his cases, as Karloff did frequently in the films. Mr. Wong is more "Americanized" than either Chan or Moto. He speaks perfect English—unlike Chan and Moto—but he frequently speaks to Chinese characters in the stories in their native language. He lives in San Francisco but not in Chinatown, although many of the cases take place in the seedier areas of Chinatown—gambling parlors and opium dens, for example.

Part of the pleasure of the Wong short stories is their brevity. Any of the twelve stories with their fast-moving action can be read in a matter of minutes. As you start to read a Wong story, there is the sense that you are jumping into a plot that has originated prior to your arrival and that there is a certain amount of "catching up" that you need to do. That catching up is craftily woven into the plot by Wiley so that presently the reader feels up-to-speed with the story. While Mr. Wong frequently uses scientific deduction to determine the villain, the stories usually end in extreme violence.

Although Hugh Wiley lived until 1968, dying that year of influenza, he never returned to his most popular literary creation, Mr. Wong, after he had completed the twelfth short story in 1938.

The Mr. Wong Short Stories

"Medium Well Done" Published by *Collier's,* March 10, 1934.

When wealthy California oil man Marshall King dies in a tragic airplane crash, an exotic Russian medium named Olga Rousseau promises his daughter Helen that she can resurrect her father from the "spirit plane" to the "earth plane" where they can be together again. The spirit voice of her father tells her that this cannot truly take place until his earthly transgressions are removed—in this case a debt owed to the tune of three hundred thousand dollars. The gullible daughter's aged cook Wong Sung, sensing a con artist at work, goes to government agent James Lee Wong and says, "Unless I am mistaken, she has been drugged with the nectar of spurious hope. Her will is broken, her reason seems to sleep. Even as an opium eater returns forever to the origin of his own hell, so has my mistress surrendered to a charlatan who gives her momentary release from the realities of her sorrow." Mr. Wong agrees to intervene and lays a trap for the mysterious medium and her cohorts.

"The Thirty Thousand Dollar Bomb" Published by *Collier's,* July 28, 1034.

Young, impulsive Senator Colton of the Committee on Foreign Relations has come to San Francisco and paid thirty thousand dollars to get his hands on an explosive secret report that could alter America's relations with several foreign countries. Colton's confidential secretary Sylvia Deane is not so sure the senator's plan to have newspaper publisher Desmond Cross release the story is a wise decision. She fears the document could be a phony that would damage international relations and hurt the senator's career. But Colton is adamant. "When Desmond Cross explodes them in his newspapers there will be enemy scalps hanging in the treetops from here to New York," he tells Sylvia.

While the senator is off to meet Cross, Sylvia calls Bradford Garnett at the State Department in Washington and asks if there is an agent in San Francisco who might help her and the senator. The name given to her is that of James Lee Wong. "Tell him Gettysburg is calling," Garnett tells her. Wong's initial reading of the document brings the comment, "If it is authentic it means that Germany and Russia are better friends than Washington thinks." Wong's scientific background comes into play as he examines and tests the paper with chemicals to determine the paper's origin and age. At the same time he sends his government operatives in search of known forgers operating in the San Francisco area. Soon Wong is ready to meet with the senator and report his findings that could start or avoid a world war.

"Ten Bells" Published by *Collier's*, August 4, 1934.

Tommy Hale is the property man at Galaxy Productions in Los Angeles where his girlfriend Sally Chapman is working in a film entitled *Death for Love* under the direction of Vernon Zenger and starring Pierre Mercer. Mercer is the problem. It seems that he has been paying too much attention to Sally which makes Tommy jealous and quarrelsome. When filming a pistol duel scene between Mercer and another actor, Walter Lodge, director Zenger in frustration asks Mercer to run the scene again with Zenger taking over the role of Lodge to demonstrate how the actor should play the scene. Property man Tommy Hale reloads the long-barreled, single-shot .38 pistols with blanks for the scene, and it commences. Director Zenger and Mercer, back to back, take five steps forward, turn, pause, and fire. Pierre Mercer falls to the ground dead—*really* dead because somehow a real bullet was loaded into Zenger's pistol. With the mysterious and tragic death of Mercer, Tommy Hale, the man who loaded the pistols and was known to be jealous of Mercer's attention to Sally Chapman, is being held by the police on a possible murder charge, and Galaxy Productions, a shoestring Hollywood studio, has cancelled production on *Death for Love* and filed with the Hazard Guaranty Corporation to collect on the two-hundred-thousand-dollar insurance policy they have on the film.

Ross Mason, the vice president of the Hazard Guaranty Corporation, asks his old Yale schoolmate James Lee Wong to investigate the curious events that have occurred at Galaxy Productions prior to paying the insurance claim. Wong's investigation leads him to conclude that the death of Pierre Mercer was a cleverly staged murder—but how to prove it is Mr. Wong's puzzlement.

"Long Chance" Published by *Collier's*, December 15, 1934.

Sam Wing, chief of aviation for the Nanking Government, calls upon his fellow Yale graduate Mr. James Lee Wong regarding the disappearance of Edgar Parmill. Wing and Parmill have come to San Francisco to meet with a representative of Meteor, an aviation company from which the duo is to purchase four fighter planes at twenty-five thousand dollars per plane. Parmill was carrying a hundred thousand in cash when he disappeared from their hotel. Sam Wing solicits Mr. Wong's assistance in finding the missing man and the money. Wong's investigation soon leads to a wealthy American named Egan Rylett, his mysterious Japanese friend Amano Kimura, a potent cocktail drink of bourbon and curacao, and, finally, to curare, a South American poison causing complete paralysis without affecting consciousness. Mr. Wong concludes the case in a shootout during which he employs a steel vest to repel his opponent's gunfire.

"A Ray of Light" Published by *Collier's*, May 25, 1935.

James Lee Wong gets a call from an old Yale classmate, Joseph Temple, asking if he might stop by Wong's apartment with the elderly Meade Capron to discuss a matter of some importance. Temple gets right to the point: "I've got a very serious charge to lay against young Warren Bayne." Bayne, Wong learns from Temple, is a ne'er-do-well playboy and is engaged to a wild social butterfly named Louise Harwood. Together they have been known to attend orgy-like drinking parties, attend gambling dens, and even frequent opium dens. But Temple's main concern is that young Bayne has purchased a sixteen-thousand-dollar diamond ring from the Temple and Peck Jewelry Company, with only two thousand down on the purchase. Peck, Temple's partner, gave Bayne a two-year credit on the balance. "That partner of mine is a fool," Temple asserts. Meade Capron, knowledgeable regarding precious jewels, goes on with their story, saying that he has recently seen Miss Harwood with the ring, and noticed that the original square diamond has been replaced with a paste one—glass. Temple speculates that Bayne has pawned the real diamond to get cash money and would like Wong to investigate—unofficially, of course. James Lee Wong's reluctant inquiry into the matter eventually brings Louise Harwood to his laboratory and a lesson in precious jewels and mere glass—and "their varying abilities to bend a ray of light."

"Jaybird's Chance" Published by *Collier's*, July 20, 1935.

The Payboy Mine has been robbed of two gold bricks and Wong Low, the Chinese cook at the mine, is being held for the crime. Melvin Armstrong, president of the Gold Rock Mining Corporation, tells James Lee Wong, "I wouldn't bother you with this case, Mr. Lee, except for the fact that the man who stole the gold is a Chinese. . . . The sheriff's men can't make him talk. We've got the goods on him, all right, but he won't open up." The "goods" are the Chinaman's fingerprints on the safe in the mine office and a recent deposit of ten thousand dollars in his bank. Mr. Wong agrees to investigate the case against Wong Low by going to the mine located about fifteen miles from Colburn, California.

Wong meets Sam Gorman, the superintendent of the mine, and several of the men who work with him: Walter Darrell, the draftsman; Tommy Miller, the time keeper and commissary boss; and the deputy game warden in the district, Jim Saunders. All of them enjoy a few rounds of poker at the end of the day, and James Lee receives an invitation to join them that evening. The poker session and the activity of a congress of Jaybirds in some mountain laurel not too far from the mining camp provide Mr. Wong with the clues he needs to identify and apprehend the real gold robber.

"Scorned Woman" Published by *Collier's*, September 14, 1935.

Chinese actor Gin Chow is suspected of trafficking in opium by government narcotics agents. When Chow's body turns up shot on a San Francisco street, the murder is at once linked to a recent shipment of opium that was flown up from Mexico. A representative of Chinatown elders, Sung Kong, calls on Mr. Wong regarding the murder and the missing opium. It seems that the elders are aware that narcotic's dealer Fang Yut arranged for the purchase of the opium, collected two hundred thousand in payment, gave the money to Gin Chow, and was escorting him to the elders when, according to Fang Yut, a man with a drawn revolver confronted them, shot Gin Chow, and fled with the money. Sung Kong informs Wong that now Fang Yut is reportedly very ill and may die—which, in fact, he reportedly does (by an overdose of opium) by the time Wong calls at the man's abode.

But all does not seem right to Mr. Wong when he observes the supposedly grieving widow, Lily Fang, tearless and eating candied coconut during the funeral procession. Soon Wong's doubts about the death of Fang Yut are confirmed when he visits his tomb and finds the coffin empty. Then there's the matter of Rose Irwin, American photographer and artist *and* undercover narcotics agent, who has disappeared. And how is Wong to deal with his knowledge of the Chinese elders' involvement in the narcotic's deal? Before Wong can wrap up his investigation, his sleuthing leads him to a gambling ring that is supplementing its income with narcotics and white slavery.

"Three Words" Published by *Collier's*, November 2, 1935.

When Alan Markham and his Chinese assistant Howard Lin returned to the United States from their expedition in Peiping, Markham brought to Berkford University a treasure of ancient manuscripts and trophies that he had recovered from the sands of the Takia Makan. Lin's job following their return is to help translate the manuscripts. A month after Markham's return, he is discovered dead in his residence. The early morning milkman discovers Markham's bloody hand caught in the window screen of his bathroom, the rest of his body awkwardly slumped partway to the floor. The coroner's report states that he died of hydrocyanic acid poisoning, and the investigation reveals that the most likely scenario regarding his death is that the junior pharmacist at Ehrmann's Pharmacy erred in Markham's prescription for hydrochloric acid to be used for dyspepsia and gave him hydrocyanic acid instead. The pharmacist, Mr. Frank Ramsay, is being held on a technical charge of manslaughter. Case closed—but maybe not.

Three days later a Japanese college student named Ota Haruki visits Mr. Ainsworth in the comptroller's office of the college and says he overheard a conversation between Markham and Howard Lin on the evening before Markham's death that may indicate murder. When Haruki leaves his office, Mr. Ainsworth puts a call through to San Francisco to Mr. James Lee Wong. "This Markham case, Mr. Lee," Mr. Ainsworth begins. "I would like to talk to you about it." Soon Mr. Wong begins his own investigation into the case.

"No Witnesses" Published by *Collier's*, February 15, 1936.

While on vacation at Sky Ridge in the High Sierra area of northern California, James Lee Wong meets Mr. Archer Long of Kansas City who is also on vacation. In casual conversation Wong learns that Long is thinking he might like to relocate to this area of California if he can find a suitable property. Several of the local inhabitants tell him of the Levi Minch property and suggest that if he put a couple of thousand dollars on the table in front of him, Minch would probably sell. Long asks Gerald Harper, the friendly college student who has been his and James Lee's waiter for their meals at Sky Ridge, to take him into town so that he can get two thousand dollars in twenty-dollar bills. Archer Long then goes to visit Levi Minch to propose the deal—and disappears. Soon the sheriff is notified and calls on Levi Minch who says that Long visited him, but that he turned the deal down and has not seen Long since; however, Long's coat and tobacco pouch are found in Minch's possession. A search is undertaken and Long's body is found in a prospect hole about a half mile from Minch's house, but no money is found. Everyone seems to think that it is an open and shut murder case with Minch the murderer—everyone, that is, except Mr. James Lee Wong.

"Seven of Spades" Published by *Collier's*, September 5, 1936.

Over Arizona, eighty miles east of the California line, the pilot of the Silver Arrow comes back to the cabin of the plane with a message for James Lee Wong from the Bureau of Investigation in Washington: BANCROFT ON DUTCH FLINT CASE MURDERED STOP YOUR ORDERS OMAHA CANCELLED STOP CALL ME LONG DISTANCE FROM STANTON. Wong's later call to his chief informs him that Bancroft, working on the Dutch Flint case, was operating undercover at Redstone as a ranger in the park service and lived with another ranger named Al Blake. Sheriff Deane has arrested Blake for the murder of Bancroft and has him in the Stanton jail near Redstone. Thus begins James Lee Wong's investigation into Bancroft's murder and the connection it has to gangster Dutch Flint's kidnapping and murder of several individuals over the last few years. Wong gets a hostile reception in Stanton from everyone he questions: From Sheriff Deane to Deputy Bill Putnam, who arrested Al Blake and runs a pool hall called the Pastime Club, to Ben Carver who owns a saddlery store in Stanton. They all want the "Chink" out of town. It soon becomes apparent to Mr. Wong that Al Blake is being railroaded and that head gangster Dutch Flint is ominously close at hand.

"The Bell from China" Published by *Collier's*, March 26, 1938.

The Gold Tiger Company on Gamblers' Alley in San Francisco handles the common merchandise of Chinatown, but enough good stuff drifts in from China to make the place good hunting for collectors of the best things in Chinese art. (There are those who feel the company handles some items that federal agents might find interesting.) Arnold Fisher, a director of the Pacific Art League, makes it his business to watch for a rare item and then to find a benefactor to purchase it for the art league. Such an item is the bell from China of the Chou Dynasty, purchased by wealthy Boad Hagardt, imported by Fung Man, the proprietor of the Gold Tiger Company, and presented to the art league. It is then discovered that the bell has a long inscription on it that needs translating, a task that Arnold Fisher feels James Lee Wong might enjoy—and he is correct. But Wong's examination of the bell reveals that it is a phony, a fact that the wily government man decides to keep to himself for a while.

Fisher invites Mr. Wong to the annual Art League Ball supported by Boad Hagardt and his beautiful Russian wife Vera. Fisher tells Wong, "You will see pearls in the show, costumes and acts and chorus groups solid with pearls." The pearl costumes, Wong learns, have been imported by Hagardt through the Gold Tiger Company. Wong begins to suspect that the pearl costumes may contain a secret that would interest the federal government.

"The Feast of Kali" Published by *Collier's*, June 25, 1938.

Denman Hale informs his elderly servant Chew Lim of his decision to end his labor problems by converting Hale Island from a thousand-acre tract of sugar beets run by his Hindu laborers to a thousand acres planted in Ladino clover where he will raise lambs. "I'm going to run that mob of rag-head Hindus out of that thousand-acre tract. . . I win on that bet two for one—get rid of the rag-heads, get rid of the beets, and cash in big on the lambs." When word gets out about Hale's plan, one of his foremen is brutally murdered and Hale himself is kidnapped by two turbaned thugs while in Stockton, California, buying sheep. He is then taken to a

Siva temple where a grave is dug for him, a grave that will be slowly filled with grains of rice in the manner of an hourglass while a robed figure of a priest in a throne-like chair will perform a ritual droning chant. In the meantime, Old Chew Lim has phoned James Lee Wong in San Francisco and told him what has happened and begs for his assistance. Wong first investigates the murder of the foreman and finds clues that lead him to the Siva temple where he must confront the turbaned thugs and save Denman Hale from The Feast of Kali.

The Mr. Wong Films

THE MR. WONG of the Boris Karloff films is more akin to Charlie Chan in his reserved demeanor rather than being a "man of action" as depicted in the short stories. In the films he is portrayed as a renowned private detective rather than a G-man. As in the short stories, Karloff speaks perfect American English—albeit with a British accent. The film Wong always wears a black fedora and black suit in public with a white boutonniere in his lapel and a neatly folded white handkerchief in his coat breast pocket. In his home he sometimes wears an oriental-style robe. He almost always carries an umbrella, inside and out, yet I don't remember it ever raining in a Wong film. None of these affectations are mentioned in the Wiley stories.

Where the Wong short stories are fast moving, the films move at a far more leisurely pace. In the films there is an attempt at comic relief in the form of a stereotypically "blustery, dumb cop," Captain Street (Grant Withers) of the San Francisco Homicide Squad. He is joined by brash and lippy cub reporter Bobbie Logan (Marjorie Reynolds) for comic banter in three of the film episodes. The short stories contain no comic relief. The films mostly take place in San Francisco and deal with criminal activity and murder connected to various types of businesses. The short stories are seamier and deal more with the underbelly of society and mostly take place in California, but not necessarily San Francisco. Because of the motion picture production code at the time, the films have far less violence than the frequently blood-soaked, vicious mayhem of the short stories.

Research into the Wong films indicates that there was little incentive for the films other than the box-office popularity of the Charlie Chan and Mr. Moto films and a desire to piggyback on their success. Boris Karloff (1887-1969) was a working actor who had gained a broad following and reputation for several horror films—*Frankenstein* (1931), *The Mask of Fu*

Boris Karloff starred as Mr. Wong in five films for Monogram Pictures.

Manchu (1932), *The Mummy* (1932), *Bride of Frankenstein* (1935)—and who saw the Wong films as a change of pace where he could play the "hero" rather than the "monster" or villain in films. In addition, it was easy and continuous revenue between the bigger-budgeted, better-quality films he could make between and after the Wong series. Right after the first Wong film, for instance, Karloff went back to Universal Pictures to film the hugely popular *Son of Frankenstein* (1939). Between later Wong pictures he made *The Man They Could Not Hang* (1939) at Columbia Pictures and *Tower of London* (1939) at Universal. There is no evidence to indicate that Karloff saw the Mr. Wong series as anything but a pathway to a regular payday and, if the films caught on like the Chan and Moto films, it could be a source of income for many years.

William Nigh (1881-1955) was a contract director at Monogram Pictures and was assigned to the Boris Karloff/Mr. Wong series by head studio producer Scott R. Dunlap. Nigh began his career in films as an actor back in silent pictures starting in 1913. Through the years he added screenwriter, director, and producer to his résumé but almost always for "poverty row" studios and especially Monogram Pictures. By 1925 he had given up acting and devoted most of his energies to directing. Detective films, a few Bowery Boy episodes, and Cisco Kid westerns were his meat and potatoes through his long career. His last film was *Stage Struck* (1948), a crime drama starring Kane Richmond, Conrad Nagel, and Ralph Byrd that he directed for Monogram Pictures. There were no really distinguishing features to Nigh's directing style. He was known chiefly for being a work-a-day director and for getting the picture done on time and on or below budget.

Phil Rosen (1888-1951), the director of the last Mr. Wong film, *Phantom of Chinatown*, had a similar directing career to William Nigh. He started his career in films as a cameraman in silent pictures and eventually became a director during the silent era. With the coming of sound to pictures, Rosen worked for most of the B studios in Hollywood, especially Monogram and PRC Pictures. He directed a number of the Sidney Toler Charlie Chan films at Monogram during the 1940s as well as other crime dramas, westerns, and other genre films for Republic Pictures, Columbia, and RKO over the years. Like William Nigh, Phil Rosen was known for being a "no-fuss" director who got the job done on time and at the lowest possible cost.

The Boris Karloff Films

Mr. Wong, Detective (Monogram Pictures, 1938) 69m.

Producer: Scott R. Dunlap, Director: William Nigh, Screenplay: Houston Branch.

CAST: Boris Karloff, Grant Withers, Maxine Jennings, Evelyn Brent, George Lloyd, Lucien Prival, John St. Polis, William Gould, Hooper Atchley, John Hamilton, Wilbur Mack, Lee Tung Foo, Lynton Brent, Grace Wood, Frank Bruno, Ed Cassidy, Wheaton Chambers, Clancy Cooper, Lester Dorr, Herbert Evans, Dick Reinhart.

Sleuth story done in lukewarm manner, despite Boris Karloff's trouping. First picture suffers from directorial and writing troubles... – Variety

PLOT/COMMENT: Simon Dayton (John Hamilton), the president of the Dayton Chemical Company, comes to James Lee Wong to seek his assistance because he fears someone is out to kill him. Sure enough, the next morning before Mr. Wong is to meet Dayton in his office, the man is murdered, but the circumstances are indeed strange: Dayton was alone in his locked office when the murder occurred—and there are no marks on the body to reveal the cause of death. Mr. Wong and Captain Sam Street (Grant Withers) of the San Francisco Police Department find only one clue: a few small shards of a broken glass vial. Soon it is determined that Dayton died of poisoned gas, but how it was administered remains a mystery.

Suspects in the case include Carl Roemer (John St. Polis), an employee who had developed a poison gas for the chemical company and feared that he was being cheated out of credit and payment for his invention; Dayton's two partners, Theodore Meisel (William Gould) and Christian Wilk (Hooper Atchley), who inherit the company upon Dayton's death; and the sinister Olga Petroff (Evelyn Brent) and Anton Mohl (Lucien Prival), foreign agents who want to get their hands on the poison gas formula for war use by their government. Soon the body count increases with two more similar murders occurring before Mr. Wong can identify the murderer and determine how the poison gas was administered since all the victims were alone at the time of their deaths.

Mr. Wong gets the drop on three suspicious characters: Olga Petroff (Evelyn Brent), Anton Mohl (Lucien Prival), and their henchman Lescardi (Frank Bruno).

This first entry in the Mr. Wong film series is a very slow-moving affair with the murder device being the most interesting aspect of the story. (In fact, it was so interesting and clever that the plot was revised slightly for the later Monogram Charlie Chan episode entitled *Docks of New Orleans* with Roland Winters.) Boris Karloff, utilizing a minimum of makeup for the Wong role, lends a dignity and seriousness to his characterization of the Oriental detective that works well as he goes about his sleuthing. The other regular in the series cast, Grant Withers as Captain Sam Street, unfortunately plays his dumb cop role to a fare-thee-well, becoming obnoxious and out of tune with the rest of the players. Director William Nigh should have recognized the over acting of Withers and brought his sharp-tongued characterization down to the level that the other actors employed. Production values are meager with skimpy sets and some scenes too dimly lighted, which was a common failing with the studio. The viewer quickly realizes that this Monogram series with Mr. Wong will not compare favorably with the bigger-budgeted Chan and Moto series at Twentieth Century-Fox. But that should not come as a surprise for knowing film fans.

Mystery of Mr. Wong (Monogram Pictures, 1938) 70m.

Producer: Scott R. Dunlap, Director: William Nigh, Screenplay: Scott Darling.

CAST: Boris Karloff, Grant Withers, Dorothy Tree, Craig Reynolds, Ivan Lebedeff, Holmes Herbert, Morgan Wallace, Lotus Long, Chester Gan, Hooper Atchley, Bruce Wong, Jack Kennedy, Joe Devlin, Lee Tong Foo, Wilbur Mack, Dick Morehead, I Stanford Jolley.

Fairly engrossing murder mystery in spite of laborious deduction in quest of solution, dreary questioning of suspects and the inescapable attitude of nearly everyone to look like the cat that swallowed the mouse. – Variety

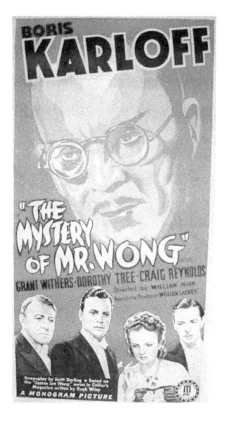

PLOT/COMMENT: The Eye of the Daughter of the Moon, the largest sapphire in the world, has been stolen in China and smuggled into the United States and is now in the hands of wealthy collector of Oriental art and artifacts, Brandon Edwards (Morgan Wallace). Edwards is well-aware of the curse of the sapphire and has received a letter with a death threat, causing him to explain the situation with James Lee Wong at a party that is taking place at his mansion. Later at the party during a game of charades, Edwards is shot dead and the sapphire vanishes. There are numerous "friends" present at the murder scene who would have no cause to weep at Edwards' death and make excellent suspects: Valerie Edwards (Dorothy Tree), the wife of Edwards, who is in love with her dead husband's secretary Peter Harrison (Craig Reynolds); Michael Strogonoff (Ivan Lebedeff), a would-be operatic singer who may also be in love with Valerie or, maybe, with the Asian maid Drina (Lotus Long), who secretly has the gem after Edwards' murder and wants to return it to China—but soon she meets the same fate as Brandon Edwards and again the gem is missing. Professor Ed Janney (Holmes Herbert), an old college friend of

Mr. Wong and Captain Street (Grant Withers) investigate the body of the
recently deceased Sing, the butler (Chester Gan).

Mr. Wong (they went to Oxford together) and a noted criminologist, is
also at the party and assists Wong with his investigation into the murders.
In typical mystery fashion all of the suspects show up at Wong's home for
the denouement.

This second Wong film is a vast improvement over the first episode in
all aspects. The script is tighter and more interesting, the production values are excellent for a Monogram Picture (especially the opulent setting
for the Edwards mansion), the acting is stronger, and the performance of
Grant Withers as Captain Sam Street is brought into focus with the other
performances—no more the blustering dumb cop. It is as if the entire
production staff and cast sat down after the first feeble film in this series
and figured out what they were doing wrong—and fixed it. Karloff's performance as Wong seems even more solidified from the first film and he
brings depth and considerable intelligence to the character. Interestingly,
it is mentioned in this film that Mr. Wong attended Oxford University. In
the Wiley short stories, as stated earlier, Wong attended Yale University. It
is likely Karloff's British accent had something to do with this change.

Mr. Wong in Chinatown

(Monogram Pictures, 1939)
70m.

Producer: Scott R. Dunlap, Associate Producer: William Lackey, Director: William Nigh, Screenplay: Scott Darling.

CAST: Boris Karloff, Marjorie Reynolds, Grant Withers, Huntley Gordon, Peter George Lynn, William Royle, James Flavin, Lotus Long, Lee Tong Foo, Bessie Loo, Richard Loo, Ernie Stanton, I. Stanford Jolley, Jack Kennedy, Donald Kerr, Wilbur Mack, Moy Ming, Bruce Mitchell, Angelo Rossitto, Guy Usher.

With careful and deliberate consideration, Mr. Wong always managed to trap the killer but in this entry the careful deliberation became almost as dull as watching paint dry. – Hans J. Wollstein, All Movie Guide

PLOT/COMMENT: The plot begins with the visit of Princess Lin Hwa (Lotus Long) to the home of Mr. Wong, seeking his help. Before Wong even enters the room where she is waiting, the princess is murdered by a poisoned dart shot from a Chinese sleeve gun through an open window. Wong, with the assistance of Captain Sam Street (Grant Withers) of the San Francisco Police Department, starts an investigation to uncover the murderer. They are joined in their search by Bobbie Logan (Marjorie Reynolds), a reporter who just happens to be the girlfriend of Captain Street. The trail leads to the princess's hotel room where her maid Lilly May (Bessie Loo) and a dwarf assistant (Angelo Rossitto) are questioned. Later Lilly May is found murdered with a poisoned dart, and the dwarf mysteriously disappears. Wong questions Captain Jaime (William Royle), the captain of the *Maid of the Orient*, the ship on which the princess arrived from China. The Oriental detective soon learns that the

Mr. Wong is too late to save maid Lilly May (Bessie Loo) from a poisoned dart.

princess came to America with a million dollars in vouchers to purchase war planes from Captain Guy Jackson (Peter George Lynn), the president of Phelps Aviation Corporation in Los Angeles. The planes were to be shipped on the *Maid of the Orient* to her homeland, but now Wong discovers that the corporation is nothing but a storefront, and the money that was deposited in Mr. Davidson's (Huntley Gordon) bank has mysteriously disappeared, apparently with the princess's forged signature. Mr. Wong travels a twisting path to discover the whereabouts of the missing money and the identity of the murderer.

This third entry in the series is plagued by a very slow-moving, listless plot punctuated by gigantic pauses between speeches that slow the pace to a crawl. Then, too, the plot veers back and forth from a murder mystery to a missing money mystery, leaving the focus blurred. Even the editing is sloppy with some bad matching of scenes, and the seventy-minute running time is excessive. The other production values—sets, lighting, and camera work—are first rate by Monogram standards.

Marjorie Reynolds joins the cast in the role of a sassy newspaper reporter and the girlfriend of Captain Street. Their repartee adds some humor and spice to the goings-on, but only for mild effect. Each of the three films up to this point has taken a different approach to the murder-mystery genre: the first, a broadly played smart detective/dumb cop format designed more for kid appeal; the second, a serious, low-key mystery format aimed primarily at the adult market; and the third, an in-between approach with a mixture of comedy and serious detective work—hopefully appealing to all demographics. This schizophrenic approach to the series may be an indication of why it only lasted for five entries with Boris Karloff. And, oh, yes, this same script was dusted off and modified slightly for the first Roland Winters Charlie Chan feature, *The Chinese Ring* (1947).

The Fatal Hour (Monogram Pictures, 1940) 68m.

Producer: Scott R. Dunlap, Associate Producer: William Lackey, Director: William Nigh, Screenplay: Scott Darling, Adaptation: Joseph West.

CAST: Boris Karloff, Grant Withers, Marjorie Reynolds, Charles Trowbridge, Frank Puglia, Craig Reynolds, Lita Chevret, Harry Strang, Hooper Atchley, Jason Robards, Richard Loo, Jack Kennedy, C. E. Anderson, Allan Cavan, Tristram Coffin, Nick Copeland, Pauline Drake, Harry Harvey, Elsa Janssen,

I. Stanford Jolley, Donald Kerr, Wilbur Mack, Bert Moorhouse, James C. Morton, Paul Scardon.

In cheap pulp fiction, characters with names like "Hardway" Harry are usually just red herrings whereas distinguished-looking pillars of society remain at all times deeply suspicious. – Hans J. Wollstein, All Movie Guide

PLOT/COMMENT: This episode in the Wong series begins with the discovery of the body of Dan O'Grady, a police officer who has worked closely with Captain Bill Street (Grant Withers). O'Grady, who was working on a smuggling racket, was shot, weighted down, and then thrown in the bay. Mr. Wong, who also knew the dead police officer, offers to help Street find the murderer. It seems that O'Grady has been on the trail of an oriental jewelry smuggling network. Clues lead Wong and Captain Street—with newspaper reporter Bobbie Logan (Marjorie Reynolds) tagging along to aggravate Street every chance she gets—to the Club Neptune, a bar near the harbor area where smuggling has been suspected. The owner of the club, a shady character named "Hardway" Harry Lockett (Frank Puglia), is well known by the police and suspected of being involved with the smuggling operation. A piece of emerald jade found in O'Grady's desk leads to the Belden Jewelry Company run by Frank Belden (Hooper Atchley) who claims that his store only handles inexpensive costume jewelry. Wong soon learns that Belden's son, Frank Jr. (Craig Reynolds), is a wastrel who is having an affair with Tanya Serova (Lita Chevret), a lady with a past who is involved with "Hardway" Harry Lockett in the smuggling operation. It's presently discovered that the Belden Jewelry Company is heavily in debt and the lawyer representing the creditors is John T. Forbes (Charles Trowbridge). Before Mr. Wong can decipher who the killer is, three more murders take place: Belden Sr. is found shot to death in his jewelry store, Tanya Serova is murdered in her apartment, and a radio performer (Jason Robards) is murdered in Captain Street's outer office. Mr. Wong must hurry to conclude the case before he runs out of suspects.

Mr. Lyons (Paul Scardon) has replied to a newspaper article requesting information on the death of Officer O'Grady. Mr. Wong teases newshound Bobbie Logan (Marjorie Reynolds) that he too is responding to her "advertisement."

This fourth episode in the series is another slow-moving affair, as all of the Wong films seem to be. Nevertheless, there are nice things that can be said about this outing in the series. The plot follows the required murder mystery format of a dead body, clues, suspects, more dead bodies, and eventually the denouement where the smart detective solves the case. Within this stock framework the screenwriters have created some atmospheric scenes in Club Neptune and the fog-shrouded San Francisco waterfront area where the smuggling is taking place. The killer's use of a "remote control" radio device to throw our Chinese detective and the police off his trail is a fascinating plot element. The production values (sets, camera work, lighting, etc.) for the Wong series—if you don't count the first episode—are impressive for Monogram Pictures. Boris Karloff's performance as Mr. Wong is first rate and always commanding, and the use of veteran character actors in the supporting cast adds to the quality of the production. The Mr. Wong films were destined and designed, of course, for the bottom half of double features in movie theatres, but they provided an hour or so of pretty good mystery entertainment filling that bill. Inexplicably, Captain "Sam" Street suddenly turns into "Bill" Street for the final two films in the Karloff series and just "Captain Street" in the Keye Luke Wong film.

Doomed to Die (Monogram Pictures, 1940) 68m.

Executive Producer: Scott R. Dunlap, Associate Producer: Paul Malvern, Director: William Nigh, Original Story: Ralph Bettinson, Screenplay: Michel Jacoby.

CAST: Boris Karloff, Marjorie Reynolds, Grant Withers, William Stelling, Catherine Craig, Guy Usher, Henry Brandon, Melvin Lang, Wilbur Mack, Kenneth Harlan, Richard Loo, Tristram Coffin, Mike Donovan, Gibson Gowland, Jack Kennedy, Maxine Leslie, Moy Ming, Angelo Rossitto, Bill Willmering.

Karloff strolls through the maze of clues as if it required only a fraction of his attention. – Hobe, *Variety*

PLOT/COMMENT: Shipping magnate Cyrus P. Wentworth (Melvin Lang) is devastated when his flagship *The Wentworth Castle* catches fire and, tragically, four hundred persons are lost at sea. Wentworth's lawyer Vic Martin (Henry Brandon) fears that Wentworth may even be contemplating suicide when he changes his will, leaving everything to his daughter Cynthia (Catherine Craig). Wentworth and his chief competitor, Paul Fleming (Guy Usher), have feuded for many years, and Wentworth is particularly upset that Fleming's son Dick (William Stelling) and Cynthia are in love and want to get married. When Wentworth is shot to death while Dick is in his office discussing the possible marriage, Captain Bill Street (Grant Withers) sees the situation as an open-and-shut case of murder, and Dick is arrested. "I'll eat my hat if he isn't the guilty one," Street asserts. Cub reporter Bobbie Logan doesn't see it that way and talks to James Lee Wong about also investigating the case. Wong uncovers a vengeful chauffeur (Kenneth Harlan), a blackmailing general manager (Wilbur Mack), and a Tong connection to the murder. Soon the Oriental sleuth discovers an attempt to smuggle one and a half million dollars' worth of gold bonds from China to the United States for safekeeping—a plan that has gone awry as unscrupulous individuals have their eyes on the money and will not even stop at murder to lay their hands on it.

Boris Karloff's last go-round as Mr. Wong is no better or worse than the episodes that preceded it. The production values continue to be good for a Monogram film, with the script slow moving but passable for the B-movie-mystery genre of the times. (The opening scenes of the burning *Wentworth Castle* were actually newsreel footage taken of the *SS Morro Castle* that caught fire in September of 1934 on a voyage from Havana to New York and resulted in many deaths.) The dumb-cop/sassy-mouthed-reporter repartee between Withers and Reynolds is ramped up in this final entry and provides the little humor there is in the story—some viewers, to be sure, would find it excessive and, ultimately, irritating. There seems to be no record of who was responsible for pulling the plug on this short series, Karloff or Monogram, but the studio decided to try a one-shot recasting on the Oriental sleuth theme—and this time with a real Asian actor.

Phantom of Chinatown with Keye Luke

Phantom of Chinatown (Monogram Pictures, 1940) 61m.

Producer: Paul Malvern, Director: Phil Rosen, Original Story: Ralph Bettinson, Screenplay: Joseph West.

CAST: Keye Luke, Grant Withers, Lotus Long, Charles Miller, Huntley Gordon, Virginia Carpenter, John H. Dilson, Paul McVey, John Holland, Dick Terry, Robert Kellard, William Castello, Lee Tung Foo, Lynton Brent, Jack Cheatham, Heinie Conklin, William Gould, Bruce Mitchell, William J. O'Brien, Victor Wong.

The yarn moves along at a sprightly clip and produces plenty of action along detective mystery lines, plus sustaining suspense in an admirable fashion. – Char. *Variety*

PLOT/COMMENT: Archeology professor John Benton is poisoned from a glass of water as he lectures about his recent expedition into the Mongolian desert where he and his team discovered the long-lost Ming emperor's tomb. One of Professor Benton's former students, James Lee Wong (Keye Luke), arrives just as Benton collapses to the floor. Captain Street (Grant Withers) of the San Francisco Homicide Squad soon arrives with his men and starts an investigation into the murder, questioning first the people who were on the expedition with Benton. They include Charlie Fraser (John H. Dilson), the cameraman who made a filmed record of their journey; Benton's daughter Louise (Virginia Carpenter); and pilot Tommy Dean (Robert Kellard) who is romantically involved with Louise. Copilot Mason (John Holland), also on the expedition, got lost in a wind storm in the desert and is presumed dead, and Benton's secretary, Win Lee (Lotus Long), was not on the excursion—but Wong learns later that she is

working for the Chinese government. It is soon discovered that Benton found a scroll in the emperor's sarcophagus that has now disappeared from his safe. The scroll is said to contain a clue to the location of the Eternal Fire, a shrine where an undying column of fire burns. Oil replenishes the flame of the Eternal Fire and there is, therefore, a potentially huge oil repository that could prove vital to the defense of China. During the investigation by Captain Street and James Lee Wong, Benton's butler Jonas (William Castello) is poisoned in the manner of Benton, then stabbed for good measure and put in the sarcophagus formerly occupied by the emperor. It's a tough case for the fledgling detective and the dim-brained Captain Street.

This film is presented as if there never were any preceding Mr. Wong features. There is no mention that Boris Karloff's Wong might be, for example, the father of "Jimmy" Wong. When Captain Street first meets Jimmy Lee Wong at the scene of Benton's murder, he does not know the young man, and when told his name, gives no indication that he might have known a Wong at any previous time. There is also no indication that Jimmy is a detective or has any ambitions to be one or has any education in criminology to cause him to become involved with the murder investigation—or that he is authorized to carry a gun, which he does. There also isn't any reason why the gruff Captain Street should include him in the investigation, which he does. I guess we're supposed to just accept all of these incongruous things because we know that it is a Mr. Wong murder mystery and the Wong character has always been a detective with a gun.

Anyway, the film is an interesting little mystery with some intriguing twists and turns involving an emperor's lost tomb, eternal fires, ancient curses, and bodies in and out of sarcophaguses. The production values are again first rate for a Monogram film, and Keye Luke and the supporting cast do their jobs handily. Given all of this, it's a bit surprising that the series didn't continue. But then, World War II was on the horizon, and the foreign film markets were already drying up—and then during those years there was the matter of some Asians being our friends and some being our enemies and the unwillingness of many American people, sadly, to tell them apart.

The Comic Book Case Files

STARTING WITH ISSUE number forty in June 1939, *Popular Comics* ran Mr. Wong serialized stories for seven consecutive issues. The comic book, published by Dell Publishing Company, had first appeared in the comic book market in February of 1936 and over the years featured a number of well-known characters such as *Dick Tracy, Terry and the Pirates, Gasoline Alley, Tailspin Tommy, Little Orphan Annie*, and *Tarzan*. For most of its run the comic was a monthly publication but switched to a quarterly in January of 1948. In all, there were one hundred and forty-five issues of *Popular Comics* published with the run ending with the July-September issue of 1948.

Popular Comics occasionally published serialized versions of movies that would have appeal to its young readers. The Mr. Wong stories in the seven issues of *Popular Comics* (issues 40-46) were adaptations of the first two Mr. Wong films, *Mr. Wong, Detective* and *The Mystery of Mr. Wong*. (Running concurrently with the Mr. Wong movie adaptations were issues featuring comic book versions of two 1937 Jack Randall western films, *Riders of the Dawn* and *Stars over Arizona*).) The surprising aspect of these movie adaptations is that the films chosen had been released to the public one to two years before the comic book versions were published. Since the Wong films and the Randall westerns were ongoing series, the immediacy of the individual films was apparently not a concern. *The Mystery of*

305

Mr. Wong, released in April of 1939, came closest to being current with the adaptation running in the October through December issues.

The Mr. Wong comic book issues credited the title of the films and then stated "featuring Boris Karloff." One has to wonder if Hugh Wiley, Monogram Pictures, and/or Mr. Karloff received any compensation for use of the character/films/name in the comic books or if the whole thing was written off as "advertising" for the Mr. Wong film series. Whatever the case, these seven issues of *Popular Comics* were the only comic book representation of the character ever published.

Afterword

MANY YEARS HAVE PASSED since the last gathering of suspects in a hushed room where Charlie Chan could utter those fateful words in his solemn manner, "You are murderer." It has been ages since Mr. Moto has hoisted a hostile ship's steward over his shoulders and flung him into the dark, murky waters below. It has been many a dark, stormy night since Mr. Wong, attired in his black suit, a white boutonniere affixed to his lapel and clutching his black umbrella, has hunched over a murder victim while contemplating the scientific deduction that will lead him to the murderer. Yes, the case files of the Oriental sleuths have been closed for many years.

Fortunately, through book reprints, the remastered films preserved on DVD, old-time radio archives, and the plethora of memorabilia available on websites such as Ebay, the original case files of the Oriental sleuths are, for the most part, still accessible and remain very popular. Some of the original memorabilia, such as movie posters and comic books, have become highly-sought-after collector's items and very expensive.

What does the future hold for the Oriental sleuths, one may wonder? Certainly someday, sometime, some year soon, an enterprising producer, director, or writer will rediscover the delight of these clever and resourceful sleuths and will create new case files for another generation's thrills and enjoyment. The body of material that exists from the original incarnations is too rich and enticing to be neglected indefinitely.

Until that time, Let us allow the words of Mr. Moto to provide our benediction: "May sleep fall upon your eyes as softly as poppy petals on a placid pool. May your soul be blessed with repose, your dreams with enchantment."

About the Author

DAVID ROTHEL IS THE AUTHOR of thirteen books, mostly in the western film history/biography genre (*Who Was That Masked Man: The Story of the Lone Ranger, The Singing Cowboys, An Ambush of Ghosts, Those Great Cowboy Sidekicks, The Gene Autry Book, The Roy Rogers Book, Richard Boone: A Knight without Armor in a Savage Land*, etc.). In the 1970s he created and hosted a daily, show-business radio program in Sarasota, Florida, entitled *Nostalgia Newsbreak* that now, years later, has served as the basis for his recent book *Opened Time Capsules: My Vintage Conversations with Show Business Personalities.* Mr. Rothel has been the Director of the federally-funded Sarasota Visual and Performing Arts Center and, in more recent years, Executive/Artistic Director of the Black Bear Dinner Theatre in North Georgia. He has been a contributor to NPR's *All Things Considered,* the BBC's *Omnibus*, and was twice featured by Leonard Maltin on *Entertainment Tonight.* He and his wife Nancy reside in Dahlonega, Georgia.

Author David Rothel

Selected Bibliography

Berlin, Howard M. *The Complete Mr. Moto Film Phile, A Casebook*, Maryland: Wildside Press, 2005.

_____, *The Charlie Chan Film Encyclopedia*, North Carolina: McFarland & Company, 2000.

Biggers, Earl Derr. *Charlie Chan, Five Complete Novels*, New York: Avenel Books, 1981.

Bojarski, Richard and Kenneth Beals. *The Films of Boris Karloff*, New Jersey: The Citadel Press, 1974.

Chin, Frank. "Confessions of a Number One Son," *Ramparts*, (Vol. 11, No. 9, March 1973).

Cox, Jim. *Radio Crime Fighters*, North Carolina: McFarland & Company, 2002.

Hanke, Ken. *Charlie Chan at the Movies*, North Carolina: McFarland & Company, 1989.

Marquand, John P. *Mr. Moto, Four Complete Novels*, New York: Avenel Books, 1983.

Nieves, Rafael and Tim Hamilton. *Mr. Moto—Welcome Back, Mister Moto*, Illinois: Moonstone Books, 2008.

Parish, James Robert, Editor-in-Chief. *The Great Movie Series*, New York: A. S. Barnes and Company, 1971.

Price, Michael H. *Mantan the Funny Man: The Life and Times of Mantan Moreland*, Baltimore, Maryland: Midnight Marquee Press, 2006.

Rothel, David. *Opened Time Capsules: My Vintage Conversations with Show Business Personalities*, Albany, Georgia: BearManor Media, 2010.

Semenov, Lillian Wurtzel and Carla Winter. *William Fox, Sol M. Wurtzel and the Early Fox Film Corporation, Letters, 1917-1923*, North Carolina: McFarland & Company, 2001.

Variety Film Reviews 1938-1942, Volume Six. New York: Garland Publishing, Inc., 1983.

Variety Film Reviews 1949-1953, Volume Eight. New York: Garland Publishing, Inc., 1983.

Vreeland, Frank. *Foremost Films of 1938*, New York: Pitman Publishing Corporation, 1939.

Youngkin, Stephen, James Bigwood, Raymond Cabana, Jr. *The Films of Peter Lorre*, New Jersey: The Citadel Press, 1982.

Zinman, David. *Saturday Afternoon at the Bijou*, New York: Arlington House, 1973.

Internet Resources/Databases:

All-Movie Guide. http://allmovie.com

Digital Deli Too, Preserving the Golden Age of Radio for a Digital Future. www.digitaldelitoo.com

Grand Comics Database. www.comics.org

Internet Movie Database (IMDb). http://us.imdb.com

Selected Index

The following index contains the major players in *The Case Files of the Oriental Sleuths* and listings of the literary, film, radio, television, comic, etc. incarnations of the case files.